Race for Revival

Race for Revival

How Cold War South Korea Shaped the American Evangelical Empire

HELEN JIN KIM

OXFORD
UNIVERSITY PRESS

Oxford University Press is a department of the University of Oxford. It furthers
the University's objective of excellence in research, scholarship, and education
by publishing worldwide. Oxford is a registered trade mark of Oxford University
Press in the UK and certain other countries.

Published in the United States of America by Oxford University Press
198 Madison Avenue, New York, NY 10016, United States of America.

© Oxford University Press 2022

All rights reserved. No part of this publication may be reproduced, stored in
a retrieval system, or transmitted, in any form or by any means, without the
prior permission in writing of Oxford University Press, or as expressly permitted
by law, by license, or under terms agreed with the appropriate reproduction
rights organization. Inquiries concerning reproduction outside the scope of the
above should be sent to the Rights Department, Oxford University Press, at the
address above.

You must not circulate this work in any other form
and you must impose this same condition on any acquirer.

Library of Congress Cataloging-in-Publication Data
Names: Kim, Helen Jin, 1984– author.
Title: Race for revival : how Cold War South Korea shaped the American Evangelical empire /
Helen Jin Kim.
Description: New York, NY, United States of America : Oxford University Press, 2022. |
Includes bibliographical references and index.
Identifiers: LCCN 2021038645 (print) | LCCN 2021038646 (ebook) | ISBN 9780367569280 |
ISBN 9780190062422 (hardback) | ISBN 9780190062446 (epub)
Subjects: LCSH: Evangelicalism—Korea (South) | Evangelicalism—United States. |
Graham, Billy, 1918-2018—Influence.
Classification: LCC BR1640 .K47 2022 (print) | LCC BR1640 (ebook) | DDC 277.308/2—dc23
LC record available at https://lccn.loc.gov/2021038645
LC ebook record available at https://lccn.loc.gov/2021038646

DOI: 10.1093/oso/9780190062422.001.0001

3 5 7 9 8 6 4 2

Printed by Integrated Books International, United States of America

For ŏmma, appa, and ŏnni

Contents

Preface ix
Acknowledgments xi
Note on Romanization and Translation xv

Introduction 1

1. Martyrs: War and World Vision, 1950–1953 22

2. Students: Immigration, Conversion, and White Fundamentalism, 1950–1960 51

3. Orphans: The Mirage of Evangelical Diplomacy, 1960–1969 75

4. Revival: Billy's and Billy's Largest "Crusade," 1969–1973 107

5. Explosion: The "New Emerging Christian Kingdom" and the Christian Right, 1972–1980 135

Conclusion 161

Notes 171
Bibliography 215
Index 225

Preface

This book began nearly two decades ago within the Korean diaspora, not with contemporary US politics and religion. In 2003, as a freshman, I became preoccupied with this book's seed questions when I walked a picket line in Los Angeles as part of Asian American Issues, a service-learning course on Asian American history, politics, and community building. We protested a Koreatown supermarket's unjust wages. I was profoundly disturbed that the supermarket did not pay its primarily Latino workers a fair wage, but offered them Sunday worship services. Such injustices not only violated Christian principles of justice, love, and peace, but also the commitments of the 1970s and 1980s Asian American social movement.

As I sought alternative pasts, to imagine new futures, I considered the legacy of Chon Tae'il (1948–1970), a twenty-two-year-old Korean factory worker, and a member of my *k'ŭnabŏji's* (eldest uncle) church.[1] Chon self-immolated in 1970, in protest of Park Chung-hee's authoritarian regime (1963–1979), which grossly violated workers' rights for the sake of rapid industrialization and developmental nationalism. Chon's suicide-protest—or, martyrdom—fueled the South Korean democratization movement to oust authoritarians like Park.[2] In the process, ministers, activists, and scholars helped to birth *minjung* (people's) theology, an indigenous Korean form of liberation theology that sought to offer a preferential option for the oppressed.[3] Such a movement of liberation also energized the ministries of Korean female pastors like Cho Wha Soon, who worked with female factory workers, in solidarity with them.[4] Had *minjung* faith—in the legacy of Chon and Cho—left a more forceful transpacific legacy, would LA Koreatown have inherited a stronger faith tradition that cherished workers and social justice?

The faith of Chon's and Cho's era did not predominate in South Korea or Korean America. Into the 1980s and 1990s, a theological and political movement, more closely aligned with evangelicalism, burgeoned transnationally from South Korea to Korean America.[5] South Korean evangelical Protestantism "exploded" through global missionary activity and megachurches, with the nation earning the title of a "regional Protestant superpower."[6] Post-1965 Korean Americans were majority Christian—about

70 to 80 percent—and fervent practitioners of evangelicalism.[7] Rebecca Kim called collegiate Korean American evangelicals "God's whiz kids," and Rudy Busto memorably dubbed Asian American evangelicals the "model moral minority."[8] Today, men of Korean descent lead flagship US evangelical institutions, from the National Association of Evangelicals to the Presbyterian Church of America.

How did evangelicalism become a predominant force in Korea and its diaspora in the United States? Was the US Christian Right responsible, given its association with "evangelicalism"? What, precisely, was the relationship between US politics, evangelicalism, and Koreans? Upon graduation, I further explored these questions with the Asian Pacific American Religion and Research Initiative, and during graduate studies, I found that a transpacific frame was necessary. Just as my questions took shape through an imagination beyond the nation-state, so too must the answers. In doing so, I found an archive remaining from a world I had not known—a testament to the power of research.

The *minjung* movement and the Asian American social movement were part of a coterminous transnational and global leftist tradition that aligned closely with communist and socialist ideals. But there was also a cadre of historical actors in the United States and South Korea who developed a transpacific tradition of evangelical piety and politics that competed with them. The politics of the Cold War in South Korea lifted them onto an unparalleled global stage. It also distanced those in the US diaspora from readily accessing alternative religiopolitical Korean narratives. To be sure, the binary between evangelical and liberationist approaches to modern Christianity is too simplistic. For it covers over gray areas where the two worlds have overlapped among both practitioners and scholars. But, as this book shows, Cold War Manichaean logic structured faith, race, and politics into binaries, pitting two worlds against each other.

Race for Revival uncovers a hidden past, which reverberates into our world today. The US encounter with South Korea during the Cold War yielded an unprecedented change in evangelical piety and politics. Two unlike worlds—Cold War United States and South Korea—became inseparable through an alliance, forged by the blood of Jesus, stained by the blood of war.

Acknowledgments

I lived around the edges of a story I could not access in books—so I wrote my own and discovered a new world in it. I entered that world with brilliant and kind scholars.

Paul Chang has been an invaluable conversation partner since I knocked on his office door as a college student at Stanford and then as a PhD student at Harvard. Marla Frederick, as a mentor at Harvard and a senior colleague at Emory, showed me how to work boldly and study people who are alive. Catherine Brekus journeyed closely through the writing, and she showed me how to run a classroom and navigate the guild. Jonathan Walton believed in me as a scholar and teacher from beginning to end, and provided crucial guidance throughout. In spring 2010, David Hempton opened up his course so I could write about transpacific evangelicalism. He is a steadfast mentor. Several nuggets of his wisdom remain: that the difficult parts of the past, while often "unwelcomed," are "still important to tell"; that dissimilar literatures and worlds would come together through me—they did! I am grateful for my Harvard writing group: Charrise Barron, Mycah Conner, Dale Gadsden, Kera Street, and especially Cori Tucker-Price, for her presence, counsel, and brilliance. Thanks to the North American Religion Colloquium, especially Brett Grainger and Elizabeth Jemison.

In spring 2013, through Princeton's Exchange Scholar Program, I studied with Gary Okihiro, Albert Raboteau, and Judith Weisenfeld, which laid the foundation for chapters 3 and 4. That term, Nikki Hoskins and Bo Karen Lee provided invaluable encouragement and I attended the Pacific Asian North Asian American Women in Theology and Ministry conference on the Korean War, which helped to structure my research, for which I am grateful to Anne Joh and Nami Kim. Shortly thereafter, I worked with Khyati Joshi, Timothy Tseng, and David Yoo on Asian American religious history, which also shaped my work.[1]

Research for this book was made possible through support from Harvard University's William R. Hutchison Presidential Fellowship, Charles Warren Center for Studies in American History, Center for American Political Studies, Korea Institute, and Graduate School of Arts and Sciences; the

National Endowment for the Humanities; the Louisville Institute; the Candler School of Theology; and, the Forum for Theological Exploration, including their incredible staff: Elsie Barnhart, Kimberly Daniel-Brister, Darlene Hutto, Stephen Lewis, Patrick Reyes, and Matthew Williams. Sem Vermeersch and Yohan Yoo hosted me at Seoul National University's Kyujanggak Institute for Korean Studies in 2016.

I received timely feedback on the manuscript at the American Academy of Religion, the American Studies Foundation's International Forum for Young Scholars in Tokyo, the American Society of Church History, the Association for Asian American Studies, Baylor University, Boston University, Chung Dong First Methodist Church in Seoul, Harvard Memorial Church, the International Association for Mission Studies, Stanford University, and, at Emory, the East Asian Studies writing group, the Candler Faculty Luncheon, and the Candler Junior Faculty Writing Group.

Many thanks to Theo Calderara, editor extraordinaire at Oxford University Press, and to my readers for their feedback. Uli Guthrie has been an amazing editor and invaluable consultant since dissertation days. I am grateful for colleagues who supported manuscript completion: Reem Bailony, Melissa Borja, Peter Choi, Alison Greene, Jehu Hanciles, Brooks Holifield, Nikki Hoskins, Jane Iwamura, Arun Jones, Nami Kim, Kwok Pui Lan, Jim Laney, Jane Hong Lee, Liz Lin, Gerardo Marti, Melani McAlister, Hyemin Na, Chris Paek, Nichole Phillips, Ted Smith, Jonathan Strom, Chris Suh, Cori Tucker-Price, Lauren Turek, John Turner, Grant Wacker, Deanna Womack, Janelle Wong, and Peng Yin. Thanks to my students, including my research assistants SeungJun Hwang, Kevin Lazarus, Seulbin Sunny Lee, and Jane Nichols.

I discovered primary and secondary source "gems" in the United States and South Korea thanks to numerous archivists, librarians, and staff at the following organizations: Steve Gray at the World Vision Archives in Monrovia, CA; Dori Ryen at Campus Crusade for Christ International Archives in Orlando, FL; Paul Ericksen and Bob Shuster at the Billy Graham Archives in Wheaton, IL; Renata Kalnins at Harvard Divinity School's Andover Theological Library; Choi Taeyuk and Park Haejin at the Institute for the History of Korean Christianity in Seoul; Yi Insu and Yi Sŭngsan at the Korean Church History Museum in Inchon; Chu Miae at the Han Kyung Chik Memorial Library in Seoul; Kim Hisu at World Vision Korea in Seoul; Choi Jinok at the World Vision Korean Children's Choir Musical Institute in Seoul; Park Sŏngmin, Chung Hisu, and Lee Sŏkho at the Korea Campus

Crusade for Christ in Seoul. I am grateful for the Korean National Archive in Seongnam and the Billy Kim Memorial Library in Suwon. Billy Jang Hwan Kim and Joy Kang shared collections with me during my visit to the Far East Broadcasting Company in Seoul.

Thank you to those with whom I conducted oral histories in South Korea: Cho Miyŏng, Choi Minok, Kim Jang Hwan (Billy Kim), Moon Ŭnmi, Moon Hyangja, Oh Chiyŏng, Oh Chint'ak, Pae Kyungha, Park Micha, Park Jong Sam (Sam Park) and Yi Hokyun. Thank you to those with whom I consulted or conducted oral histories in the United States: Marilee Pierce Dunker, Judy Douglass, Gertrude Phillips, Jerry Sharpless, Bailey Marks, and Ed Neibling. Rhie Deok Joo shared his expertise on the history of Korean Christianity through his course History of Korean Theological Thought at the Methodist Theological University.

I am grateful for early mentors and friends. Carolyn Wong advised my college thesis, and her activism and expansive mind helped me to believe I could become a scholar. Roy Sano, one of the historical subjects of that thesis, was a crucial mentor. Russell Jeung and Sharon Suh, of the Asian Pacific American Religion and Research Institute, were gracious *sŏnbaes*. Friends provided laughter, wisdom, and care: Stephen Behnke, Laura Cheifetz, Sarah Fleischer-Ihn, Chris Hong, Antonio Houston, Bomi Kim, Larry Kim, Kelly Lee, Su Lee, Melanie Long, Derlyn Moronta, Karen Nga, Maytal Saltiel, Jung Eun Shin, Helen Shi Stafford, Esther Whang, Nicole Wubbena, the Wednesday Neighborhood Group, Irene Yang, Ivanna Yi, and Jason Yung.

I could not have written this book without my family. Thank you for their wisdom and hospitality, especially while I conducted research in Korea: Kim Yelee, Kim Jinu, Kwon Kyŏngsoon, the late Kim Donghwan, Choi Soonyang, and Kim Yongduk. Thanks especially to Yi Hayŏng for her laughter and Kim Kelee for her guidance. My *ŏmma* and *appa*, Hee Soon Kwon and Hong Ki Kim, have been my courage. Words cannot contain the measure of their love and their commitment to my self-actualization. In his retirement, my father visited me in the archives, cooked delicious meals, painted pictures to spur me on, and engaged me in wide-ranging debates and discussions about ideas that filled me with joy. Writing this book coincided with my mother's tenure as a pastor in the San Francisco Bay Area. Her wisdom always came at a timely moment, her insights helped me to see beyond challenges, and her pioneering life set the ultimate example. Thanks to my *ŏnni*, Esther Ryoung Kim, for her courageous life and fierce sisterhood.

Note on Romanization and Translation

Korean names and words were Romanized using the McCune-Reischauer system. Exceptions were made for names, places, and organizations with standard or official English spellings (such as Syngman Rhee, Kyung Chik Han, and Joon Gon Kim). Following Korean custom, surnames precede given names, excluding names that reference English language publications. Translations from Korean into English are mine unless otherwise specified.

Introduction

On June 3, 1973, Billy Jang Hwan Kim (1934–), a South Korean minister with Baptist and Carolina roots, just like Billy Graham (1918–2018), joined the white southern evangelist at a wooden pulpit custom made for two (figure I.1). Billy Kim, just a few inches above five feet, mounted a wooden booster to match Billy Graham's towering height of over six feet. On this day, they preached to 1.1 million people, their largest "crusade."[1] Graham had gained global fame as a revivalist, an adviser to US presidents, and the leader of modern evangelical America. He attracted vast crowds, and one might reasonably assume that Graham preached this, his largest crusade, at a southern football stadium or a Sun Belt megachurch. Yet it was in South Korea that Graham, with the help of translation, preached to 1.1 million. Why South Korea, of all places?

On this "scorching hot" June Sunday, the record-breaking crowd sat on the hot concrete with sheets of newspaper for cushioning as they awaited Graham's sermon, the high point of that afternoon. Throngs of Korean men and women, young and old, as well as Korean and US soldiers, gathered in Yoido Plaza, a barren strip of land typically used for military training. Billy Kim was Billy Graham's "good voice," without which he would have been "absolutely nothing" in South Korea.[2] He translated into Korean Graham's sermon, "Love of God," based on John 15:13: "Greater love has no one than this: to lay down one's life for one's friends." The two men opened this revivalist apex in twentieth-century history with memories of the Korean War (1950–1953), the first "hot" war of the global Cold War, or, as Grace Cho puts it, "the first and last conflict of the Cold War, whose beginning is uncertain and whose end has not yet arrived."[3] The two Billys sacralized the Korean War, deeming it a costly but holy war, as they conflated the image of the US soldier's blood sacrifice with Jesus's martyrdom on the cross.

The two preachers concluded the crusade with an invitation to make a "decision for Christ"—to accept Jesus as their Lord and Savior or renew a previous decision. That afternoon, seventy-three thousand people rose from their seats, many solemnly with bowed heads, some weeping, and made

Figure I.1 Billy Graham and Billy Kim, Seoul, Korea, June 3, 1973
Source: Folder 54 "Korea Photos," Box 140, Collection 17, BGEA—Crusade Activities, Archives of the Billy Graham Center, Wheaton, Illinois.

public a "decision for Christ." It was the largest group of converts and faith renewers in any crusade hosted by the Billy Graham Evangelistic Association (BGEA) since its 1950 founding.[4]

What did it mean that Graham held his largest crusade beyond US borders? Two other global evangelical nonprofits, or parachurches, shared center stage—Campus Crusade for Christ and World Vision.[5] Why were World Vision, Graham's organization, and Campus Crusade, in particular, present at this revivalistic apex? Was this the triumph of American evangelical empire? Or was it a showroom moment for local Korean Christianity? What role did US Cold War empire building in Asia play in this moment of transpacific revival?

In part, this revivalist apex signified what evangelicalism had become in the Cold War era—a white and male-led movement, made by the global masses. It was also a movement that would stop at nothing for the sake of the world's conversion, even allying with authoritarians. Indeed, as will be discussed, without the consent of South Korean president Park Chung-hee, an authoritarian despot, this crusade could not have been organized. Piety and politics intertwined, hardening evangelicalism on both sides of the Pacific into a religion of heart and hierarchy.

For a more complete answer, one must suture two parallel and otherwise disconnected stories. The first is of early twentieth-century modernists and liberals who believed that the backward fundamentalist strain of Christianity in the United States would fade away. They were wrong. Instead, a cadre of primarily white fundamentalists reformed themselves into a more culture-friendly "neo-evangelical" movement in the 1950s and 1960s, and then, having gained public attention, into mainstream evangelicalism in the 1970s. *Newsweek* magazine declared 1976 to be the "Year of the Evangelical." Republican Ronald Reagan's election as president in 1980 reflected in part the rise of this once-reticent evangelical subculture to mainstream power.

The re-emergence of evangelicalism in the United States paralleled the growth of non-Western Christianity in general and the "explosion" of Christianity in South Korea in particular.[6] This is the second story. When the Korean War stumbled into an inconclusive armistice in 1953, North and South Korea remained divided. The North, the original hub of Korean Christianity, soon espoused *Juche* ideology, and the South, Christianity.[7] Between 1950 and 1980, South Korea's Christian population grew from less than 5 percent to 20 percent of the population.[8] The nation was deemed a "regional Protestant superpower."[9] Now, in the twenty-first century, South Korea sends out more missionaries per capita than any other country in the world.[10] The Yoido Plaza of crusade fame has been replaced by the Yoido Park. But it remains a landmark of revivalism: Cho Yonggi, or David Yonggi Cho, the founding pastor of the Yoido Full Gospel Church—the largest church in the world—houses his office in front of the park, not far from where the church stands today.[11]

Historians have studied these parallel stories—of US evangelicals and South Korean Protestants—as independent narratives. But they were actually tightly intertwined.[12] The BGEA, World Vision, and Campus Crusade are best viewed as border-crossing networks stretching especially across the Pacific Ocean. They allied themselves with similar movements in South Korea long before they became "multinational corporations," as Darren Dochuk puts it.[13]

The presence of all three—along with a million people—in Seoul was a culmination of a transpacific history with millions of participants spanning two continents and beyond. Since the outbreak of the Korean War, Cold War South Korea and the United States had been intertwined in a "religious Cold War" against global communism—matters of faith permeated the war as a political struggle for legitimacy and a global rivalry between divergent ideas of governance in Cold War America's battle against the Soviet Union.[14] In spite of Harry Truman's (1884–1972) and Dwight D. Eisenhower's (1890–1969) vast political differences, Eisenhower shared Truman's belief that Cold War America had a divine mandate to save the world from "the spiritual evil of atheistic communism."[15] That religious Cold War extended into communist Asia.[16] It culminated, in part, at this transpacific revivalistic apex, with the two Billys, World Vision, and Campus Crusade at the helm, as they sought to win a holy war through fulfilling the Great Commission, the total evangelization of the world. Mapped onto that divine mandate was a Manichaean logic of "good" versus "evil" that created a transpacific religious, racial, and political fault line, not only empowering the global rise of South Korean Christianity, but also, in part, shaping a niche and dying white fundamentalist America into the US evangelical empire. A transpacific historical lens reveals that the rise of modern evangelical America—and the explosion of South Korean Christianity—depended on America's religious Cold War in Asia.

Race for Revival is the first book to use a transpacific lens to interpret US evangelical history, politics, and race. Historians have recently written global histories of US evangelicalism, providing a fresh lens to understand old stories.[17] Yet this is the first to set the history of modern US evangelicalism in the Asia-Pacific. To that end, I connect a triad of previously self-contained conversations. I link modern American evangelicalism with Korean Christianity, and connect these religious histories to the backdrop of the Cold War in Asia. I tell this story by studying World Vision, the Billy Graham Evangelistic Association, and Campus Crusade for Christ. Spurred on in part by the global Cold War—which is still symbolized by the 38th parallel, dividing communist North Korea and democratic capitalist South Korea—a vast group of mid-twentieth-century white fundamentalists became evangelicals by converting, disputing, and allying with transnational South Korean Protestants, whom they viewed as racial "others," anticommunist allies, and models in converting the world to an evangelical form of Christianity.

Furthermore, when one follows the historical trail on both sides of the Pacific, an immense transpacific canopy of evangelical conservatism comes into view. Not until the 1980s and 1990s did the Christian Right solidify in both the United States and South Korea, but the history of these three organizations between 1950 and 1980 describes the rise of a potent array of non-state actors. No single narrative can capture the full web of connections that converge to bring about large-scale historical change, but the fabric of both South Korean Protestantism and US evangelicalism would have a different texture and feel today were it not for the story that this book tells.

Since the early nineteenth century, white Protestant missionaries had been venturing across oceans to places then virtually unknown to most

Americans. It seemed that only one force could stand in their way—their own disunity. Though at the turn of the twentieth century white Protestants were sending out more missionaries than even imperial Great Britain, with its colonies all over the globe, the evangelical consensus that fired their imaginations was about to implode. The fundamentalist-modernist controversy, which pitted theological liberals, or "modernists," against fundamentalists, was largely responsible for the implosion. While white liberals accepted German higher criticism of the Bible and scientific theories of evolution, white fundamentalists held onto biblical literalism (often with a seven-day creation), redemption by the blood sacrifice of Christ, and an imminent return of Christ to judge the wicked and save the righteous. Along the way, they also rejected Darwinian evolution.

Though the 1925 Scopes Trial symbolized the ensuing split, the real battles occurred within the denominations, where the fundamentalists usually lost and then separated to form their own small empires.[18] These separatist groups viewed not only theological liberalism but also the global rise of communism as threats to the mission to evangelize the world.[19] They were not content to remain in small separatist havens. White fundamentalists hoped to recover their dominance in American society and extend it to the rest of the world.

For white fundamentalists in the twentieth century, "Revival in America" meant "the evangelization of the world."[20] To that end, they created one institution after another, from national evangelical associations to schools such as Bob Jones University and Fuller Theological Seminary and new missionary networks like World Vision, Campus Crusade, and the BGEA. Global missionary work continued despite the postwar decolonization movements that lashed out against Western missionary imperialism and sometimes thwarted Christian missions.

White fundamentalists were little moved by postcolonial activists and nation builders who organized against colonialists.[21] They stormed the world. Because fundamentalists adhered to a literal reading of the Great Commission in Matthew 28:18–20, they streamed into Asia, Africa, the Americas, and even Europe to "make disciples of all nations, baptizing them in the name of the Father and of the Son and of the Holy Spirit." By 1952, half of the 18,500 North American Protestant missionaries came from evangelical agencies.[22]

They could do so, in part, as Cold War America extended its reach into Asia. Unlike the British Empire, Cold War America extended global influence through its image as a nonimperial power and as a democracy espousing racial equality. Eisenhower encouraged everyday Americans to forge close ties, including religious friendships, with people in noncommunist Asia as a way of bridging racial and national differences.[23] For white fundamentalists, close ties entailed proclamation of the gospel. People-to-people diplomacy aligned with the heart-to-heart encounters required of the work of conversion, which fundamentalists had already prioritized. Eisenhower's vision for cultural diplomacy merely amplified what white fundamentalists had already longed for in their embrace of noncommunist Asians—to bring them into their fold.

At this time, "parachurches" were key—one cannot understand modern US evangelicalism without parachurches. They expose the movement's DNA in terms of its structural foundation, boundary-making work, and theological impulse. "The organizational structures that house the throbbing heart of evangelicalism are not denominations at all," Nathan Hatch argues, "but the special purpose parachurch agencies that sometimes seem as numberless as the stars in the sky."[24] "Parachurch" describes interdenominational, voluntary evangelical networks that conduct missionary and humanitarian work *alongside* churches.[25] In 1950, as a white fundamentalist, Graham used his parachurch to introduce a new brand of global evangelicalism during a time when old denominational structures were flagging.[26]

Most studies of modern US evangelicalism have tended to study parachurches within a nation-state frame, but these organizations are mostly global or aim to be global, as historians are increasingly showing.[27] Indeed, as this book shows, some of the largest parachurches responsible for the making of late twentieth-century evangelicalism had transpacific beginnings.[28] Such voluntary networks embodied the evangelical activist impulse hearkening back to the eighteenth century.[29] Since its origins in the eighteenth century, evangelicalism had been a diffuse and borderless network that spanned national and linguistic borders. Without a pope to send doctrinal orthodoxy down a chain of command, the network centered around key charismatic leaders as well as the masses. Eighteenth-century evangelicalism had coherence and power even then as a religion of the heart in the age of the Enlightenment because it was the religion of the people. Revivals were key meeting grounds. Revivalistic texts and testimonies were pivotal sources.

Just as eighteenth-century evangelicalism cannot be understood without a transatlantic frame, only a transpacific frame, as I show, can reveal the forces that empowered twentieth-century evangelicals. In the 1950s, stepping confidently into the hotbeds of the global Cold War, a new generation of white fundamentalists built evangelistic networks with South Korean Protestants. They did so in part by aligning with the new US military and political project to save the world from communism, which only magnified their world vision, altering religion and politics on both continents.

But the religious "crusaders" in this story were crusaders because they were religious in a particular way. When they acted in the political arena, they first desired to form an empire of the Spirit—even as their religious ideas became entangled with the politics of nation-states. To say as much is not to provide an apologia for their politics, but to clarify one of their key tools: the power of their religious ideas, no matter how muddled or misdirected they seem to critics. Had these religious "crusaders" operated with different ideas—say, primarily feminist theologies—would this story be sung to a different tune? Yes. It is the strong hold of religious ideas on both sides of the Pacific that makes this story possible—the Great Commission, or the evangelization of the world, was an indispensable religious impulse that propelled this story.[30]

Moreover, South Korean Protestants were not "duped" by white hot-gospelers and cold warriors. The Koreans, no less than the Americans, envisioned a future marked by world evangelization. They latched onto Cold War expansionism and white-led evangelicalism and used them for their own vision of a Korea-centered Christian empire. As Nami Kim argues, missionary forms of Korean Christianity cannot be understood merely as "western export" or "indigenous response free from global power structures."[31] The following is a "betwixt and between" narrative, as it exceeds the binary of accommodation versus resistance. Americans and Koreans both wanted to change the world, particularly when war linked them in a permanent and shape-shifting network. Billy Kim and Billy Graham, standing before more than a million people in 1973, hint at the force of a transpacific network, signifying the rise of the US evangelical empire *and* the changing face of world Christianity, in the context of an ongoing war.

The Rise of US Evangelical Empire and the Korean War (1950–1953)

As most scholars know, "evangelicalism" is difficult to define. The most frequently cited definition is the Bebbington Quadrilateral, upheld by the following four pillars: first, *conversionism*, the belief that lives need to be changed, one must turn away from sin toward Christ in faith and through repentance; second, *activism*, expressing the gospel in vigorous effort, including, but not limited to, evangelism; third, *biblicism*, revering the Bible as the Word of God, the source of all spiritual truth, some may believe in its infallibility and inerrancy; fourth, *crucicentrism*, the cross and substitutionary atonement are central; Jesus paid the penalty for humanity's sins.[32]

Yet, historically, "evangelicalism" is pluriform, paradoxical, and fractured—at once unified and diverse; tradition-bound yet adaptive to culture. Some have used the metaphor of "patchwork quilt" or "kaleidoscope" to describe the diversity embedded in evangelicalism.[33] Others distinguish between "religious" and "political" evangelicalism to create a sharp line between those who identify with it as a faith tradition versus those who use it as a politically expedient tool.[34]

"Evangelical" is also often synonymous with white evangelicals, the US Christian Right, Trump followers, and white Christian nationalists. Though the conflation between "evangelical" with Republican or white supremacist politics tends to break down when factoring in race, the US evangelical Left, and global evangelicals, scholars are also simultaneously careful to highlight the whiteness embedded in "evangelicalism," as the term has escaped racialization for too long.[35] As Anthea Butler argues: "Racism is a feature, not a bug, of American evangelicalism."[36] Thus, scholars studying nonwhite evangelicals have distinguished the unique social location that their subjects inhabit compared to white evangelicals.[37] As Janelle Wong shows, contemporary Asian American evangelicals overlap in their politics with white evangelicals on abortion and same-sex marriage, but not on race and immigration.[38] Still others argue that, especially in the wake of the 2016 and 2020 elections, "evangelical" as a moniker and movement is comatose and should not be revived, all the more so as it is intertwined with white supremacy and militant masculinity.[39] As seen, "evangelical" is a polysemic term, employed in multiple contexts, though it is often used as a monosemic term.

Race for Revival takes a snapshot of evangelical America and South Korean Christianity from 1950 to 1980, with a transpacific Cold War lens. Herein, evangelicalism is a movement on the move, a shape-shifting network based in transnational one-on-one relationships that have religious, racial, and political consequences.[40] Furthermore, *Race for Revival* examines how these networks then went onto shape modern evangelical America into an empire as it reveals how white and nonwhite people built its global infrastructure, but with varying degrees of ownership. Indeed, as this history shows, modern evangelical America was built by many hands—a multiracial and multinational group of people. Yet key segments of it have defended its whiteness, rendering invisible the very people who constructed it and upon whom its vision and mission depend. It is a reflection of the American experiment itself: while the nation was made by the hands and feet of a multiracial and multinational group of people, key constituents insist on its white nationalist character.

Militarized Transpacific Highway

Korea became central to the making of modern evangelical America because the Korean War triggered unprecedented movement across the Pacific between the United States and Korea, which aligned with the evangelical impulse for movement. Following the fall of the Japanese empire, the US military established a permanent presence in Korea, while expanding a Cold War regime throughout Asia, which increased US Protestant access to Korea.[41] By 1953, a "stable cold-war structure" was in place throughout East Asia, including an "anticommunism-pro-Americanism structure." That structure supported anticommunist autocracies, stalled the post–World War II decolonization process, and constructed East Asian subjectivities "heavily colored by the favor of American influences."[42] With the end of Japanese imperialism, the "cold war mediated old colonialism and new imperialism" through US military expansion into East Asia.[43]

Scholars and practitioners have often depicted the rise of evangelical Christianity in South Korea with a wonder akin to the way scholars describe the economic "miracle of the *han*." But on a more mundane level, evangelicals succeeded in South Korea in part because, as Christina Klein notes, in the 1940s and 1950s, "hundreds of thousands of Americans flowed into Asia . . . as soldiers, diplomats, foreign aid workers, missionaries. . . . Never had American influence reached so far and so wide into Asia and the Pacific."[44] Just as war bound together the United States and the Philippines, so too the United States and South Korea became permanently inseparable.[45]

The war created and fortified a militarized highway across the Pacific Ocean. Ideas, goods, and people traveled in both directions on this *militarized transpacific highway*. While the Cold War's duration, geographical breadth, and geopolitical import varied from region to region, in the Asia-Pacific, the Cold War "resulted in real wars and in the destruction of communities at the grass-roots level."[46] The body count was devastating. Between 1950 and 1953, South Korea suffered 1,312,836 casualties and 415,004 deaths. North Korea sustained more than 1.5 million casualties, including about one million civilians and 520,000 soldiers. In total, 36,940 Americans died in Korea. About four million people lost their lives, half of whom were civilians, exceeding the proportion of civilian deaths in both World War II and the Vietnam War.

Though white Protestant missionaries had traveled to Korea since the late nineteenth century, twentieth-century fundamentalists, unlike their predecessors, followed US military routes. White fundamentalists traveled to Korea for evangelistic and humanitarian reasons, and Koreans traveled to the United States as part of post–Korean War immigration. Migration across the Pacific was highly intertwined with the US military presence in Korea. Thus, during the Asian exclusion era, a limited number of Koreans, especially orphans, military brides, and students with connections to US soldiers were granted permission to immigrate to the United States.

Among the first to see the potential of these militarized routes of connection were white and South Korean Protestants. South Korean evangelists Kyung Chik Han (1902–2000), Billy Jang Hwan Kim, Joon Gon Kim (1925–2009), and the World Vision Korean Orphan Choir traveled to the United States.[47] White evangelists, including Bob Pierce (1914–1978), Billy Graham, and Bill Bright (1921–2003) traveled to Korea on this militarized transpacific highway—they were only some of the best-known figures among a host of others. These American evangelists and South Korean Protestants traveled back and forth on this bloodstained highway with the dream of evangelizing the world.

World Vision was established in Korea in 1950, just months after the outbreak of the Korean War. Its initial aim was to provide emergency relief and aid for Koreans and to help meet the material needs of widows, orphans, and the impoverished. But its founders also sought Korean converts. They helped Graham become acquainted with the Korean peninsula when he traveled there for the first time during the war in 1952, an experience that prepared the way for the massive crusade two decades later. The BGEA, also founded in 1950, had broad aims, but it hoped to attain them through organized mass evangelistic crusades. Campus Crusade, founded in 1951, sought to attract students, staff, and faculty at colleges and universities. It established early connections to the peninsula by opening its first international chapter in Korea in 1958.

No one was more influential in reviving the moniker "evangelicalism" in modern America than Graham. He was the star who helped transform the American image of "backward" fundamentalists into mainstream and respectable "evangelicals." Campus Crusade and World Vision were also core to that revision. All mid-twentieth-century innovations, these organizations established transpacific networks stretching back to the Korean War, which was key for their global success. Though called the "forgotten war" in US history, remnants of the war remain in US evangelical institutions, which South Koreans helped to build. The modern US evangelical empire was made on the route to US Cold War expansion in Korea. That hidden war story requires exhumation if we are to understand the full meaning of evangelical America.

At the 38th Parallel: Religion, Race, and Politics

For further background, the division of North and South Korea at the 38th parallel rendered Korea's civil war a minitheater in the global war between Soviet communism and American democratic capitalism.[48] The 38th parallel was not only a fault line between two seemingly incommensurable political economies, vying to be the next global superpower; it was also a transpacific racialized and religious fault line. The 38th parallel was and is, in part, a US border insofar as the US military had a forceful hand in drawing it and has remained to defend it. Thus, transnationalism and racialization go hand in hand at the 38th parallel, fueling a process through which modern American evangelicalism became revived at this Korea-US border.

At mid-twentieth century, Eisenhower's Cold War America was dubbed "God's Country," intensely devout with a religious revival across traditions and denominations.[49] The reach of this revival was global, as it dovetailed with a Cold War expansionism that made no postcolonial apologies for intervention in non-US territories. At this time, the rise of Mao Tse-tung in 1949 was detrimental to the US foreign missionary enterprise, as Christian missionaries were ousted from China. South Korean Protestants, however, did not disappoint. The US militarization of Korea in the aftermath of World War II and the onset of the "religious Cold War," thereafter, connected a new generation of white fundamentalists to South Korean Protestants, who were key evangelistic and Cold War allies. Their stalwart anticommunist narratives encouraged white fundamentalists to believe in world evangelization, in spite of emerging critiques from communist and decolonizing nations. These new transpacific networks not only remade institutions that exemplified modern evangelical America but also renewed the racial politics that accompanied their revival.

America's revival as a Christian nation occurred through the Cold War embrace of noncommunist Asia, and in the fire of that war, transpacific racism fueled revival. As scholars have shown, modern evangelical America came to power through a white supremacist process that depended on the subordination and exclusion of Black Americans.[50] *Race for Revival* shows that Koreans' racial erasure, integration, and model minoritization were three key transpacific racialized processes that also propelled a niche and fledgling form of white fundamentalist America into the US evangelical empire. Scholars have studied race and Asian American evangelicals in the contemporary United States, but a historical and transnational frame has not been utilized to understand how the US encounter with Asia transformed evangelical America.

Cold War South Koreans and Race: Erasure, Integration, and Model Minoritization

The South Korean martyr, student, and orphan were three transpacific Christian figures through which the racialized politics of inequality between Cold War South Korea and the United States were mediated, empowering the whiteness that propelled the growth of the US evangelical empire. Mid-twentieth-century white fundamentalists not only engaged in a race for revival against global communism, but also positioned themselves as the race that held the mantle for revival through the racialized and mediating figures of the Korean martyr, student, and orphan. *Race for Revival* shows the crucial role that US fundamentalist, neo-evangelical, and evangelical networks played in circulating and mediating US ideas of race in Korea and Korean America.

As discussed, the Korean War prompted white evangelists such as Bob Pierce and Billy Graham to travel to Asia for the first time. In following their stories across the Pacific, one can see that the origins of World Vision cannot be told without its Korean and Korean War origins, especially the death, or martyrdom, of Kim Ch'anghwa. The story of his wife Paek Okhyŏn, and their pastor, Kyung Chik Han is also key. However, rendered martyrs of religious sacrifice instead of the tragedies of war, their stories were erased from the annals of World Vision history in particular and US evangelical history in general. Forgetful storytelling requires not only a correction to include new narratives, but also an understanding that the US evangelical empire grew by rendering Korean stories invisible.

The Korean War also prompted the second wave of Korean immigration to the United States, where South Korean students forged new networks with white fundamentalists through institutions of higher education in the Jim Crow South and Southern California, namely Bob Jones University, Fuller Theological Seminary, and Campus Crusade. Inhabiting a racially interstitial position in a primarily Black and white racial hierarchy, Joon Gon Kim and Billy Jang Hwan Kim's conversion narratives as student immigrants bridged affective gaps between the Cold War United States and noncommunist Asians, in alignment with Eisenhower's Cold War emphasis on US-Asian integration. Through the costly racial logic of Korean integration, these Christian students' narratives portrayed an image of racial equality in a liberal democracy, even as those American fundamentalist and neo-evangelical institutions maintained a system of racial inequality, in which Black students were excluded and Koreans were divided into "good" and "bad" racialized categories.

These student networks became the basis for massive Korean revivals in the 1970s, but not before these transpacific networks forged in the 1950s had devastating effects, especially upon the children of Korea in the 1960s, as revealed in the World Vision Korean Orphan Choir and individual choristers' stories, such as those of Oh Chiyŏng and Kim Sang Yong, nicknamed "Peanuts." Throughout the 1960s, Korean orphan choristers toured the world, including the United States, and helped listeners, especially white Protestants associated with the "new evangelicalism," to believe they espoused, and *could* espouse, racial democracy through individual financial donations, sponsorships, and the practice of humanitarianism. The intertwining of religion, race, and diplomacy embedded in the image of the World Vision Korean Orphan Choir facilitated the transformation of the image of a new American evangelicalism. Yet, racialized as "models," the paragons of piety, Korean orphans were exploited in the process.

Indeed, Manichaean Cold War logic divided "bad" communist Koreans from "good" noncommunist Koreans at the 38th parallel—so did midtwentieth-century white fundamentalists who made clear divisions between saints and sinners, saved and unsaved. Communism represented godlessness, and to some, North Korea posed an existential threat as the Antichrist.

Anticommunism led to a series of political, theological, and racial binaries—good versus evil, saved versus unsaved, good Asian versus bad Asian, Black freedom versus Asian peace. These deleterious binaries energized anticommunist white fundamentalists to recast their "backward" tradition in alignment with a whiteness that signaled American respectability.

Race for Revival: South Korean Christianity and the Christian Right

At the same time, fulfilling the Great Commission became a process through which South Korean Protestants attempted to thwart evangelical America's rising status as the US evangelical empire by forging their own status as the leaders of a new modern Christian empire. Massive revivals, led by South Korean Protestants, that exceeded the scale of those led by US evangelicals showed outsized growth and attempts to replace US Christian power. Embedded in those South Korean Protestants' large-scale attempts to save souls was a challenge to the US evangelical empire—to replace it as the "new emerging Christian kingdom." Indeed, even as white fundamentalists' and neo-evangelicals' racialized encounters in part revived modern evangelical America, that process also stoked Cold War South Korean Protestants' ethnic nationalist faith in a Korean-centered empire of the Spirit. Cold War South Korean Protestants sought to supersede the US evangelical empire as they advanced their own vision for global evangelization to higher heights. With a staggering power imbalance between the United States and South Korea, Cold War South Korean Protestants' choices were highly circumscribed. Yet they were not mere props or victims in the face of US Cold War power: they colluded and negotiated with it, seeking to also supersede it.

So, then, what of South Korean agency? Amid war, national division, US Cold War expansionism, and racialized encounters with a new generation of American evangelicals, to what extent were South Korean Protestants in charge of crafting their own lives and stories? How do scholars take them seriously as historical actors? To address these questions, an overview of Korean religious history and the debate over local agency versus cultural imperialism, as it pertains to Korean Christianity, is helpful.

Korea is historically a religiously diverse nation, with a deep Buddhist and Confucian past and present. As the "very model of religious pluralism," the contemporary South Korean religious landscape consists of Buddhists

(25.3 percent), Protestants (19.8 percent), Catholics (7.4 percent), Confucians (0.3 percent), Won Buddhists (0.21 percent), and others (0.75 percent); the remaining report no religious affiliation.[51] In particular, the Christian growth in the twentieth century is a notable outlier in Asia, as South Korea developed into the most Protestant nation in the region. Christianity first entered Korea in the eighteenth century through Catholicism, which faced persecution due to strict neo-Confucian governance, resulting in thousands of martyrs. In the late nineteenth century, American Protestants found more traction in planting their religion in Korea, significantly shifting the religious landscape of Korea. The adoption of Korean Protestantism at high rates can be explained through the indigenization process as well as the nationalist use of Protestantism, including to protest Japanese imperialism.

In 1884, when the first American Protestant missionaries, including Presbyterian Horace Allen and Methodist Henry Appenzeller, landed in Korea, they were successful in converting Koreans, in part because of the support of King Kojong of the Choson dynasty. As well, the Nevius method emphasized Korean self-rule, self-propagation, and self-initiation.[52] Koreans helped to translate the term "God" into the Korean language as *Hananim*, and they modified ancestor worship rituals and ideas about shamanistic demonology to Korean Protestantism, to make it their own tradition. The Pyongyang revivals (1905–1907) marked a watershed moment as Koreans formed their own practices, such as *t'ongsŏng kido* (audible prayer in unison) and *saebyŏk kido* (dawn prayer), both well-known traditions today.[53]

Protestantism also gained esteem in Korea as it was used for nationalism and anti-imperialism. Soon after the Pyongyang revivals, Japan colonized Korea (1910–1945), enforcing Shinto as the religion of the peninsula. After 1938, Korean Christians were forced to worship at Shinto shrines, in tandem with the empire's larger vision for the Japanization of its colonies: it suppressed Korean and promoted the Japanese language, changed personal names from Korean to Japanese, and recruited Koreans into the Japanese military, and the Japanese Shinto priesthood acted as missionaries to its Korean colony.[54] Yet a significant segment of the Korean independence movement leaders used their Christian faith to protest imperial rule—of the thirty-three signatories of the March First Movement for Independence, half were Protestants.[55]

By comparison, modern Japan had neither experienced explosive Protestant growth nor used it as a means for nation building. With the opening of Japan to the West, and in the midst of the national instability with the end of the Tokugawa government, Christianity seemed to gain greater footing in Japan. But with the rise of the Meiji empire, Shintoism dominated the nation's collective consciousness, spurring nationalism and modernization. Seen as a Western religion, and at times castigated as evil, Christianity remained of little interest, adhered to by about 1 percent of Japan's population. With the arrival of the US occupation forces upon the Japanese empire's World War II defeat, there was some greater interest in Christianity, as General MacArthur encouraged an increased missionary presence, but Christians still never exceeded 1 percent of the nation.[56]

Koreans, instead, made Protestantism their own. To be sure, Christianity in the non-Western world in general, and in Korea in particular, has been critiqued as a source of cultural imperialism, a "colonization of consciousness."[57] At the same time, the field of world Christianity has had a long-standing conversation about the force of local agency among non-Western Christians in general and Korean Christians in particular. Stressing non-Western Christians' power to translate Christianity into their own contexts, scholars have argued against the cultural imperialism thesis, positing Christianity as a global movement with multiple centers of power.[58] Historians have argued that early Korean Protestantism, in particular, was a hybrid form of "Korean religious cultures, Chinese Protestantism, and Anglo-American Protestantism," and a "third way" representing a uniquely Korean form of Christianity.[59] Even in the Cold War era, South Korean Protestants cannot be reduced to Western puppets and automatons.

Cold War South Korean Protestants were not mere pawns of US empire because they brought their own nationalist vision to supersede US Christian dominance through organizing massive revivals—in a race for revival against the United States.[60] In the Cold War era, South Korean Christianity "exploded" from less than 5 percent to nearly 20 percent of the population by 1980, a phenomenon that reflects the long evangelical inflection of Korean Christianity.[61] But it needed to be reinvented with every generation. Highlighting Cold War South Korean Protestants as full-fledged historical actors shows they contended with national inequalities by employing a revivalistic form of Christianity as a strategy for their ascendancy in the world order. Even as they allied with the US evangelical empire, they also sought to oust it through the power of their own nationalist version of Korean evangelical Protestantism, which was "explosive" in its fervor and reach. They saw their nationalist faith in Korean ascendancy realized through revivals hosted throughout the 1970s, including the 1973 Billy Graham Crusade, Explo '74, and the 1980 World Evangelization Crusade. US evangelists like Graham and Bright increasingly saw Korea as an evangelistic center to which they would need to submit their attention, resources, and power.

At the same time, South Korean Protestants were not free global agents, unencumbered by US empire, either. They were ultimately entangled historical subjects. South Koreans would go on to send out the most missionaries per capita in the world, rendering them a powerhouse in the Christian missionary world, but they would still contend with US race and imperialism. In the study of "reverse missions"—the non-Western effort to evangelize the West—Korean missionaries have sought to influence America, but their efforts have been circumscribed.[62] Korean missionaries in the United States wield a distinctly Korean faith, but their intention to convert white Americans, seen as the most prized of converts, is largely fruitless, because as immigrants they cannot overcome the US racial hierarchy.[63] These findings provide an empirical basis for what Jehu Hanciles has concluded: "*While non-Western Christians now represent the face and future of global Christianity,*" due to prevailing attitudes of Western superiority, "*the church in the non-Western world does not yet constitute its main driving force.*"[64]

In the 1970s, South Korean Protestants' nationalistic vision for revival was ultimately threatened by the transnational antidemocratic politics with which they were intertwined. South Korean Protestants' nationalistic revivals, throughout the 1970s, centered individual conversion as the primary mode for social change in the nation. In so doing, their faith activities opened them up to antidemocratic politics in both the United States and South Korea, forging a transpacific Christian Right. The South Korean Protestant Right had its "earliest activation" during US military rule from 1945 to 1948, when Protestants and communists were pitted against each other.[65] The South Korean Protestant Right of the 1990s echoed the fundamentalism of the US Christian Right in its emphasis on biblical inerrancy, anxieties over gender and sexuality, and the synchronicity in the founding of major conservative organizations in both nations, such as the Christian Council of Korea and the Christian Coalition of America, founded by Pat Robertson.[66] *Race for Revival* highlights the connections between US and South Korean evangelical conservativism. The evangelical surge in Cold War South Korea planted the seeds for the rise of the South Korean Protestant Right, even reinforcing US evangelical politics.

The war brought new racial dynamics, diplomatic maneuvering, and conservative politics and religion, and these, in turn, lifted World Vision, the

BGEA, and Campus Crusade onto the global stage. It also stoked Cold War South Korean Protestants' aspirations for ascendancy.

To study the organizations and to locate them in their global setting is to recognize that this influence has never flowed in only one direction.[67] In the Pacific world, as in the Atlantic, influence moved both ways, however unevenly.[68] US Cold War expansionism reached into the Asia-Pacific partly through religious agencies; but at least in the instance of South Korea, they used the same agencies to reach back. Yet, without the cessation of war, South Koreans remained entangled in American political demands, even as they sought to use religion to circumvent that power. Insofar as that project was embroiled in antidemocratic politics of Korean authoritarianism and its connections to the US Christian Right, they fought a battle for the souls of the world that continued to relegate them to a subordinated status. Without an end to the unending "forgotten war," attempts to rise in the ranks of the world left their goals unfulfilled. The religious Cold War not only compelled South Korean Protestants to build bigger revivalistic movements to outpace the US evangelical empire, but also entangled them in its inner workings.

Ultimately, the evangelical America they helped to create imagined a small space for them to inhabit in the hinterlands of its empire. World Vision was never seen as founded by Han, Campus Crusade's Korean history was usually lost, and the BGEA never reveals it was made by the masses. As "multinational corporations," they mimicked the capitalist structure in which the metropole extracts resources from the periphery, without giving credit where credit is due. The Cold War South Korean Protestant vision for social change, as rooted in individual conversions alone, proved to undermine their creative contributions to modern evangelical America. Yet remembering the stories on the underside of this transpacific past may serve as a corrective, for in telling a forgotten and erased past, scholars and practitioners may imagine a new future.

The Transpacific Turn

What follows is part of a broader historiographical effort that has directed professional historians toward a transnational turn in American history.[69] *Race for Revival* questions the predisposition to narrate the history of modern American evangelicalism with a nation-bound focus.[70] At the same time, it also resists a nation-bound approach to South Korean Protestantism, as "We must understand every dimension of American life as entangled in other histories. Other histories are implicated in American history, and the United Sates is implicated in other histories."[71] In this vein, the story I tell is not a history of US-South Korean relations, but a transpacific history of American religion.[72]

To tell this story, I have conducted archival research and oral histories in English and Korean in the United States and South Korea.[73] A bilingual and binational approach to the topic is illuminating partly because in much of American religious history—and the history of Christianity—Korean names appear only in passing and rarely as the main subjects of study. Especially in the Western academy, the transnational South Korean Protestant stands at the edges of these historical accounts, even when they treat evangelicalism. I uncover these historical figures who have crossed the Pacific, and I place them squarely in the narrative of American religious history. They are not merely blips on the historian's radar but active agents in the making of US religious history. They were historical figures who conserved and contested the US institutions of which they were an indelible part. Many of the archival sources that inform my story have never before been used in either Korean- or English-language scholarship, largely because until now much of the history of Korean Christianity in English and in Korean has been a story of the late nineteenth and early twentieth centuries or of Japanese colonialism. Fewer works have covered the late twentieth century, and even fewer the parachurch institutions.

Transpacific history is concerned with "transnational processes, persons, and events within and across the Pacific Ocean" and tends to bridge "two or more conventional fields, including histories of the American West, US immigration and ethnicity, US diplomatic and international relations, Asian American Studies, East Asian Studies and Pacific Islander studies."[74] This emerging area of research takes seriously the assessment that the United States is a Pacific as well as Atlantic civilization.[75] In this view, the United States is not merely an ever-expanding frontier but also "an island surrounded by lands north and south, but also oceans, east and west. As an island, unlike the imagined insularity of the agrarian tradition and frontier hypothesis, the US must be viewed properly as a center with its own integrity but also as a periphery and a fluid space of movements and engagements that resist closure and inevitable or final outcomes."[76] The United States becomes one island among many others in the Pacific, a perspective that diminishes narratives of US exceptionalism and dominance and instead creates an analytical framework for bringing to the fore historical figures otherwise left invisible, including those who are on the receiving end of the postwar US empire in the Asia-Pacific region.[77]

At the same time, to write transpacific religious history is also to engage in an implicit critique of Orientalism and an unmasking of inequalities. The task of transpacific American religious history is not merely the acknowledgment of unrecognized historical actors, or even a geographic turn, but more fundamentally an understanding of the conditions of inequality that have rendered these subjects invisible in history. In so doing, this book takes the "Orientalism before Asian America" perspective seriously, and in the process takes up transnational modern Korean history and Korean religious history as a core part of that retelling of the past.[78] Such a transpacific approach has largely been absent in studies of America's past, including its religious past.

Puritans fleeing the state Church of England have occupied center stage for more than a century, with a corresponding interest in an Atlantic-facing Protestant narrative.[79] Though historians have suggested alternative tropes, few have redirected the "spatial vector" toward the Pacific. "All that most of us know and learn about American religion," writes Laurie Maffly-Kipp, "keeps us firmly moored in an east-to-west framework, and the farther west we go, the less important the religious events seem to become, in part because the vast majority of us know much less about them."[80] In her seminal essay "Eastward Ho! American Religion from the Perspective of the Pacific Rim," Maffly-Kipp calls for a Pacific turn in the field of American religious history, a turn that will bring us, by incremental steps, closer to a "world history of American religion."[81]

The field of American religious history, however, may have proceeded in far too incremental a fashion. For it is not only the South Pacific islands and their interchanges with the United States that remain understudied.[82] Histories of American religion have privileged European American and Judeo-Christian subjects sometimes because the original sources have seemed more copious and accessible.[83] At the same time, religion has not been a primary category of analysis for transpacific historians. It is possible that histories of Asian Americans have tended to neglect religious subjects because many authors have been influenced by a Marxist labor history, which has little use for religion. Yet since the late twentieth century, an interdisciplinary group of intellectuals has criticized the separation of Asian American histories and histories of US religions.[84]

Original sources are more readily available and allow us to look at religious histories within Asian homelands, to discern transnational connections, and to understand better the history of American Orientalism. What would it look like for scholars to read historical figures from the Pacific Rim and the Asia-Pacific as central to the making of American religious history? How might the history appear when historians set their gaze on the Asia-Pacific before returning it to America? How would this change the story of America's religious past?

US evangelical parachurches were an outgrowth of the "other Cold War," a war that persists today.[85] The unending Korean War, which paused in an armistice in 1953 and not a peace treaty, has left a transpacific fault line that animates US evangelicalism today. It is no accident that Billy Kim and Franklin Graham, Billy Graham's son and the current head of the BGEA, were planning for yet another crusade, or "festival," for Seoul in 2020, had it not been for the Covid-19 global pandemic.[86] US evangelicals and South Korean Protestants seek still to "win over" North Korea as a necessary step in the evangelization of the world. Transpacific networks still elevate the hope of Christianizing the world, a hope that has religious and political consequences. This book investigates a hidden history, but its traces surround all of us.

1

Martyrs

War and World Vision, 1950–1953

World Vision is an organization that began with the idea of Kyung Chik Han (1902–2000), which Bob Pierce (1914–1978) then incorporated into a 501(c)(3).[1] Two months before the outbreak of the Korean War—traditionally, recorded as June 25, 1950—Han, a northern Korean Presbyterian minister, met Pierce, a white evangelist from the fundamentalist Sun Belt, in the southern region of Korea. Pierce had formative transpacific encounters as a missionary in China, but his alliance forged with Han, annealed in the fire of war, was arguably the most impactful in his career, as Han bequeathed to him the idea to create a large evangelical humanitarian organization. Though Pierce carried greater national status as a representative from the "big brother" nation of the United States, Han, a pastor twelve years his senior—a significant marker of rank in Confucian societies—tutored Pierce in the business of evangelical humanitarian care.[2]

Korea was indispensable for the revival of modern US evangelical institutions like World Vision. Yet World Vision's founding is usually solely attributed to Pierce. World Vision's origins in Korean creativity and suffering is a largely forgotten story. Along with that memory loss, the history of war—the Korean War origins of World Vision—has been underanalyzed in the organization's founding narrative.[3] That forgetful storytelling was core to the formation of the modern US evangelical empire. This chapter corrects that oversight, narrating the rise of World Vision through the inconvenient history of Cold War America's entanglements with Korean people in a war turned "hot," unspeakably bloody and tragic, on Korean soil.

In Seoul, Han and Pierce preached revivals and engaged in humanitarian work that drew thousands of Koreans. Han and Pierce sought to care for Korean Protestant martyrs' families, especially Kim Ch'anghwa's and Paek Okhyŏn's, the inaugural family that World Vision financially sponsored. The blood shed by Kim Ch'anghwa, his martyrdom, sowed the seeds for the creation of World Vision. Thus, World Vision's origins were connected to the rise of world Christianity in the non-Western world, especially in Korea. Pierce leaned on Han's ideas and Kim's sacrifice to make his Christian humanitarian vision a reality. Thus, highlighting the story of Korean Protestants like Han Kyung Chik, Paek Okhyŏn, and Kim Ch'anghwa modifies the myth that World Vision was created by one white man and reveals how much Pierce needed them. So indebted was Pierce to Korea that, even at the end of his life, when he had contracted leukemia, he painfully longed to be buried in South Korea, with Han at the helm of his funeral. Han persuaded him to be buried in California and spoke at his funeral.[4]

However, World Vision was built upon a troubling paradox. The US militarization of Korea in the aftermath of World War II, and the onset of the "religious Cold War" thereafter, connected a new generation of white fundamentalists to the peninsula, which not only remade institutions that would exemplify modern evangelical America, but also renewed the racial politics that accompanied its rise as a religious phenomenon. As mentioned, World Vision expanded into the BGEA. After Eisenhower's election as president in November 1952, Han, Pierce, and Paek spent Christmas in Korea with Graham, who, with the Pentagon's support and accompanied by Youth for Christ (YFC) friends Grady Wilson and David Morton, traveled across the Pacific for the first time. Graham's preaching at the Korean War battlefront was a key cultural force that helped to sacralize whiteness on South Korean soil through nonstate transpacific networks, linking white Jesus, white soldier, and white evangelist.

As a result, while Korean Protestants founded and built World Vision and were glorified for doing so, they were simultaneously erased, their narratives and faces nowhere to be seen in the organization's origins. Indeed, Pierce's and Han's reliance on the superiority of the salvific power of the American Cold War state short-circuited the full effect of the transnational, intimate, and existential exchanges between two men from vastly different worlds. When Pierce translated what he saw in Korea to a white audience in the United States, as in his film *Dead Men on Furlough*, he regrettably mistranslated the story of Kim Ch'anghwa and his wife Paek Okhyŏn, representing them as flat characters who perpetuated racial stereotypes about Asians. Kim Ch'anghwa's death was rendered Christian martyrdom with little acknowledgment of the tragedy of war. Han was also made a martyr as he was erased from this film, nowhere to be seen in the image of the emerging US evangelical empire, which World Vision would help to build.

A new generation of white fundamentalists and Korean Protestants transnationally remade evangelical America through conserving American ideas of race and politics, which relied on both the glorification and the martyrdom of non-Western, nonwhite Korean Protestants. Accordingly, this story adds to the study of US empire building during the Korean War, accounts of which have primarily focused on the Cold War origins of international adoption, transracial global families, immigrant Korean GI wives, and US military prostitutes.[5] Though underanalyzed, Protestantism was an ever-present connective tissue, a transpacific force of cultural diplomacy, that mediated US–South Korean Cold War relations.[6] White-led US fundamentalism transformed into the US evangelical empire, in part, because it held growing cultural and diplomatic power in the Asia-Pacific in general and in Korea in particular.

World Vision's Korean Founder: Kyung Chik Han

Pierce is widely known as the founder of World Vision. However, his daughter Marilee Pierce Dunker named Kyung Chik Han as its progenitor. She recalls: "Pastor Han was already doing the work of World Vision when my dad met him, and Pastor Han was someone who showed my father how to meet the practical needs of the hungry and homeless and the widows and the orphans." Having had a near death experience while living abroad in the United States, Han had used this experience to serve the disadvantaged in northern Korea. When Han was a pastor at Second Sinuiju Presbyterian Church, he met Bok Soon, an orphaned child who had lost one of her legs. Inspired by her story, he created *Borinwŏn*, a home for orphans, which launched his lifelong social welfare ministry.[7] He also created a *kyŏngnowŏn* (community center for the elderly).[8]

Amid the war, and in the southern region of Korea, Han continued to translate these social welfare ministries into Tabitha *mojawŏn*, or Tabitha Widow's Home, established for families whose male head of household was martyred during the war.[9] Han recalled: "During the Korean War . . . so-called fatherless families came into being more in the church. As they lost their husbands, the church had to take care of them, that is, widows."[10] Pierce Dunker remarked that when Pierce arrived during the war, "Pastor Han had already begun the arduous task of organizing the church to feed, clothe and care for the homeless and the widows and the orphans."[11] Han showed Pierce how to connect US resources to war-torn Korea. Pierce Dunker concluded: "So, you see, my father's vision to engage the world . . . to provide for the needs of those who have not, my father received his education about how to do that from Pastor Han."[12]

Pierce came to Korea with Christian American ideas of heroism and rescue. But he also encountered seasoned Korean Protestants like Han, whom he described as a "Korean saint," a spiritual role model, whose "depth of patience" he marveled at, and who he observed "hour upon hour." He studied Han "tirelessly" evangelizing, ministering "to the multitudes," caring for "men's souls irregardless of their station in life," and showing "mercy to refugees."[13] Han tutored Pierce in evangelical humanitarianism, laying the groundwork for World Vision.

Pierce also described Han as a man of "slight stature." As he juxtaposed Han's grand faith, which would "stagger any clergyman I know in America," with his smaller physical build, Pierce painted Han in extremes, romanticizing his faith as exceptional, placing him on a pious pedestal, in stark contrast with his diminutive body. Indeed, US Protestants like Pierce looked to Han with admiration, as he was "an early sign of the evolving relationships between the two groups," in which Americans "increasingly looked to Korean Christianity as a source to revitalize their own institutions and congregations at home."[14] But that desire to emulate also entangled him in a paradoxical process of Korean glorification and erasure that would haunt Han and Pierce's alliance, and therefore, the founding of World Vision.

For further background, Kyung Chik Han emerged out of the lineage of Protestantism in northern Korea. Born and raised on a farm near Pyongyang, he attended a church founded in 1907 by Samuel Moffett (*Mapo Samyul*), an early American Presbyterian missionary to Korea. As Han grew up under Japanese colonialism (1910–1945), he was raised to use Protestantism for Korean nation building. Han attended Osan High School, which was known for its nationalist leaders, including Cho Mansik, the school's principal. Yi Sŭnghun, another Korean independence leader, was a key teacher and role model for Han. Han vividly remembered how Yi Sŭnghun showed students his wounds from the 105 Persons Incident in December 1911, when he was tortured by the Japanese. When Yi helped lead the March First Movement for Independence in 1919, the Japanese government burned down Osan High School.[15]

Han went on to Soongsil College in Pyongyang, where Moffett was president. While Han initially studied science, he had a transformative spiritual experience that shifted his interest to theology. Contemplating his future near the ocean at Hwanghae Do, he pondered what he could do for his nation, at which point he stopped to pray. He reported hearing a divine voice urging him to shift his educational focus: "If I want to serve my country's people, rather than science, I need to, more fundamentally, devote my life to help revive their mind and spirit."[16] He decided to study theology, in part as a tool for national uplift. Yun Chi'ho (1865–1945) helped Han with the fees to travel across the Pacific, and he studied education and religion at the College of Emporia in Kansas. After receiving his master of divinity at Princeton Theological Seminary (1926–1929), he had hoped to attend Yale for his doctoral studies, but he shed those dreams when he caught tuberculosis, spending two years in a Presbyterian sanatorium in Albuquerque, New Mexico.

Upon returning to northern Korea, which was still occupied by the Japanese, he became a pastor at the Second Presbyterian Church of Sinuiju.[17] Eventually, with the outbreak of the Korean War, Han would meet Pierce, who traveled to South Korea in the spring of 1950. They preached in the cities of Pusan, Taegu, and Seoul, and Han helped translate his sermons and Bible studies from English into Korean. They reportedly attracted hundreds of people. They often preached open-air revivals, including at Namdaemun Park in Seoul.[18] To understand the historical forces that led to the unlikely meeting of the two men, which would transform modern evangelical America, one must understand the larger backdrop of war.

The Historical Backdrop of Korean Nationalism, Division, and War

In 1945, Japan surrendered. As Koreans shed the shackles of colonialism, they rid the nation of Shintoism, such that "nothing remain[ed] of Shinto" in Japan's former colonies.[19] Though the 1919 March First Movement for Independence had begun to lay a foundation for a movement for Korean sovereignty, most Koreans could only imagine their liberation. So few had expected to actually see their liberation that some Koreans actively collaborated with the Japanese, finding favor in their eyes, and with it elevated status, even as their fellow Koreans suffered the empire's brutality. With the end of the empire, those Korean collaborators experienced a reversal of fortune, now being deemed traitors. Those who had protested the lure of empire and its privileges, even engaging in the most public forms of protest, were rewarded respect as nationalists, and they rose to the ranks of leadership in postcolonial Cold War Korea as they jockeyed for national power. These leaders included Kim Il-sung and Syngman Rhee, both part of the Korean provisional government during the imperial period.

Kim Il-sung and Syngman Rhee had divergent ideas about national leadership for postcolonial Cold War Korea. Whereas Kim pursued a vision aligned with international socialism, Rhee pursued one aligned with international democratic capitalism. Some scholars have seen Rhee's and Kim's adoption of these divergent worldviews as evidence that they were puppet leaders, manipulated by the United States and Soviet Union. Though this point has been extended to scholarship that rendered the Korean War as nothing more than a proxy war for the United States and Soviet Union, Bruce Cumings strongly critiqued this position, viewing the war as rooted in a civil war between forces of revolution and antirevolution, national liberation and reactionary forces, represented respectively by North and South Korea.[20]

Rhee and Kim were influenced by the United States and Soviet Union respectively, but as others have shown, their drive for a unitary nation-state, or ethnic unity, previously thwarted by the 1945 division of the nation, was a key factor in the outbreak of war. The North's and the South's respective desire to liberate the other from foreign powers, whether US or Soviet, with the goal being national unity; thus, ousting those "black sheep" deemed national traitors was a core impetus for war within a relatively ethnically homogeneous nation.[21] As Gi Wook Shin writes: "Seen in this way, the Korean War was a war of national liberation of fellow nationals from foreign powers and their collaborators for *both* Kim and Rhee."[22]

But, of course, the two superpowers cannot be ignored in the matrix of the causes of the Korean War. As Korean leaders debated the direction of the nation, with large differences surrounding Kim Il-sung and Syngman Rhee, the United States and Soviet Union also intervened in 1945. As a result of the 1945 Potsdam Conference, Korea was divided at the 38th parallel, with the Soviet Union and the United States taking respective control of the northern and southern regions. By 1948, two separate nations were created: the Democratic People's Republic of Korea in the North and the Republic of Korea in the South. Korean War novelist Susan Choi writes:

When each nation set about establishing a Korean government under its own auspices, on its own terms, and in its own zone, the thirty-eighth parallel ceased to be a line and became a border, and soon was not only a border, but one made of mirrors. Each Korean government claimed sole legitimacy. Each noted that it was sovereign over the entire peninsula, and that its borders coincided with those that had always been Korea's. Being made to disappear in this way, the line revealed itself as entrenched.[23]

The polarizing beliefs among Korean nationalists—those espousing international socialism versus capitalist democracy—were exacerbated by the intervention and military presence of the two rival superpowers that represented those worldviews, the United States and the Soviet Union.

When North Korean leader Kim Il-sung, with the support of Stalin, attempted on June 25, 1950, to force North and South Korean reunification, he believed the skirmish would likely last three days, not result in a three-year war. Kim Il-sung and Stalin had not anticipated that the United States, under the auspices of UN authorization, would defend its interests in the Korean civil conflict as one of its first efforts to contain communism in the region. Historically, the United States had few political interests in Korea, the nation sandwiched between China and Japan. In fact, through the Taft-Katsura Agreement (1905), the United States permitted Japan's annexation of Korea in exchange for colonial rule over the Philippines.[24] In the aftermath of World War II, however, the geopolitical landscape of Asia shifted. Thirty-five years of Japanese imperialism in Korea ended, and the United States relinquished colonial rule in the Philippines. The US military then occupied Korea in 1945.

With Mao Tse-tung's 1949 communist triumph in the People's Republic of China, the United States eagerly sought to contain communism through its new military position in South Korea, which moved the Korean civil conflict onto the global stage of the Cold War.[25] Sheila Miyoshi Jager reflects on the significance of Korea in the early days of the global Cold War:

> The former Japanese colony that few had ever heard of and had been on the periphery of America's post-war interests suddenly became the epicenter of America's first armed confrontation against communism. Truman had drawn the line in Korea between freedom and slavery. Haphazardly and fatefully, Korea's local civil war morphed into a war between the centers of power in the post–World War II order.[26]

On April 7, 1950, the US Department of State's Policy Planning Staff issued National Security Council Paper NSC-68, entitled "United States Objectives and Programs for National Security," a top-secret fifty-eight-page report, which was declassified in 1975 and is among the most influential documents drafted by the United States during the Cold War. Its authors argued that one of the most pressing threats confronting the United States was the "hostile design" of the Soviet Union. They concluded that the Soviet threat would soon be augmented by the addition of more weapons, including nuclear weapons. To respond to this threat, NSC-68 argued that the optimal course of action for Truman was a massive buildup of the US military and its weaponry.

Syngman Rhee and Kim Il-sung espoused divergent philosophical and religious commitments. Both Rhee and Kim grew up Christian, though the former remained a Methodist and the latter developed the ideology of *Juche* as his core political and philosophical frame.[27] Where they agreed was in their adamant rejection of state Shintoism. Yet South Korea forged a close relationship between nation building and Protestantism, not unlike the United States. Koreans' use of Protestantism for nation building was formidable in strengthening the tradition's presence in the peninsula. Moreover, Han strongly sided with the model of Western capitalist democracy as a path toward Korean liberation, not only because of his education in the United States but also because of his particular religious commitments. Prior to the outbreak of war, Han had established the Christian Democratic Social Party to defend Christianity and democracy against communist ideals in northern Korea.[28] "Considering our ideology had nothing in common with theirs and none of our members agreed with their socialist ideals," Han recalled, "there was no way for us to not fight them at every step."[29] Han's party, however, was unsuccessful.[30] In November 1945, Korean Protestants clashed violently with the Korean communist army in the North, rendering many a martyr on both sides of the conflict.

Han and his family fled from the northern city of Sinuiju to Seoul. Other northern Korean Protestants followed suit. Amid the waves of southern migration, Korean Christianity's center shifted from the North to the South.[31] By 1968, a majority of the missionary organizations in South Korea—that is, forty-seven out of fifty—had been founded after 1945.[32] "No other mission field, not even Taiwan, is so completely dominated by American Missions," J. Herbert Kane noted.[33] With the United States in South Korea, Protestantism became a connective tissue between the two nations. The power of Protestantism became ever more concentrated in South Korea as the nation came under the influence of the United States. Han translated his religious vision against communism into politics, revivalism, and humanitarianism, activities through which he met Pierce.

New Transpacific Networks: From Bible Belt to Sun Belt and across the Pacific to Asia

The war forged a militarized transpacific highway between the United States and the Asia-Pacific, built not only upon a militaristic foundation but also that of anticommunist faith.[34] Via this highway, anticommunist Protestants in South Korea and white fundamentalists from the US Sun Belt and Bible Belt fused their ideas and practices, with Han and Pierce serving as a prime example. Orientalist fascination, humanitarian interest, and fear marked the US gaze toward the Asia-Pacific at mid-twentieth century. Sunbelt evangelicals, located in California, the "gateway to Asia," were eager to spread the gospel to mitigate the communist threat to their sunny, free world.[35] California's proximity to Asia fueled their anticommunist political fervor and religious anxiety, solidifying a desire to preserve their ideas about religion, race, and free market capitalism.

At this time, anticommunist sentiment was commonplace among Americans and religious Americans in particular. US Catholics, under the leadership of the pope, were among some of the most fervent anticommunists.[36] The meaning of communism and the degree to which it was feared, however, differed among US religious traditions. Liberal Protestant leaders such as Reinhold Niebuhr held communism at arm's length for unjustly manipulating the poor and for failing to "understand the ambiguity of all human virtue and the foolishness of all human wisdom."[37] He critiqued those Christians who professed faith "but claim[ed] [God] too simply as an ally of their purposes." He had the moralism of US secretary of state John Foster Dulles in mind, and he suggested that some Christians, too, were people "who bring evil into the world."[38]

Americans associated with fundamentalism, and the emerging neo-evangelicalism, believed anticommunism was inextricably linked with soul saving.[39] They differentiated themselves from the social gospel orientation of their liberal counterparts and framed soul saving as an alternative to communist (and secular) identity.[40] Moreover, the psychological menace of "Red China" and California's proximity to Asia fueled not only anxiety but also action on the part of white fundamentalists. For instance, while preaching at Church of the Open Door in Pasadena, California, Pierce first heard about the outbreak of the Korean War, after which he rushed preparations to return to Korea.[41] Sunbelt fundamentalists like Pierce traveled to South Korea for evangelism, humanitarianism, and alliance building. They met with American missionaries and soldiers, Korean Protestants and soldiers, as well as US and Korean government officials, to combat communism through Christian conversion.

Unlike modern Judaism or Hinduism, evangelicalism has been, since its eighteenth-century origins, a missionary religion seeking global converts; for twentieth-century fundamentalists like Pierce, ideally the whole world would heed his understanding of faith—that Jesus Christ is the only means to humanity's salvation and freedom from the damnation of sin. When white fundamentalists had seemingly lost in the fundamentalist-modernist controversy, they sought revival not only through domestic but also global allies beyond the US nation-state. Accordingly, movements like YFC, a missionary organization with roots in the fundamentalist strand of the fundamentalist-modernist controversy, remained core for young fundamentalists. In spite of the post–World War II concerns that the evangelical thrust of Western Christianity was, in part, responsible for propagating imperialism, YFC continued to send out missionaries due to its stalwart faith in biblical literalism and, therefore, the literal command to follow the Great Commission to make disciples of all nations.[42]

White fundamentalists who believed their worldview to be universal truth nevertheless sought confirmation that this was so. Global missionary organizations like YFC could not advance their vision without nonwhite partners in the Third World who were interested in their evangelically inflected vision. As they were coming of age and finding their footing, white fundamentalists found in South Korea a glimmer of hope. At mid-century, postcolonial resistance in the Asia-Pacific, including in India, China, North Korea, and North Vietnam against Western Christianity as the handmaiden of imperialism, was an overwhelming force. Yet South Korean Protestants fervently argued for the necessity of fulfilling the Great Commission to evangelize the world. In doing so, they confirmed the validity of white fundamentalists' global cause, but also, perhaps surprisingly, instilled new ideas in white fundamentalists, helping them generate ideas about how to move forward. Not only from the Bible Belt to the Sunbelt, but also across the Pacific, white fundamentalists revived their conservative tradition through partnership with South Korean Protestants. World Vision is a prime example.

While from two different nations, with vast power differentials between them, Han and Pierce shared the belief that the Korean War was a religious war between good and evil. Though relatively unknown pastors, from Seoul and the Sun Belt, Han's and Pierce's vision aligned with Cold War America's faith-based argument against communism, amplifying their power as non-state actors. Once in Seoul, Han, together with twenty-seven other northern Protestant refugees, founded a new church called Young Nak Presbyterian Church.[43] "Young Nak" meant "everlasting joy" and signified their belief that, though they had "lost everything," they still possessed "everlasting joy in Jesus Christ."[44] If the war was a religious war, Han believed that with each new church, the South grew stronger as a nation, and Pierce believed the same.

World Vision's Korean War Origins, 1950

With the emerging global Cold War, the geopolitical landscape of East Asia shifted, and with it, the US missionary presence in the region. In light of the communist triumph in China in 1949, the "communists were kicking everyone out," including Pierce, who was working in China as a YFC missionary.[45] For Pierce, the geopolitics of the emerging Cold War in Asia restricted access to China, but also paved new routes into South Korea. Pierce first traveled to Korea when, in the summer of 1949, Oriental Mission Society missionaries invited him to join them—they believed he knew "how to reach across the pulpit to touch the people."[46]

US dominance was never more powerful in Korea than in the midst of the Korean War. Yet at mid-twentieth century, Koreans were not merely potential converts for white fundamentalists. Korean Protestants had for decades indigenized their tradition, making it their own through revival, ritual, and anti-imperial protest.[47] Pierce basked in the experience of learning Korean Christian practices such as *t'ongsŏng kido* (audible prayer in unison) and *saebyŏk kido* (dawn prayer).[48] He recalled: "Attending those prayer meetings was an indelible experience. These people pray with fervency, with a faith that reaches out and believes God from the moment of a prayer's utterance."[49]

Pierce's vision for revival intensified because of his encounter with Korean Protestants' spirituality. Pierce reflected: "Do you wonder why I have such an overpowering love for these dear people? They are my seniors in the Gospel! They walk with God in a fellowship which I yet long for! To think that they yet cry out so hungrily for more of His power! After I had witnessed some of these things, it was not difficult to believe that there is not a more vigorous church on the face of the earth." In casting Korean Protestant spirituality as more mature and earnest than his, he gained greater hope for a revived church. But his admiration also cast Koreans as exceptional: "No wonder the Koreans, differing from all the Orient, sent missionaries to fellow lands like China. No wonder the Korean church is so staunchly indigenous."[50] Pierce was especially impressed with how Korean Protestants' faith had been proven through "great testing," especially under Japanese imperialism and North Korean communism. He reflected, "No wonder I so constantly found myself feeling embarrassment, as I realized what they had done for the Lord in comparison to the scant service I, and so many of my fellow Christians back in America, have offered in appreciation of Calvary." From the perspective of the work "for the Lord," Pierce believed Korean spirituality to be exemplary for Americans. But that exceptionalism also served as a means of rendering them invisible and martyrs in the eyes of white fundamentalists. At the same time that Pierce genuinely learned from Korean Protestant fervor, the exceptionalist lens through which he viewed them also romanticized their spirituality. But that very dance, between Korean Protestant exceptionalism and white fundamentalists' romanticization of them, sustained the embrace between the two nations.

In spring 1950, Han introduced Pierce to Kim Ch'anghwa, a northern Protestant refugee and elder at his Young Nak church, who helped Pierce lead Bible studies.[51] On June 25, 1950, one month after the outbreak of the Korean War, North Korean communist officials arrested Kim Ch'anghwa. Pierce declared in pamphlets that because he had established a Bible study with him, he was accused of collaborating with "American imperialists," replacing "ancient oriental culture" with the "new Western superstition of Christianity." On August 4, 1950, Kim Ch'anghwa was executed.[52] When pressured to recant his faith publicly, he resisted, with Pierce later recounting that Kim declared: "I do believe that Christ himself and his truth are the hope of the world, and I believe in everything that I taught these young people and I'm willing to die for the hope I have in Christ."[53] Pierce hailed Kim's death a "tragic—yet heroic," a martyr's death. Kim Ch'anghwa martyrdom connected closely with the US fundamentalist vision of Protestantism in terms of the belief that faith could, indeed, call for the sacrifice of one's whole life. Korean martyrdom also served as a first line of Christian defense for Americans who feared the international threat of communism. Kim Ch'anghwa's death triggered Pierce to shortly thereafter, in September 1950, incorporate World Vision as a 501(c)(3), described as "an evangelical inter-denominational missionary service organization meeting emergency world needs through established evangelical missions."[54] Pierce opened a small office in Portland, Oregon, and the work of World Vision began.

Kim Ch'anghwa's death was glorified as martyrdom, but it was undoubtedly also a tragedy. He left behind his wife, Paek Okhyŏn, and their four young daughters (figure 1.1). In January 1951, when North Korean troops pressed harder into the South, Paek Okhyŏn and her four daughters fled the advances of the North Koreans for Pusan, the southernmost city of South Korea. She carried her youngest daughter on her back and held hands with her two middle daughters, while the eldest carried a bundle of

Figure 1.1 Paek Okhyŏn and her four daughters (top left). Paek's husband Kim Ch'anghwa was martyred during the Korean War. This photo is prominently displayed on the first floor of the Korean World Vision office in Seoul.
Source: Photo by author.

coverlets on her back.⁵⁵ With their home now twice demolished because of national division and then war—from Sinuijui to Seoul, and now Pusan—Paek Okhyŏn placed her daughters in an orphanage called Home of Birds while she sold rice cakes on the streets of Pusan.⁵⁶ She found an alternative means of financial survival when she discovered that Han, whose church she had attended in Seoul, had established Tabitha Widows Home for war widows. At Tabitha, Paek Okhyŏn relied on the paternal comfort of her heavenly "Father's house."⁵⁷ The war rendered her dependent on Han's patriarchal hearth.

Kim Duck Hei was also a northern Protestant refugee who resided at Tabitha Widows Home as a result of her husband's martyrdom. She recalled 1946 as a "very blessed" year because her first son, Chul Woong, was born and thirty-five years of Japanese imperialism ended. "We shouted 'hurrah' as loud as we could, filled with unbounded happiness to have our freedom. Even now, the ecstatic scene of that time rises before my sight. . . . But who would have wished our country be divided into two with [the] 38th parallel?" During the war, Kim Duck Hei ultimately became a "heroine" of "a novelistic tragedy." Her husband had left their home to flee from the Communist Party and never returned. The war was a "great wound," and her son Chul Woong became fatherless at the age of four.⁵⁸ Kim Duck Hei and her husband left their home due to religious persecution, much like Kyung Chik Han, Paek Okhyŏn, and Kim Ch'anghwa.

In June 1951, Pierce visited Tabitha Widows Home in Pusan with Han, where he met Paek Okhyŏn and her four daughters. Upon learning of her husband's death, Pierce immediately sponsored Paek Okhyŏn and her daughters for fifteen and then twenty-five dollars per month.⁵⁹ It is unclear if Pierce felt especially eager to commit to them because his association with Kim Ch'anghwa led to his death. What is clear is that he did so in part as a result of Han's request. As Pierce recalls, Han, the pastor of "the largest Presbyterian Church in Korea, was the first to ask me, 'Can you find someone in America to sponsor some of the widows and orphans that my church is trying to help?'"⁶⁰ Paek Okhyŏn used this money to purchase burlap bags and army uniforms, which she unraveled to sell as thread at marketplaces and war-torn streets in Pusan.⁶¹ The money Paek Okhyŏn received was insufficient to challenge the US interests in Korea that fueled the war or the polarizing vilification of communists and Christians. It did, however, provide a temporary means of financial survival.

Ever the evangelists, Han and Pierce shared their world vision with others, including their networks within white, fundamentalist America. In December 1952, with Han's and Pierce's help, Graham spent Christmas in Korea, exposing himself to Asia for the first time, and shaping the BGEA's world-making vision as a border-crossing institution. Yet that very process of expanding its transpacific networks also erased its Korean origins. "Christmas in Korea" shows how nonstate networks, like that of Graham's BGEA as it was linked to World Vision, played a key role in sacralizing whiteness on South Korean soil. Moreover, Graham's sacralization of whiteness gave license to the erasure of Koreans in Pierce's mistranslations of Koreans in the print and visual media he circulated in the United States.

Billy Graham's "Christmas in Korea," 1952

"The burden of Korea was particularly heavy," Graham noted, as missionaries, chaplains, Christian GIs, and Korean Christian leaders urged him to visit war-torn Korea.[62] Forgoing the comforts of a southern Christmas with his family, including his wife, Ruth Graham—who, as a child of missionaries, was born in China and schooled in northern Korea—Graham embarked on his first travels across the Pacific, with the Pentagon's approval, one month after Eisenhower's election in 1952. He spent this holiday preaching to US soldiers and Koreans on the battlefront, on makeshift outdoor podiums, and in churches, including Han's.

Graham, Wilson, and Morton visited prisoners of war, injured civilians and soldiers, refugees, and orphans and widows, including Paek Okhyŏn. Graham, Wilson, Morton, and Pierce's first stop in Pusan was to preach to the US military and then to visit the Tabitha Widows Home. Paek came out of her home wearing a *hanbok* (traditional Korean dress) to greet them.[63] Tabitha, the home for war widows, became a transpacific site where Pierce and Han launched the first World Vision sponsorship, and where Graham began to forge relationships with local Koreans. Graham and Han also preached a series of revivals on the streets of Pusan, sharing the podium on a rugged, wooden platform constructed by the military. Koreans at the Pusan revivals hungrily extended their hands for the literature distributed that night, the Gospel of John.[64] Graham recalled that at the first gathering at Pusan, nearly six thousand people attended, including eight hundred American GIs, and that nearly eight thousand people attended on the last evening.[65]

On Christmas Eve, Graham traveled to the battlefront to preach to US servicemen, an evening he said he would never forget. While most military pulpits were barren, marines adorned the pulpit with artwork that day. A US marine prepared a six-foot painting of Jesus, depicted as a meek white man with long flowing hair, wearing a white robe draped around his shoulders (figure 1.2). Under a dark and ominous sky, the meek white Jesus watched over a tired and discouraged white marine who, while holding his rifle, crouched down on the ground in front of a traditional Korean tile-roofed house (*kiwa-chip*). Yet, in the background, behind this large painting of the white Jesus and white marine, hung southern flags from North Carolina, Arkansas, Texas, Alabama, Mississippi, foregrounding the US South in this moment of Southern Baptist preaching on Korean soil. The white South and South Korea, white Jesus and the white marine, merged in this preaching hour, as it conjured up nostalgia for home, stoked white southern regional pride, and knit together the triad of Jesus, soldier, and evangelist.

As Graham stood confidently at this pulpit, he breathed life into these otherwise lifeless material objects and deflated figures. Graham served as the

Figure 1.2 Billy Graham at the Korean War battlefront, 1952.
Source: Billy Graham, *I Saw Your Sons at War: The Korean Diary of Billy Graham*, Minneapolis: Billy Graham Evangelical Association, 1953, 50. Archives of the Billy Graham Center. Wheaton, Illinois.

transpacific linchpin that fused the white Jesus, soldier, and evangelist together. Sociologist Nadia Kim argues that Koreans most thoroughly learned the American racial hierarchy of white supremacy through mass media and military culture, in the aftermath of World War II, with the arrival of the US military in Korea.[66] Though she does not highlight the role of religion, or religious material culture, we see here the crucial role that anticommunist American evangelists like Graham played in activating and circulating US ideas of race through the sacralization of whiteness, as the images of white Jesus, white soldier, and white evangelist were strung together on the Korean War battlefront.

The conservation of domestic racial lines on foreign soil did not detract from Graham's revivalistic message, but only boosted it. Though the white marine was defeated, he would soon rise with the help of the meek white Christ, and so would Graham, the white evangelist, adorned in military garb and ready for battle as a soldier for Christ. The preaching hour was not just a performance, but became animated in the lives of soldiers. Graham declared: "Never in my ministry have I preached with more liberty or power. The Spirit of God seemed to fall on the meeting." Many of the "big, strong, tough Marines" were "weeping unashamedly" because of their "sins and their need of a Savior." One of the "big" marines who had calloused hands from years of fighting gripped Graham's hand and thanked him with "tears streaming down his face." Graham associated this marine's spiritual awakening and emotional release with increased masculinity: "I was proud of him, and proud of every one of those men, the finest of American youth. Everyone was a rugged he-man. Everyone was a courageous, red-blooded American."[67] Not only did this moment reflect the militarized masculinity that pulsed at the heart of modern evangelical America, as Kristin Du Mez suggests, but it also highlighted its racialized dimensions as it sacralized the white soldier alongside the image of the white Christ, emboldening Graham, the white evangelist, across US borders.[68] Graham's presence not only elicited this performance of sacralized whiteness on Korean soil, but also animated the white Jesus, soldier, and evangelist against communism, a war he understood as holy.[69]

Graham linked white Jesus, white evangelist, and white soldier as martyred figures in the crucible of the Korean War, which he circulated back to the United States through publications and preaching. When he returned stateside, he published *I Saw Your Sons at War: The Korean Diary of Billy Graham* (1953) and the *World Vision Pictorial* ran a special section titled

Figure 1.3 Album cover, Billy Graham, *Talking Pictures: The Hour of Decision in History / Let Freedom Ring*, 1953. This cover is also featured in the first-floor exhibit of the Institute for the History of Korean Christianity, Seoul.
Source: Photo by author.

"Billy Graham—Christmas in Korea," centering photos that displayed scenes of the war.[70] Moreover, when Graham returned from Christmas in Korea, his understanding of revival as the solution to combating communism and solving international affairs strengthened. In 1953, on the Independence Day following his Korean trip, Graham preached in Texas:

> Communists are doing their deadly work in government and education. . . . There's only one way that the stars and stripes can continue to wave above the land of the free and the home of the brave, and that is for a great spiritual revival to break out in America. If we would have true repentance and

an individual turning to Christ . . . our international problems would solve themselves.

When this sermon was distributed as a phonograph record, a photo of Graham sitting with the South Korean president, Syngman Rhee, taken during "Christmas in Korea," further legitimated Graham's ideas (figure 1.3).[71] Graham imagined that saving souls one by one could solve foreign affairs; his experiences in South Korea, forged through preaching to US Marines at the Korean War battlefront, underscored this vision during his preaching in the American South. For Pierce's part, he mistranslated Koreans in his cultural productions, erasing their narratives and names. Thus, South Korean Protestants were not just martyrs to religious sacrifice or the tragedies of war, but also, ultimately, martyrs to white supremacy in a religious Cold War.

Korean Erasure and *Dead Men on Furlough*, 1954

If a transatlantic network of communication was crucial for the eighteenth-century growth of evangelicalism in the Anglo-American world, then the transpacific network forged between the United States and Korea depended on skillfully leveraging visually based media.[72] Pierce relentlessly gazed upon and involved himself in ameliorating suffering, especially that of children, and it led to an oeuvre of tracts, films, and photos. In the midst of the war, one could often see him connecting with an orphaned or bedridden child, or kneeling down to sympathize with malnourished babies sleeping on the floor. He used technology to see more closely: dark-rimmed spectacles, a camera, and a Pathé brand three-lens video camera, which he carried around with his bare hands even in the dead of winter.[73] Yet the projects that Pierce produced to portray the people of Korea reflected his own theological imagination and entrepreneurial impulse more than the empirical stories and ideas of Koreans themselves—though much of his American audience embraced the veracity of his work. His very best effort to see clearly ironically resulted in a blurry image of reality. A prime example is his translation of the story of Kim Ch'anghwa and Paek Okhyŏn in the black-and-white film *Dead Men on Furlough*. In spite of his attempts to "see," Pierce was often blind to the geopolitical nightmare of the Korean War.

When Pierce returned to the United States, he publicized Kim Ch'anghwa's martyrdom to elicit action, especially from fundamentalist Christians. He created *Dead Men on Furlough* (1954), a forty-minute film based on the symbolism of Kim's Cold War martyrdom, directed by Dick Ross of Great Commission Films.[74] Ross noted that "Pastor Chai," the protagonist, is "'really Mr. Chang Hwa Kim, but names and places have been changed to protect the innocent from Communist retaliation.'"[75] As a work of creative nonfiction, the film was a "factual dramatic story," as the media reported, an early version of the "docudrama."[76] The film is a 35 mm black-and-white drama, the only World Vision movie shot in black and white, which the moviemakers thought was "better suited psychologically to some story lines," those that had "a lot of Cold War era rhetoric." A poster for the film declared: "See the growing struggle between godless Communism and Christianity!"[77] Publicity excitedly suggested that Pastor Chai's "confession . . . will thrill the hearts of the audience in the stand against Communism."[78] *Dead Men on Furlough* is a window onto Pierce's understanding of the war. He used it to motivate fundamentalist Americans into action.[79] The film imagines a polarized debate that conflated a binary fundamentalist theology of good versus evil with the Cold War politics of democratic capitalism versus communism.[80]

The anonymity of Kim Ch'anghwa's story provided considerable creative license. Thus, loosely based on Kim's story, the plot centers on the North Korean military's infiltration of South Korea during the Korean War, when Pastor Chai, Mrs. Chai, their newborn, and the rest of the villagers in their town are captured by North Korean officials. Pastor Chai encounters the North Korean official Major Koh, who tries to force him to recant his faith to save his wife and child; when Pastor Chai refuses to recant, he is killed by the communists, leaving behind his family and the villagers who, nevertheless, are proud of him for defending his faith. The polarized debate between Pastor Chai and the North Korean army official exemplified the theological battle that Pierce imagined between the Cold War enemy and ally.

Because Pastor Chai and his community refuse to follow Major Koh's directions, they engage in a tense theological and political argument that pits communism against Christianity, and socialism against capitalism. Koh's and Chai's polarized theological and political differences are apparent through their dress and expression. Whereas Koh is angry, wears dark military garb, and holds his fists tightly, ready for battle, Chai is calm, wears white, traditional Korean civilian garb, and stands peacefully, as if a pacifist. Major Koh and Pastor Chai engage in a vigorous debate driven by their seemingly irreconcilable differences, framed primarily as a theological battle between Christianity and communism.

Major Koh attempts to persuade Pastor Chai to give up his faith, since Koh sees communism as liberation from the "yoke of capitalism" and "bourgeois tyranny." Chai's Christian worldview is an opiate of the masses, he says. In spite of Koh's challenge, Chai believes that preaching and stalwart belief in "God's word," which "never changes," is the most powerful antidote to Koh's atheistic belief system. As they continue to debate, Chai argues that Koh's communist worldview is a form of enslavement, a denial of the "spirit" and "soul" of man, who was "made in the image of God." Koh, however, articulates that the re-education system in "labor camps," as Chai calls them, or "hospitals," as Koh calls them, are the best means to "heal" the "sick" from "capitalistic disease." Both believe they have an antidote for the other's sickness, a means of salvation for the other's sin.

The climax of the film is when Pastor Chai arrives at the podium to declare the central motivating message of the film. He will not renounce his faith for godless communism. Pastor Chai's defense against the communists is a declaration of faith, but more specifically, a theological declaration in the belief that the "Bible is God's word" and that Jesus Christ is "the way, the truth, and the life." Pierce then looks into the camera and challenges viewers: "This camera in front of me is meant for me to make a confession. . . . But I will not lie for them. I cannot deny Christ and his truth. He is the way, the truth, and the life." He goes on to defend the Bible: "The Bible is God's word and his promises are true. And I am willing to die . . . for righteousness . . . for the Savior . . . the one true hope of the world. God's day of judgment will come. But all of us must make some kind of decision now. Jesus said, 'He that is not with me is against me.'" He further linked theology with anticommunism, revealing his belief that faith, in the tradition of fundamentalism, was a core strategy for Americans who sought to win the Cold War: "There are times when no man can be neutral, when the choice is between democracy and communism, God and devil. On these issues no man can just decide not to decide. The faith of the communist must be surpassed by our deeper faith, their labor by our harder and better labor, their consecration by our greater consecration."

Pastor Chai became a symbol of the Christian triumph over communism and, relatedly, the global triumph of democratic capitalism over Sino-Soviet communism. Pierce's theological paradigm that divided God and the devil, democracy and communism, capitalism and socialism, made a clear, binary challenge to other fundamentalists who desired to be on the side of God. Moreover, in an era when the inerrancy of the Bible and Christianity as the sole path to salvation was debated in liberal and conservative theological communities in the United States, Pastor Chai represented a defense of a conservative interpretation of Christian scripture. When Pastor Chai is killed, he dies not only for defending the Christian God against godless communism, but also for being a transpacific spokesperson for fundamentalist Christianity in the United States.

But note that the sacralization of a Korean martyr depends on multiple racial elisions and erasures. Though the film is set in war-torn Korea, it uses the English language from beginning to end. The Korean language and Korean actors and actresses are not central. In an article titled "Communism in Korea Portrayed by Film," *Torrance Press* reported that *Dead Men on Furlough* would feature "a number of Hollywood's most competent actors and actresses, including Keye Luke, Richard Loo, Jean Wong, Don Harvey, Victor Sen Yung and scores of all ages from a Korean colony in Los Angeles."[81] While the article notes the names of the prominent actors, it does not mention they are all Chinese American. Ross recalls that these actors "were hard to direct and 'unresponsive,'" and found "their delivery of lines somewhat stilted."[82] Their "stilted"—unnatural or wooden—lines were as stilted as the racial imagination in the film that imagined that English-speaking Chinese Americans could stand in for Kim Ch'anghwa and Paek Okhyŏn, the foreign "others." The film associated Chinese American actors with war-torn Korea, a nation in which they had no roots, relying on the extant racial imagination of Asians in the United States as "perpetual foreigners," unassimilable and ineligible for American citizenship.

Han is also nowhere to be seen in the film. Instead, Pierce plays the role of narrator and actor. Pierce shifts between these roles in a scene in the Korean village of Inkok, encouraging villagers to "live for godliness as the communist lives for godlessness," and to follow and rely on their leader, Pastor Chai, a "man of godliness." "Follow him as he follows Christ," Pierce declares. The Korean flag in the background and the Koreans wearing traditional clothing indicate that the scene is set in Korea; however, the western cowboy straw hats that the villagers wear betray that *Dead Men on Furlough* was filmed in the United States, and most likely in a Southern California studio. Pastor Chai's first words are a hymn sung in English, titled "I Must Tell Jesus All of My Trials": "I must tell Jesus all of my trials; / I cannot bear these burdens alone; / In my distress he kindly will help me; / He ever loves and cares for his own." The film makes the normative assessment that, like Pastor Chai, "good" Koreans are those who rely on Jesus in the midst of the trials of war, who sing hymns that reflect this belief, and who combat godless communism with Christian faith. Pastor Chai seems to be a stand-in figure not only for Kim Ch'anghwa but also Kyung Chik Han, but neither are actually documented as historical figures in the film, rendering both martyrs for the transnational Christian cause against communism.

Dead Men on Furlough also mapped transpacific Cold War geopolitics onto local Chinese American bodies, including them in the craftsmanship of molding "good" Cold War racial subjects. Chinese Americans feared during the Korean War that they would be racially targeted for their associations with China, especially as Mao's government allied itself with North Korea.[83] The film associates the Chinese American actors, who act like anticommunist Korean Christians, with "good" Cold War American citizens. Thus, fundamentalist theology was a crucial pivot on which transpacific racial myths turned at mid-century. The geographies of the Soviet Union, the Korean peninsula, and Chinese America collapsed into one Cold War racial frame, such that World Vision's transpacific networks, spanning the United States and Korea, also helped to facilitate the racial disciplining of Chinese Americans.

Han and Pierce's alliance had a seesaw effect. At its highest point, Korean Protestants like Kyung Chik Han and Kim Ch'anghwa served as an example to Americans; at its lowest point, Korean Protestants like Kim Ch'anghwa and Paek Okhyŏn were not only reduced to caricatures, but also hidden from the American gaze. As much as Pierce and Han's partnership complicated the white-over-Korean hierarchy, they could not escape the Orientalist trappings of the Cold War era. When Pierce communicated his message to other white fundamentalists, he did so, in part, through stilted and inaccurate renderings of their lives. As historian William Yoo has noted, Han possessed a "rising stature" with greater American attention to the proliferation of Christians in the global South; yet he was also the "object of American affection" because Americans could "project their values" onto him and "advance their agendas at home."[84]

As Han and Pierce's alliance cut in paradoxical directions, the role of the Korean War martyr was further underscored by what Josephine Park calls a Cold War "friendly." Park defines a "friendly": "An adjective first turned into a noun to describe unthreatening natives, 'friendlies' became military terminology most often used to distinguish among raced others."[85] The "friendly" is "fully cognizant of neocolonial designs," but instead of indicting it, "she seizes upon it. . . . It is the friendly's task to shield her friends from the charge of neocolonialism, even though her very existence perpetually belies such attempts. Yet though she may be devastated by superpower interests, she also knows and insists upon her centrality to the Cold War's logic of integration."[86] Han's "friendly" status as a South Korean Protestant was contingent upon his identification with other Korean "martyrs" like Kim Ch'anghwa and his family.

At the same time, he leveraged his "friendly" status to expand his church—an embattled Korean War church—to make it the first megachurch in South Korea. When Han met Pierce, he found an opportunity to channel his desire to care for war-torn families by connecting Korean needs with US resources. For approximately the first decade, a majority of World Vision's budget was devoted to Korea, beginning with sponsoring Paek Okhyŏn's family.[87] World Vision's sponsorship program became its bread-and-butter project even as it globalized in future years. As World Vision has reported, "Pierce traveled across America collecting donations while Rev. Han and others worked fervently to establish orphanages and clinics in urgent need. The earliest projects World Vision helped to fund were overseen by Young Nak Presbyterian Church."[88] Park Jong Sam (Sam Park), a past president of World Vision in Korea, noted that Pierce and Han's partnership "connected the American dollar and indigenous evangelical Korean Christianity."[89] From 1959 to 1973, World Vision donated an estimated $14,520 to "Dr. Han / Young Nak Presbyterian Church."[90] With separate donations in 1951, 1953, and 1954, the total was $22,892.[91] Han and Young Nak Presbyterian benefited from Pierce's connections to US financial support; thus, the seeds of the first South Korean megachurch began in the Cold War era, with the backing of white fundamentalists within the emerging US evangelical empire.[92] These transnational financial networks were possible in part because Pierce's and Han's influence penetrated deep into white fundamentalist networks.

Outsized South Korean Protestant growth would match its haunting invisibility from American purview as Han was erased from World Vision's origins. The trope of martyrdom both glorified and erased South Korean Protestants from the narrative of the emerging American evangelical empire, as sacrificing one's self—via invisibility—was hailed pious amid a holy war. As South Korean Protestants were both glorified and forgotten in the eyes of Americans, World Vision grew as a global organization.[93]

Mythmaking and the Problem of Historical Memory

Yet, as noted, World Vision's "founding myth" does not usually begin with Koreans or the Korean War. Rather, narratives about World Vision's beginning may focus on Pierce, whether it be his humanitarian compassion, evangelical heroism, or paternalistic Orientalism, thinly addressing the transpacific and US Cold War context out of which World Vision emerged.[94] Moreover, White Jade, a Chinese woman, usually takes center stage in the founding myth. Multiple versions of the White Jade myth exist, but most go something as follows: Pierce began his missionary work abroad with YFC in China, where he was invited in 1947 by Dutch Missionary Tena Hoelkeboer to preach in Amoy to four hundred female students. When one of the girls, White Jade, told her father that she had converted to Christianity, legend has it that her father beat her and kicked her out of the house. "What are you going to do about it?" Hoelkeboer challenged Pierce. Each account of this story recounts Pierce giving White Jade a different sum of money—five dollars, ten dollars, fifteen dollars, or all of the money he had—but all the accounts agree that Pierce gave generously in response to White Jade's religious persecution.

In Pierce's own account, he recalls that White Jade's mother was the one who opposed her attending a Christian school, and he makes no mention of an angry father; when Pierce gives White Jade fifteen dollars, she is able to pay for school, an answer to her prayers.[95] Given the multiple versions of this story, it is hard to pin down what is empirically verifiable versus legendary. Moreover, it obscures the social history of White Jade's context and her role as a historical actor, as she is cast as a mythological figure, vulnerable to the whimsy of the storyteller.

Those internal to the organization recall World Vision's Korean origins. In "World Vision Began in Korea," past World Vision president Dean Hirsch notes the Korean contribution to the organization's founding: "No one could possibly have imagined 50 years ago that a friendship between an American evangelist and a Korean pastor would result in what would become the largest Christian relief and development organization in the world." He goes on to name Han's and Pierce's shared vision, in spite of their differences: "The Rev. Bob Pierce and the Rev. Kyung-Chik Han had little in common beyond a shared commitment to Christ and a passion to do something for suffering children." Hirsch notes that they first translated their humanitarian hopes into "an organization through which American Christians supported Korean orphans by becoming their personal sponsors. Their donations were used to feed, clothe and shelter these abandoned children"[96] He continues: "Child sponsorship of poor and vulnerable children soon grew beyond America and beyond Korea. A half-century later, World Vision donors sponsor nearly two million children in developing countries and poor communities around the globe."[97] Indeed, that World Vision is the largest evangelical humanitarian organization in the twenty-first century should not obscure its origins as a small transpacific network forged in Korea.[98]

Not only is this story usually overlooked, but the larger context of war is often underanalyzed. "If the Korean War had not happened, then World Vision would not exist," said Lee Hokyun, a member of the World Vision Korean Orphan Choir.[99] She continued: "Korea is the root country of World Vision . . . it started by supporting orphans and widows."[100] Here Lee not only names Korean contributions, but also intimates that forgetting World Vision's Korean origins leaves out the brutality of war and the US military intervention in Korean affairs that rendered them in such dire need. Park Jong Sam recalled: "They started [World Vision] in Oregon but legalized it in California. . . . So, legally, the organization started in the US but the original idea and the labor for the organization started in Korea." He continued:

> If you think about it in a less formal way, then you go to the story of Kyung Chik Han and Korean Christian leaders, working with Bob Pierce. . . . World Vision itself was made solely for Korea. . . . If you want to get technical about it, it was an organization that was created solely for the orphaned children of Korea—100 percent. You have to think that World Vision began for Korea . . . for the orphaned children of Korea.[101]

Park's ethnic nationalism infuses his adamant view that World Vision was "100 percent" created for the "orphaned children of Korea." His defense of Korean origins points to a sense of loss of that ownership as World Vision grew to become a global organization, and Americans took the reins. Park's reflections also point to a critique of war—without US empire-building projects launched in Korea in 1945, there would have been no need for World Vision.

Note that Han and Pierce disputed the origins of World Vision, but ultimately also identified Han as the progenitor. When Han recounted World Vision's origins, he related its indelible transpacific origins. He named the location of the organization's founding in Seoul during "the spring of 1950 when the Korean War broke out." And he named the "young Pastor Pierce" as the founder. Han told Pierce: "Even though I told you that World Vision was needed and I told you that we should do World Vision in your name, you are the one who founded World Vision." Pierce replied: "No, you, *hyŏngnim* [older brother] are the founder of World Vision." Yi Kwangsun recalled that they "went back and forth like this" and "at the end, Pierce said you were the one that came up with all of these ideas . . . that this world needs World Vision . . . and that World Vision is a name that Rev. Han created. But [Han said that] since Han is a Korean person, I cannot do this work. He told Pierce to do it in his name. . . . That's how today's World Vision was created."[102] Han saw that Pierce's national status as an American could make his vision a reality. Han and Pierce influenced each other, however unevenly.

Yet when Korea is named in World Vision's history, scholars and practitioners have tended to obfuscate its role, rendering Korean names and contexts as phantoms hovering over the real historical drama.[103] To forget this history or to write it out of World Vision's history mainly serves to highlight Pierce's heroism and to imagine a figure like White Jade as an exotic idea more than a historical figure. Moreover, in Marilee Pierce Dunker's essay on the history of World Vision in Korea, "Korea Is Transformed into a Nation That Blesses Others," she traces Korea's history through a developmentalist arc. When Korea becomes the "12th strongest economy in the world" and "one of World Vision's top 10 donor nations," she describes the country as "blessing others with the same spiritual hope and practical help they once received."[104]

Yet Koreans have been "blessing" World Vision from the beginning through their martyrdom, which was not just a religious sacrifice, but a war tragedy. The developmentalist narrative that ranks nations from least to most developed contributes to the mischaracterization of Korea in the organization's history. Moreover, to omit the Korean origins of World Vision is to overlook the geopolitics, including Cold War America's interests in Korea, that gave rise to it, as well as the racialized dimensions that ultimately led to Korean erasure.

Indeed, to forget Korean names such as Kyung Chik Han, Paek Okhyŏn, and Kim Ch'anghwa in the historical origins of World Vision is to forget the Pacific-facing career of the US Cold War empire in Korea, including the ways in which white fundamentalist America preserved domestic ideas of race on foreign soil through institutions like World Vision and the BGEA. As much as these institutions benefited from, and glorified, South Koreans for their contributions, they also respectively sacralized whiteness—linking white Jesus, white evangelist, and white soldier—and erased Korean narratives and names from their publications and productions, whitewashing their institutions even as they depended on nonwhites like Koreans to build them.

Though often called the "forgotten war" in American history, the Korean War was memorable for fusing the fates of South Korea and the United States, including their religious histories. Korean Protestants and American fundamentalists realized a vision of global revival in later decades that had its origins in networks forged through war. The war, then, birthed not only World Vision but also a transpacific network that was critical for spawning a world vision that fueled the survival of American fundamentalism and its eventual reformation into mainstream evangelicalism. Yet, even though World Vision became the world's largest faith nonprofit, one built upon the creativity and suffering of Koreans, Koreans have never really been part of the organization's history and have largely been lost and forgotten, much like the Korean War itself. Though Han had the idea for World Vision, Pierce, by virtue of his national identity, had power in terms of resources. This chapter has corrected and critiqued the historiographical omission of Korean and Korean War narratives from World Vision's history. It has expanded knowledge about Cold War America's entanglements with South Korean Protestants, nonstate actors who helped to mediate US-Korean Cold War relations, including through World Vision, a key institution that remade modern US evangelicalism.

Han and Pierce believed that the Korean War was not only a war between Soviet communism and US capitalist democracy, or North and South Korea, but fundamentally also a war between God and atheism, which was of diplomatic import for US efforts to contain communism in Asia. Moreover, they were ignited by the outbreak of war, as they saw this as a potential barrier to the Great Commission. The transpacific militarized highway between Korean Protestants and white fundamentalists was built upon a shared sense of faith, but these roads were also paved by the US militarization of Korea. When Pierce went on to translate his messages to Koreans, he reinscribed values of hierarchy that justified the US military presence in Korea. In so doing, Han became a martyr of history—as a "friendly," he was both a saint and invisible. His story was embedded in a war that never had in mind the humanity of Koreans themselves.

Yet Han's stature as a Korean Protestant patriarch only grew further. Though at mid-century Korean Protestants and white fundamentalists were still weak powers in their respective nations, the transpacific networks they built were foreboding. They grew an empire of piety that flexed its transpacific muscles to strengthen the evangelical movement in South Korea and across the Pacific in the United States. They laid the groundwork for the founding of World Vision, Campus Crusade's first international partnership, and for the Billy Graham Evangelistic Association's largest "crusade." The networks created in the wake of war continued to expand, not only drawing more Americans to Korea but also Koreans to America, as we will see next.

2

Students

Immigration, Conversion, and White Fundamentalism, 1950–1960

Americans like Pierce and Graham traveled to Korea at an unprecedented rate during the Korean War. The war also triggered a new wave of Korean immigration to the United States through which South Korean Protestants and white fundamentalists forged new transpacific networks. Often called the "post–Korean War immigration" period, this moment brought not only Korean military brides and orphans but also students, especially men like Billy Kim and Joon Gon Kim, from Korea to the United States for their education. Chang Ahn, or Chuck, is a notable fictional figure from this time period, as the male protagonist in Susan Choi's acclaimed novel *The Foreign Student*. As an immigrant at the University of the South in Sewanee, Tennessee, he rooms with the son of a Klansmen and falls in love with Katherine, a white southern woman, all while battling the trauma of the Korean War.[1] Chuck's fictional story parallels Billy Kim's and Joon Gon Kim's narratives of immigration and conversion as students who inhabit "racial interstitiality" in a Black and white racial hierarchy, respectively in the 1950s Jim Crow South and in Southern California.[2] Their stories remain distinct, however, as they highlight student immigration and conversion at white-led fundamentalist institutions, namely Bob Jones University, Fuller Theological Seminary, and Campus Crusade for Christ.[3]

In 1951, when a white soldier, Sergeant Carl Powers, encouraged Billy Kim to immigrate from South Korea to the United States, he answered yes "without hesitation."[4] Powers and Billy Kim were not at the time Christians. But Powers enrolled him at a private Christian school in the heart of white fundamentalism, Bob Jones University. In lieu of his childhood dreams of becoming a politician, Billy Kim rose to global fame as a Baptist evangelist, baptizing Powers in the Jordan River and translating for the BGEA's largest crusade. During the war and its aftermath, immigration to the Jim Crow South and conversion at Bob Jones University redefined Billy Kim's life.

As for Joon Gon Kim (1925–2009), encountering Campus Crusade for Christ while he was a student immigrant at Fuller Theological Seminary activated his faith as never before.[5] Joon Gon Kim met Bill Bright, who founded Campus Crusade in 1951 at UCLA. They sought converts, like the quarterback who later became Ronald Reagan's pastor at Bel Air Presbyterian Church. Like Bright, Joon Gon Kim quit Fuller and, after one year, returned to South Korea to launch Campus Crusade in 1958. He was the first nonwhite partner, and he established the first international site for the organization.

It was not as if Korean integration into Cold War American institutions was seamless. The outbreak of the Korean War ignited suspicion of a communist overthrow from within the United States. As part of a national sweep of aliens suspected of subversive communist activity, two Korean men, David Hyun and Diamond Kimm, were arrested for their respective engagement with labor activism and the publication of a pro-communist newspaper.[6] Under the auspices of the 1950 McCarran Act, Koreans who questioned US democracy's capacity to ensure freedom and equality for all were arrested and even deported. Yet if the US government suppressed viewpoints like those of Hyun and Kim, other narratives, like those of Joon Gon Kim and Billy Kim, were highlighted. In alignment with the Eisenhower administration's Cold War emphasis on US-Asian integration, Joon Gon Kim's and Billy Kim's narratives bridged affective gaps between the United States and noncommunist Asia through nonstate institutions within fundamentalist America. Cold War America favored these Korean narratives that intertwined a commitment to the Great Commission—world evangelization—with racialized anticommunism.

By the same token, white fundamentalist America's survival depended on the integration of nonwhite and noncommunist Koreans whose life narratives reflected a commitment to a racialized and religious Cold War.[7] Bob Jones, Fuller, and Campus Crusade were institutions founded by white Protestants who emerged out of the fundamentalist strand of the fundamentalist-modernist controversy. They targeted white students to fulfill their respective missions, but throughout the 1950s, they also prioritized the inclusion of students of Asian descent, more than any other nonwhite race, reflecting the racial and foreign policy priorities of Cold War America. Joon Gon Kim's and Billy Kim's narratives of conversion into these institutions portrayed an image of racial equality in a liberal democracy, even as those white fundamentalist institutions maintained a system of racial inequality, in which

Black students were excluded and Koreans were divided into "good" and "bad" racialized categories.

Espousing these narratives of faith, however, did not mean Billy Kim or Joon Gon Kim achieved equality within white fundamentalist America. Their integration relied on Cold War Orientalist dynamics that subordinated them. Even as Billy Kim was granted educational privileges at Bob Jones, it alienated him from his actual contributions to world Christianity. As for Joon Gon Kim, his story required a polarization of Christian versus communist that exacerbated a divisive line between "good" and "bad" Korean. As racially interstitial student immigrants who were neither white nor Black, Billy Kim and Joon Gon Kim were characters in stories that ultimately found "uneasy resolution."[8] Through integration into white fundamentalist institutions, their narratives as survivors of the Korean War were both celebrated and suppressed.

White Fundamentalism, Cold War Orientalism, and Racial Segregation

America's Cold War rise to global power was complicated, as nationalists throughout Asia were fighting for decolonization from Western domination. As Christina Klein asserts, the cultural problem became "How can we define our nation as a non-imperial world power in the age of decolonization?" One of the litmus tests for American democracy, and by extension, the nation's legitimacy as a global leader in the Cold War era, was its claim to racial equality. Projecting to the world that America championed racial equality was crucial for saving face on the Cold War stage, precisely because of the internationally publicized racialized violence against African Americans throughout the 1950s, which communist nations used against the United States. As Klein notes, an imagination of the United States as a racially diverse nation played a critical role in the nation's Cold War expansion: "The United States thus became the only Western nation that sought to legitimate its world-ordering ambitions by championing the idea (if not the practice) of racial equality. In contrast to European imperial powers, the captains of American expansion explicitly denounced the idea of essential differences and hierarchies."[9]

America's relationships with noncommunist Asians became a critical way to globally circulate an image of racial democracy. Eisenhower's administration encouraged everyday Americans to engage in people-to-people diplomacy that forged personal attachments with noncommunist Asians through "structures of feeling" that sought "sympathy—the ability to feel what another person feels."[10] Policymakers declared that "differences of language, religion, history and race could be bridged" through an "inescapable interconnectedness."[11] Klein's concept of Cold War Orientalism shows that such narratives, "far from undermining the global assertion of U.S. power, often supported it."[12] Intimate bonds between Americans and noncommunist Asians reinforced "the famed 'Cold War consensus,' the domestic hegemonic bloc that supported the postwar expansion of US power around the world."[13]

White fundamentalists closely aligned with Eisenhower's vision to establish heart-to-heart connections with noncommunist Asians. The Protestant missionary enterprise, in particular, created a "worldwide institutional infrastructure that enabled millions of Americans, especially in isolated Midwestern and rural communities, to understand themselves as participating in world affairs," and to feel "bound to the people of Asia and Africa" in spite of their differences.[14] For white fundamentalists in particular, heart to heart connections had long been prioritized for the sake of the heart's conversion to Christ, a core means for fulfilling the Great Commission. At mid-twentieth century, white fundamentalists insisted on the world's total evangelization, in spite of the critiques of Western missionary imperialism and liberal denunciations of literalist interpretations of the Bible. They were aided by Cold War America's military, economic, and political expansion throughout the world.[15] Bob Jones, Fuller, and Campus Crusade were key institutional forces in that global effort. While these institutions are often thought of as local institutions with a domestic focus, they were globally minded from their inception, with close connections to non-Western people, including noncommunist Koreans.

Bob Jones was founded in 1927 on antimodernist values, in the aftermath of the fundamentalist-modernist controversy. Graham, who emerged out of the fundamentalist thread of that controversy, matriculated in 1936, though he transferred because of Bob Jones's strict institutional rules. He held onto fundamentalist values and sustained a close relationship with Bob Jones Jr., occasionally visiting the campus to meet with students.[16] In the 1940s, a reformation movement from within fundamentalism emerged, called the "new evangelicalism," a term coined by Harold Ockenga, the founder of the National Association of Evangelicals (NAE). By 1947, Bob Jones gained further momentum in South Carolina. Fuller was founded as an institutional base for an otherwise loose network of "new evangelicals," or neo-evangelicals. When Fuller was founded, it held onto its fundamentalist roots. The real schism between "ultraseparatist fundamentalists" like those at Bob Jones and "new evangelicals" like those at Fuller did not occur until nearly a decade later, in 1957, with Graham's New York Crusade.[17] In the 1950s, the "new evangelical" movement seeking fundamentalist reform from within was still in the making; fundamentalists and neo-evangelicals shared the twin goals of national revival and evangelization of the world. Campus Crusade was intimately tied to these institutions.[18]

These institutions insisted on global expansion as the state was refashioning its national identity as a global Cold War power. As much as missionaries went overseas to establish connections with nonwesterners, war abroad also triggered new immigration routes to the United States that created new networks, as in the case of Korean people. Koreans, in part, integrated into fundamentalist networks through the second wave of Korean immigration from 1950 to 1964.

Korean immigration in US history is segmented into three major waves. Most widely known is the third wave of immigration, which began with the 1965 Hart-Cellar Act and continues today. With the Hart-Cellar Act's elimination of national origin as a criterion for immigration, Koreans immigrated to the United States, mostly as highly educated, middle class, and professional. From 1965 to 1977, 264,000 Koreans entered the United States, of which 13,000 worked as physicians, nurses, pharmacists, and dentists. These demographics contrast with the first- and second-wave immigrants, who arrived in the United States as semiskilled or unskilled workers and as a result of the hardships of war. In the first wave, from 1903 to 1905, immigrants from Korea, approximately 7,226 people (6,048 men, 637 women, 541 children), traveled to Hawaii as laborers on sugar plantations. Korean immigration to the United States effectively halted after the 1908 Gentleman's Agreement, with the exception of approximately one thousand women, known as "picture brides," who arrived between 1910 and 1924 to marry Korean men.[19] Korean male laborers discovered harsher working conditions than expected on plantations, and picture brides married husbands more impoverished and elderly than they were led to believe.[20]

In the second wave, from 1950 to 1964, of which Joon Gon Kim and Billy Kim were a part, limited immigration routes opened, with about fifteen thousand Koreans immigrating to the United States. Largely through personal connections with US citizens, about six thousand students immigrated from Korea. The National Origins Act of 1924 barred Asian immigration to the United States, and two high-profile Supreme Court cases, the *United States v. Thind* (1922) and the *United States v. Ozawa* (1923), rendered Asians as "aliens ineligible for citizenship."[21] In the 1950s, when the second wave of Korean immigration ensued with the onset of war, Asians in the United States lived under that precarious legal status in an age of Asian exclusion.[22] Yet, throughout the 1950s, Cold War America cultivated Korean leaders—ambassadors of goodwill—through education.[23] The State Department Leadership Grants program, the Defense Department, and private foundations sponsored education for thousands of Koreans and trained hundreds of Korean professionals, exposing them to American-style modernity and capitalism.[24]

Most Korean international students during the 1950s would transfer their immigration status from nonimmigrant to permanent resident, settling in the United States as professionals. Joon Gon Kim and Billy Kim, however, returned to Korea, forging transnational networks between white fundamentalists and South Korean Protestants through Fuller Seminary, Campus Crusade, and Bob Jones University. In an age when Cold War America feared communist infiltration, their stories of student immigration and conversion as nonwhite and noncommunist Koreans gained transpacific significance, as they cohered with Eisenhower's broader call for people-to-people diplomacy.

These institutions practiced racial segregation and Black exclusion. Bob Jones remained racially segregated, rejecting Black student admissions until 1971, and out of fear of interracial dating and marriage, did not admit unmarried Black students until 1975. Students donned blackface at school events called "Special Days" at the same time that they evangelized Black people in the African continent through the African Fellowship.[25] While the school excluded Black admissions well past *Brown v. Board of Education* (1954), throughout the 1950s, it admitted approximately 355 nonwhite students, and about 72 percent of them were of Asian descent (254 students) from Asia and within the United States, which included Billy Kim in 1952.[26]

As for Fuller, the school was founded by a nearly all-white faculty and white student body. Fuller's starting class had approximately thirty-two men, nearly all white, with one man of Asian descent. In the 1950s, approximately 105 nonwhite students attended Fuller, of which approximately 93 students (89 percent) were of Asian descent. In 1956, the first Black student attended Fuller, and thereafter, about five more attended throughout the decade. Approximately four Latino students attended in the 1950s, and of all the nonwhites, about ten were Asian women. Though Fuller did not practice strict racial segregation, as with the case of Bob Jones, the Confederate flag made its way into public school gatherings.[27] As for Campus Crusade, the organization's founder, Bright, discouraged staff and student involvement in the civil rights movement, espousing a more individualistic and heart-centered approach to change, and belatedly created its Black student-centered campus ministry in the 1970s. Yet it forged its first nonwhite partnership with Joon Gon Kim, a Korean national, as early as 1958.

Throughout the 1950s, white fundamentalist institutions, core to the formation of modern evangelical America, and later, the US Christian Right, depended on the Cold War Orientalist politics of Asian integration and the segregationist politics of Black exclusion. As racially interstitial student immigrants, Billy Kim and Joon Gon Kim were incorporated into transpacific networks with white fundamentalists insofar as they sought to fulfill the Great Commission and celebrate the United States as a racial democracy. The elements of their lives that aligned more closely with the racial alienation of Black students and Black civil rights activists were suppressed.

Billy Kim at Bob Jones: From War-Torn Korea to the Jim Crow South

US soldiers stationed in Korea during the war nicknamed Jang Kwan Kim "Billy." And while working for them as a "houseboy," he met Powers. He recalled: "I lived with them; I ate with them; I shined their shoes and I made their beds."[28] He ran errands for US soldiers in exchange for Hershey's chocolates and Lucky Strike cigarettes, which he sold on the black market to support his impoverished family. While flipping through Sears catalogs in military barracks, Billy Kim learned of the privileged life one could find in the United States. In November 1951, amid the war, he set sail from the southern coast of Korea to the United States. Three months later, in January 1952, by way of San Francisco, he arrived at Powers's farm in Virginia.

Later that year, Powers enrolled Billy Kim in school at Bob Jones, located in Greenville, South Carolina. Billy Kim was productive in his eight years in the United States, graduating with his bachelor's degree in biblical studies and master's degree in theology from Bob Jones. He was also ordained as a Baptist minister, and before the school banned interracial dating, he dated and married white classmate Gertrude (Trudy) Stephens, with whom he returned to South Korea in 1959.[29] He fulfilled his dreams of education, career, and marriage through immigration and conversion in the heart of white fundamentalism. Yet his narrative reveals his consternation about whether the United States would be a land of opportunity or exploitation.

Student or Slave?

Billy Kim was uncertain as to how he would be accepted in the United States—as a student or a slave?[30] While first traveling with Powers from Korea to the United States, Billy Kim worried: "*He is taking me to use as a slave.*"[31] He had recalled that Powers' parents were farmers, who, he imagined, would exploit him for labor. He "could not sleep" and doubted: "*Will I really be able to go to school?*"[32] He may have imagined the lot of the male workers from the first wave of Korean immigration to Hawaii, who labored on sugar plantations with few opportunities for educational mobility.[33] When he arrived at Powers's secluded Virginia farmhouse, Billy Kim "fell into despair." The "glitter of San Francisco," the port at which he first docked, he feared, was "just a mirage to lure him to this dark place." "Behind the gentle smile of Carl," he worried, "was the crafty scheme of a farm owner." He was "convinced that they [had] brought him here as a slave. He was in despair—there was no school around anywhere. The admissions letter of acceptance might have been fake." In using the word "slave" to refer to labor, Billy Kim may have wondered whether he would be racialized as Black or white in the Jim Crow South. Which racialized narrative would hold true for a Korean man, with regard to educational access and attainment?[34] After all, Asians in the US South experienced "extreme fluctuations" in accessing education in segregated schools, which often exposed the arbitrary and illogical character of Jim Crow as a racial regime.[35] His fears also likely emerged from his encounter with the US military in Korea, as "one of the key sources of racialization of Asian ethnics is US imperialism in Asia since World War II."[36] That first night, Powers's magnanimity seemed deceptive: "As he sat around the dinner table with Carl and his family, he smiled as if nothing was wrong, but his doubts and fears grew bigger and bigger, as the family's laughter and kindness increased."[37]

Educational segregation was a common form of racial subordination that Asians had experienced in the United States. As legal scholar Angelo

Ancheta recounts: "In 1860, California barred Asians, blacks, and Native Americans from attending the public schools. Twenty-five years later, after the law had been declared unconstitutional, segregated schools were established in California. San Francisco set up 'Oriental schools' for Chinese students and other Asian students. A federal court upheld the constitutionality of the segregated schools in 1903."[38] At the same time, there was variability depending on the state and local context. In the US South, for instance, "Jim Crow laws were clear in stating the limitations for black students, but when it came to Asian Americans, there was more maneuverability and access to white schools throughout the South."[39] Chinese Americans, who were the largest Asian population in the US South at mid-twentieth century, were "once seen as an acceptable oddity, a group of others who tended to their businesses in the black sections of town" and who were also, in small numbers, accepted at white schools.[40] Yet, in the wake of anti-Asian sentiment in the 1920s and 1930s and the National Origins Act (1924), Chinese American students were deemed unacceptable at white schools. Ultimately, in *Lum v. Rice* (1927), the Supreme Court ruled that Chinese placement in a segregated Mississippi school for "colored races" did not violate the Constitution. *Lum* was not overturned until *Brown v. Board* (1954).

As for Billy Kim, his fearful narrative about exploitation and enslavement took a quick turn when he gained access to education at Bob Jones. "Ninety-nine percent of our worries do not become a reality," he confidently stated. "And so, on February 3, 1952, just weeks after arriving at Carl's home, Billy was able to start school. Carl's promise was real, and Billy's worries were not," he continued. For a mere houseboy, access to education as Powers promised was key to assuaging Billy Kim's fears. Yet he was granted admissions to one of the most notoriously segregationist schools in the United States, with Senator Strom Thurmond on its board of trustees. In fact, Bob Jones was one of the institutional linchpins that gave rise to the US Christian Right.

Using the case study of Bob Jones, Randall Balmer has debunked the myth that the US Christian Right mobilized due to *Roe v. Wade* (1973), showing, instead, it emerged out of a racial protest against desegregation. On June 30, 1971, the district court for the District of Columbia handed down a ruling in *Green v. Connally* that, in light of the Civil Rights Act of 1964, segregated religious schools in Mississippi would lose their tax-exempt status. The IRS targeted Bob Jones since it had not admitted African Americans until then. When the IRS rescinded Bob Jones's tax exemption on January 19, 1976, due to unlawful racial segregation, Balmer shows that the Republican Party "finally had the issue that would motivate evangelical leaders."[41]

What is the significance of Billy Kim's admission to an institution responsible for the rise of the US Christian Right? The white fundamentalist supremacy undergirding Bob Jones arose through Black segregation *and* Asian integration. Billy Kim inhabited a position of "racial interstitiality" in which he simultaneously benefited from the school's anti-Black admissions policies and was subjected to the Orientalist culture at Bob Jones.

In the year *Brown v. Board* passed, the school maintained segregationist practices, and went on to publish an "Oriental" themed yearbook, reflecting the school's Orientalist culture. Stating that just as the "artists of the West" found "in the ancient pagoda lands of the Orient that 'different something'" to "revitalize their own" art, Bob Jones had been revitalized because of the East. In "a period of twenty-seven years," it had "extended to the four corners of the globe." Using art from Bob Jones Jr.'s personal collection, the yearbook, called the *Vintage*, chose to "compare the unusual influence of the East with the unusual program of Bob Jones University," using Asian artifacts and images of people to elevate its sense of distinction as an antimodern and fundamentalist institution.[42] Though a majority of their nonwhite students were of Asian descent, the school imagined them through the dehumanized lens of artifacts and exotic images of geishas, rendering the East as effeminate, ready to submit to the West to aid its revitalization.

Asians were reduced and integrated for the sake of the institution's vitality. Bob Jones dramatized its reverence for "Oriental" culture in terms of a regal lord, a "debtor" to his female servant imagined as a diminutive geisha penciled in as a caricature of Asian people. Employing the Christian gospel to instantiate this racial message, *Vintage* analogized the East to Christ, and hyperbolically imagined the East as the West's savior. In step with this simultaneously diminutive and idealistic imagination of the East, local newspapers infantilized Billy Kim, portraying him as a "Korean War victim," a "Korean refugee," and "the young Korean protégé of Carl Powers." As a refugee, victim, and protégé, he depended on funds from Dickenson County in Virginia to attend Bob Jones.[43] Yet, just like Eastern art, the student from the East became a vital symbol for Bob Jones, used to prop itself up, displaying the image that Bob Jones was a moral US institution with global influence in the Cold War era.

Perhaps because of this racialized context, Billy Kim recalled that his Bob Jones high school dormitory felt like a prison. He wrote: "Surrounded by the four walls of the dormitory, Billy felt caged inside a dark, narrow, and tall-ceilinged box, all alone." He remembers his estrangement from his Korean family and culture: "He cried in intense loneliness. 'Mom, Mom, Mother!' He missed his mother. He yearned desperately for his mother's homemade bean stew. He felt as if someone had cut open his heart and was rubbing it with a tough pot scrubber. Billy was extremely homesick."[44] When he shared a Korean meal with two Korean students at Bob Jones, he experienced brief relief, but "his aloneness became worse and even deeper."

He described his pain at length. He recalled the "mere falling of an autumn leaf would bring tears to his eyes." Gazing into the "moonlit night would intensify the aches in his heart," reminding him it was the "same as the moon from the night sky of his homeland, and he could almost see his mother's face on the glowing moon." While tearing, he recalled "a song back home: 'Gazing at the glowing moon, not even the loneliness passes soon.'"[45] Even though he was admitted into a school in South Carolina, he was still alienated from family and culture, exacerbated by the rupture amid his migration from South Korea to Jim Crow South.[46]

A Heart for Christ and Democracy

But all of this changed swiftly, according to his narrative, when he accepted Christ into his heart. Shortly following his conversion, the "light of democracy" also began to "shin[e] in my heart." Though he feared America, his heart was won for Christ and American democracy. He learned to honor, at the deepest level, Jesus and democracy in the spirit of the Cold War. Billy Kim's evangelical conversion through an intimate and interracial one-on-one encounter with roommate Jerry Thompson, in which he offered salvation through Jesus as a solution to his despair and tears, gained heightened political import because of the Eisenhower administration's Cold War expansionist aims that appealed to US-Asian integration on the level of the everyday. The conversion of a nonwhite and noncommunist South Korean like Billy Kim suggested to white fundamentalists at Bob Jones that the global mission to evangelize the world was still possible. His conversion provided an image that the institution reflected the democratic ideals of racial equality, even as it preserved the logic of white supremacy within its very foundations. He would go on to weave a transpacific Cold War network between the United States and Korea that interlaced conversion to

Christianity with a belief in America as a racial democracy, in spite of evidence to the contrary, most firmly revealed in the case of his own school, Bob Jones University.

Shortly after arriving at Bob Jones, Billy Kim experienced conversion. Daily chapel service had seemed like an "unfamiliar ritual of a foreign religion," yet when his roommate Jerry Thompson introduced him to the Christian scriptures, John 3:16, he "felt a rush of emotion he had never felt during chapel or dorm worship."[47] He was "captured by a vague expectation that perhaps the 'One called Jesus' could quench his urgent thirst for home and mother." He confessed to his roommate: "Jerry, I cry every day. I can't study anymore. I think I'll go insane this way. Do you think that this 'Jesus' can help me?" Jerry responded, "Jesus will most definitely help you. Believe in Jesus, and you will not cry in such despair anymore." Jerry shared the salvation message: "God sent His only Son to this world to save sinners and chose death on the cross in their place. He then rose again from death and ascended into heaven to forgive all our sins." He assured Billy Kim that if "anyone believes Jesus did this to save them, they will eternally, forever be saved and will be blessed as God's own child."[48]

In Jesus, he could find the solution to his anxiety and despair, the alienation he experienced upon migrating to a foreign nation, a nation where he was an "alien ineligible for citizenship."

He believed Jesus had the power to eradicate his despair, forgive his sins, and include him in a new family as a child of God. Kim accepted Jesus Christ as his savior. In this moment, it was as if even the linguistic and racial barriers between Billy Kim and Jerry Thompson were dissolved. In spite of language differences, they prayed: "God I am a sinner. I accept Jesus who died on the cross for my sins into my heart right now. Please forgive my sins." Billy Kim recalled that accepting Jesus into his life had a healing effect on his "heart": "At first, it seemed awkward, but as he continued, his heart started to melt. The divine One who had called Billy to Bob Jones was now personally touching Billy's despairing, aching heart and his weary soul, at that very moment."

When the prayer was over, Jerry confirmed he had gained salvation: "Billy, you just accepted Jesus Christ as your Savior. . . . You have been saved. You are born again." His conversion had an emotional effect; he "felt immersed in an indescribable sea of peace" and was "not alone anymore." Billy Kim renarrated his immigration experience as facilitated, not by the US soldier Carl Powers, but God: "The 'One' who had called Billy to Bob Jones Academy was with him." With certainty of his salvation, Billy Kim stated: "There, Billy met God. There, Billy was saved. There, Billy became a child of God. He now knew the truth: 'To all who received him, who believed in his [Jesus's] name, he gave the right to become children of God (John 1:12 NIV).'"[49] Through his heart's conversion, Billy Kim became a Christian.

Kim's conversion had multiple effects and its spiritual geography many consequences. In addition to an "indescribable sea of peace" in his "aching heart," he discovered a new identity as a child of God that assured him that he was not alone. His new belief that he was directed by divine powers to attend Bob Jones resulted in a new vision for his life, including a career change: "It had seemed to me I wanted to be a politician when I first came to America. But a few weeks after my conversion to Christ, it seemed as if God were saying to me, 'I want you to go back to Korea and carry this great message to the teeming millions like yourself who have never heard.'"[50] Kim's conversion provided a sense of resolution and purpose to the inexplicable tragedies of the Korean War, and became an affective response that ameliorated and relieved the contradictions of war. If his psychological anxiety and existential despair were rooted in the alienation of the immigration experience, then a religion of the heart rooted in belief in Jesus, he suggested, could collapse difference, even racial difference.

One of the trajectories of Kim's conversion was a defense of US democracy. In 1955, at the age of nineteen, Kim became the South Carolina winner of the "Voice of Democracy" contest. Though Bob Jones was a racially segregated private Christian school steeped in Orientalist culture, Billy Kim argued that access to education was a key factor as to why he believed in democracy. He went on to represent the state in the national contest and attended a Democracy Workshop in Williamsburg, Virginia, along with four cowinners and thirty-two other state winners.[51] "Education is for all," Billy Kim declared. He confirmed the superiority of American democracy: "Only democracy can give the individual rights, a higher standard of education and better education." He quickly made the connection between access to education and the legitimacy of the expansion of American democracy, including through military force, as he declared his gratitude to "Uncle Sam for sending the boys to my country and allowing me to find democracy." Kim's conversion to Christianity occurred with his acceptance of the myth that American democratic capitalism championed equality. As a nonwhite person, he became the face for publicizing the image of the United States as a racial democracy.

Billy Kim's immigration narrative tested whether the United States could legitimately serve as a global leader in the postwar era, and whether American democracy was, indeed, a more ideal form of governance than Soviet communism. The first line of Kim's speech, a potent line, revealed his main argument. "I am a Korean and I speak for democracy," he declared. That a Korean like Billy Kim could represent democracy suggested its universal reach, legitimating US Cold War expansionist aims, including in the Asia-Pacific region, the last US frontier.

His experience with American GIs especially testified to the merits of democracy: "In my tent were white people with German and French accents; short Hawaiians, and a few of the GIs were black skinned, yet they seemed to come from the same race and had much respect for each other." Billy Kim found an example of racial unity and equity among whites, Blacks, and Hawaiians that exemplified the American democratic values justifying the Korean War and the US military presence in Korea: "I began to understand why they came to our country to fight. That they might keep that freedom and liberty for their country and share it with us too."[52]

Soldiers who knelt to read their Bibles and pray, who gave out chocolate and other food, and who helped children who were wandering homeless and helpless convinced Billy Kim that American GIs were a benevolent rather than an oppressive force: "As I watched those things my heart began to convince me that these GIs were different from forces of other countries who tried to suppress the Koreans. . . . Now the light of democracy shines in my heart." Not unlike the heartfelt conversion that led him to accept Jesus as his savior, Billy Kim expressed his heartfelt conversion to American-style democracy. He ultimately won a television from the state of South Carolina in this competition, and he gave it to Powers as a gift, repaying his benevolence.

He discovered a belief in Jesus and American democracy that converted his despair and alienation into hope, though it did not address the conditions of US Cold War empire building in South Korea that prompted his migration to the US South. When he returned to Korea in 1959, he not only went on to serve in Christian ministry, but also hosted a similar "Freedom and Democracy" speech contest, sponsored by the 314th Air Division, an event that began with an invocation and devotion by an American military chaplain and a Korean chief of police. In spite of the racial contradictions and hierarches that haunted his story, Billy Kim carried not only the torch of a "religion of the heart" but also the torch of American democracy with him to Korea.

Even as Billy Kim affirmed the United States as a racial democracy, representations of his immigration and conversion narrative instantiated racial hierarchy. In a two-part comic series called "My Chum," *Christian Story Magazine* retells Carl Powers's and Billy Kim's story.[53] The comic strip begins: "Carl was a Christian. He tried to teach English to Billy. Carl told Billy about life in America. But Carl didn't know how to get Billy to know Jesus as his savior."[54] Then, one day, Powers asks Billy Kim to immigrate to the United States, where, the comic assumes, he could discover Jesus as his savior. The comic strip begins with assumptions about the hierarchical and unilateral direction in which Christianity moved triumphantly from the United States to the world, revealing an imperial imagination of America as the benevolent provider not only of the English language and abundant resources, but also of the truth of the gospel. Billy Kim actually converted Powers after he became a Christian at Bob Jones. Billy Kim baptized Powers in the Jordan River (figure 2.1), defying the lines of racial hierarchy that the comic strip meant to instantiate through religion. Christianity did not

Figure 2.1 Billy Kim baptizing Carl Powers in the Jordan River, 1979. The "Christian Culture Ministry" Exhibit, Seoul, Far East Broadcasting Company.
Source: Photo by author.

always move west to east, or from the United States to South Korea, but also bidirectionally. Yet their story continued to reflect the racialized thinking of US exceptionalism.

Joon Gon Kim, Fuller Theological Seminary, and Campus Crusade for Christ

If Billy Kim's narrative came at the cost of his disavowal of his racial alienation in the Jim Crow South, Joon Gon Kim's narrative came at the cost of perpetuating a racialized anticommunist binary of dividing Koreans into "good" and "bad" racialized categories. The year that Billy Kim left for the United States, Joon Gon Kim witnessed Korean communists from his village kill his wife and father, which led to a conversion more powerful than his initial Christian commitment: "The starting point of my Christian life began when I faced persecution and death under the Communist occupation," he recalled.[55] While enrolled at Chosun Seminary in Korea to become a Presbyterian pastor, he became disgruntled with Korea's growing theological liberalism. In 1957, he immigrated to Pasadena, California, where he attended Fuller.[56]

Joon Gon Kim was born and raised on the southwest coast of Korea, on Jido Island. He grew up in a Confucian family but had heard of Christianity through a cousin who tried to evangelize his mother. He studied agriculture and became a successful and wealthy agricultural administrator, managing farming operations in Manchuria. During his time in Manchuria, he began to attend a small congregation called Mokneung Church, where in 1943 he became a Christian at the age of nineteen. By 1958, he had immigrated to Pasadena, California, to attend Fuller, where he met his contemporary, Bill Bright, the founder of Campus Crusade for Christ.

Bright, born in Oklahoma, had grown up in a family with an influential Methodist mother. In his adult life, however, he was more interested in running a successful candy business than in any religious activities. Bright moved to Los Angeles to begin his company, California Confections, which marketed delicacies such as fruits, candies, jams, and jellies through exclusive shops and major department stores nationwide. While running his business venture in Southern California, he experienced spiritual rejuvenation. From the moment they first met in 1957, Bright and Joon Gon Kim were purported to be like "two prongs of a tuning fork . . . ; when one was struck with a strategy he believed was of God, it motivated the other, right on pitch."[57]

Korea Campus Crusade staff worker Oh Chint'ak recalled that Bright and Kim were "spiritual sojourners" as well as "rivals" who "encouraged and challenged each other."[58] By 1974, they had organized Explo '74, the largest revival in Campus Crusade's history.

Given that they came from markedly different backgrounds, how did they come to establish a transpacific partnership in the Cold War era? First, a shared theological anxiety about modernism brought white fundamentalists like Bright and South Korean Protestants like Kim across the Pacific. The fundamentalist-modernist controversy in the United States was not only a national theological dilemma, but also one that Christians elsewhere, including in Korea, shared. That Kim shared the critiques of modernism, communism, and liberalism with Bright and those at Fuller allowed him to extend the work of Campus Crusade internationally. Second, Kim's anticommunist conversion narrative in the midst of the Korean War cohered with Cold War concerns for the containment of communism among white neo-evangelicals, which distanced Joon Gon Kim from the "red" cause of North Korean communism. Relatedly, the racial implications of his conversion narrative cohered with Cold War America's vision to integrate noncommunist Koreans, distancing him from the "red" cause of civil rights.

The Critique of Theological Liberalism

Bright had become a Christian at Hollywood's First Presbyterian Church, a wealthy suburban church in the Sun Belt.[59] At Hollywood Presbyterian, he met Henrietta Mears, the influential Christian educator, under whose tutelage he experienced spiritual renewal. He recalled his conversion experience: "She ended her message by saying to us, 'When you go home tonight, get down on your knees, and say with the Apostle Paul, Lord, what would you have me do?' Well, I did exactly that." For Bright, this was not an instantaneous change but the beginning of a journey. "It wasn't a profound prayer," he writes, "but the Lord heard it, and he changed my life—not dramatically in an instant, but gradually."[60] Bright continued to stay active at Hollywood Presbyterian, and in 1946, with Mears's encouragement, he began his seminary education at Princeton Theological Seminary.

Just one year after beginning his studies, however, Bright returned to California to revive his candy business. Fortuitously, in that year Fuller was founded, and Bright transferred from Princeton to join its inaugural class. For

Bright, "Effective ministry equaled effective evangelism," and he did not think he learned how to become an effective evangelist through seminary.[61] True to his proclivity for the practical over the scholastic, it was while he was studying for a Greek exam that he was interrupted by a spiritual vision. He later wrote: "The experience of Forest Home was repeated. I suddenly had the overwhelming impression that the Lord had unfolded a scroll of instructions of what I was to do with my life."[62] God was calling him to begin a nationwide ministry for college students. In 1951, Bright began his campus ministry at UCLA, the first chapter of hundreds, under the name Campus Crusade for Christ.

Joon Gon Kim, on the other hand, matriculated at Fuller in 1957 in order to gain a stronger sense of "intellectual Christianity." He was interested in studying Christian philosophy because he attributed his lack of evangelistic success among college students and youth to his inability to "make the intellectual mind satisfied." Moreover, "liberal influences," he said, had brought "great trouble" to the Korean churches for the past ten years, "chiefly through students who studied at liberal seminaries in the United States."[63] Joon Gon Kim was referring especially to the theological tensions at Chosun Theological Seminary, where he initially enrolled in 1946.

American theological institutions were experiencing fundamentalist-modernist rifts, and the Korean theological landscape was shifting along similar lines. Chosun Theological Seminary, founded in 1940 by Korean theologians such as Kim Jae Jun, rejected biblical literalism and sought an alternative to the theologically fundamentalist Pyongyang Theological Seminary. In 1947, the same year Fuller was founded in Pasadena, fifty-one Chosun seminary students, including Joon Gon Kim, signed a petition denouncing its theological liberalism. By July 1952, this fundamentalist cadre established the Korean chapter of the NAE.[64] Those following Kim Jae Jun's theological orientation created in 1959 a new Korean Presbyterian denomination, historically the most left-leaning in Korea.[65]

Though Kim had hopes of finding both a spiritual and an intellectual Christian tradition that would give him the key to evangelistic success and to remedying liberalism in the Korean church, he was skeptical of the spiritual condition in the United States—was America a secular or a Christian nation? "Frankly speaking," he wrote, "I had never expected to acquire spiritual power from this country."[66] But when Joon Gon Kim arrived at Fuller, he entered a new center for American fundamentalism, one that increasingly reformed itself into the "new evangelicalism."

While at Fuller, Joon Gon Kim met Campus Crusade staff, including Bob Kendall and Bob Johns, who introduced him to Bright, who had already heard about "Kim from Korea."[67] Kim attended their meetings, conferences, and even met Mears. His former prejudices about the US spiritual landscape were transformed when he encountered the organization, for it provided him with the keys to unlocking his failures in evangelism. At the annual staff training conference in the summer of 1957 at Mound, Minnesota, Kim "discovered something which [he] had not realized before."[68] He had failed to proclaim the "basic message" as Campus Crusade had done. The staff members were asked to memorize a twenty-minute evangelistic tool, "God's Plan for Your Life," a precursor to Campus Crusade's signature document, *Four Spiritual Laws*.[69] The message spoke of "the Lord Jesus Christ, the new birth, the Holy Spirit [and] of prayer, and of Scripture." But "quite contrary to my expectation, it was an intellectual discussion," which was important, given the critique of fundamentalism's anti-intellectualism. Kim had been searching for an evangelical message that would satisfy the minds of college students and youth, and in Campus Crusade he believed he found it. It appealed to the intellect, but it was not a form of philosophical or theological jargon. As a "simple, basic message," he believed it to be the "key that God could use to open the hearts of men." He learned that instead of persuading a person philosophically, appealing to the person's mind through a simple, basic evangelistic communication tool could chart a path to the heart's conversion. Kim wrote: "I said to myself, 'Here it is, this is the only key to winning the lost souls to Christ.'"[70] Bright's entrepreneurial knack for packaging the gospel in a simple, reason-based message was relevant for Koreans. As a result of his encounter with Campus Crusade, Kim was convinced to turn from a philosophical to a pragmatic approach in sharing the gospel. In 1958, he worked to internationalize Campus Crusade by establishing its first chapter in South Korea.[71]

There were distinctive theological divisions in mid-twentieth-century Korea and the United States, but Bright and Joon Gon Kim were both dealing with similar problems of modernity and the Bible. They were looking for similar solutions to keep a classical evangelical tradition alive in the midst of the critiques of biblical higher criticism and the arguments posed against biblical literalism. These theological conflicts led to institutional divisions but also the motivation to begin a new institution like Campus Crusade across the Pacific.

Conversion and Racialized Anticommunism

In meeting Bright at Fuller, Joon Gon Kim engaged in a transpacific network conserving a biblically literalist tradition of Christianity in a modern moment that seemed to threaten the viability of this tradition. These conversations could have been had largely within the boundaries of each nation, but they happened across the Pacific because of the Korean War and postwar immigration, which paved unprecedented routes between the United States and South Korea. Kim's anticommunist Christian narrative of physical, spiritual, and psychological rebirth also served as a foundation for establishing a transpacific network with Campus Crusade. The fact that Kim and his daughter survived the war revealed to him and evangelicals in the United States the possibility of the triumph of Christianity over communism.

While for Americans anticommunism was rooted in a distant but lingering fear, Joon Gon Kim's anticommunism was rooted in his Korean War experience, specifically of witnessing his family die at the hands of communists. Klein notes the fear that occupied the imagination of Americans in cultural productions: "According to *The Manchurian Candidate*, contact with Asians, either at home or abroad, could only weaken the nation. While American participation in the Korean War halted the spread of communism in northeast Asia, it also opened up a hole in the nation's defenses, allowing the Asian menace to invade and corrupt America."[72] Thus, Bright believed that the "evangelization of Japan and South Korea would inoculate other Asian countries against the contagion of communism."[73] Joon Gon Kim's conversion narrative was relevant to Cold War America, as it assuaged the fears of Americans, showing them that communism could be contained through South Korean Christians like him. Similarly, Kim believed that Korea was the key to saving Asia from communism. He declared, "As Chiang Kai-shek remarked, 'The one who conquers Korea will conquer Asia.' Her position is important not only from the political standpoint, but the spiritual standpoint also."[74] Kim analogized his spiritual strategy to Chiang's political strategy. Henrietta Mears, Bright's mentor, echoed this sentiment when she warned her parishioners at Forest Home in 1947: "There must be a Christian answer to the growing menace of communism." Mears consequently resolved, "God is looking for women and men of total commitment," and an uncompromising proclamation of the gospel was the solution.[75] South Koreans like Joon Gon Kim were crucial noncommunist Asians who could protect Americans from the menacing communist Asians. Kim's anticommunist conversion narrative revealed that he was a trustworthy Cold War ally.

During the war, Joon Gon Kim was in his hometown on Jido Island when Korean communists occupied the region for three months: "Our executioners were fellow villagers who had joined the communists, and they began with my father." He recalled witnessing his father's brutal death: "Just a stone's throw away from me, my father was struck on the head several times and fell dead." He then witnessed his wife's death: "Then my wife, trying to keep back her tears, said goodbye to me and said she would see me in heaven. Before my eyes, she was brutally killed."[76] Joon Gon Kim recalled that he also "just waited to be killed," and that during the three-month massacre, he "overcame twenty-one instances where [he] almost died."[77]

The three-month massacre at Jido Island resulted in the death of 10 percent of his town's population of twenty thousand. From his family, only he and his baby daughter survived. The choice between life and death shaped Kim's theological commitments. Given his experiences, he realized that one could not hold a theological middle ground or nuanced imagination of a theologically gray area when faced with life-or-death situations and their associated theological choices. For him that choice was between Christianity and communism. Though he had become a Christian at the age of nineteen, he recalled that the real "starting point of my Christian life began when I faced persecution and death under the Communist occupation."[78] After witnessing his family's death, he structured his theology in opposition to communism, as if communism represented an alternative religious belief. Joon Gon Kim's faith came to life under communist persecution. On the Korean War battlefield, he had a "born again" experience, which cohered with the Christian idea of resurrection, that the dead could come back to life.

While his life was spared, Kim not surprisingly reported facing near psychological and spiritual death in the aftermath. "I was so heartbroken that I began to question God," he recalled. "My spiritual livelihood was also dying at that time. My consciousness came and went for days at a time. . . . I was also dead psychologically because I had no hope."[79] If communist ideology did not convert Kim to atheism, then the brutality of war nearly did. "I had stopped praying or expecting God to answer and I had no desire for eternal life," he remembered. "I lost sight of God, and within my soul I was complaining and trying to cut myself off from him. I experienced the total despair and darkness of spiritual death, which was a feeling of complete separation from God. It was unbearable," he recalled.[80]

Yet in the midst of his near psychological and existential death, he was renewed. He recalled, "But in the valley of death, God called my name." When Kim was seemingly abandoned, God called on him personally, and suddenly he "realized that my lips had begun to move in prayer to God." A source outside of himself, which he identified as the Holy Spirit, compelled him to engage in prayer: "That prayer was begun on my lips by the Holy Spirit, and ended in my heart." At this moment Kim declared that he "passed from death to life." He then "turned to my Savior," who gave him "great peace and joy," which "sprang from my heart like a river." Kim centered on the resuscitation of his "heart," a key metaphor in the evangelical tradition, often called a "religion of the heart."[81] His "heart" had the power to move him from psychological and spiritual death to life. Moreover, in the same way that "peace and joy" sprang from his heart in lieu of death, so too his heart "burned" with a sacred desire to overcome hatred: "My hatred for the Communists vanished, and there burned in my heart a desire to please God, to glorify his name and to do his will."[82] The "heart" was the spiritual organ through which Kim gained a second chance at life after losing his family and fleeing the brutality of war.

Though his "hatred" for communists "vanished," Kim's religious experience suggested clear options: communism versus Christianity, death versus life. The division of North and South Korea along the 38th parallel exemplified the binary theological options available.

The ideological and theological battle that white fundamentalists and emerging neo-evangelicals fought in seminary classrooms and suburban pulpits had an urgent life-and-death battleground on the stage of the Korean War, which made Kim's conversion narrative especially compelling to white fundamentalists. During Graham's and Harold Ockenga's Boston rallies in the 1950s, communism served as a symbol of satanic and secular influence. They feared communism not only as a threat to the evangelization of the world but also as an apocalyptic sign of the end times. Moreover, intertwined with the Cold War anticommunist theology of this age was an argument against the "red" cause of Black civil rights. In the 1950s, white fundamentalists, or emerging neo-evangelicals, like Graham did not side with King's cause for civil rights because of their individual-centered vision of sin and social change. Graham's conversion-focused individualistic theological paradigm eschewed the institutional change.[83] Graham argued that King moved too fast and should put the brakes on racial reform.

Anticommunism exacerbated white fundamentalists' individualistic theological resistance to civil rights reform. Unproven theories connecting

Bolshevik radical activities to Black activists' opposition to white supremacy continued into the 1950s red scare, when King's and other civil rights activists' vision for racial equality was cast as communist and therefore un-American or anti-American.[84] When Graham preached about the "communist threat" in the 1950s, he linked the fear of communism with the "fiery concern about the Black civil rights activists who were, to their way of thinking, promoting communist ideas and socialism." He connected "communism with civil rights work" and "fear of the end times and the Antichrist," which "instilled fear and determination in evangelists and evangelical listeners alike."[85]

On one hand, the Cold War propelled racial progress in America. As Cold War and civil rights historians have shown, international pressures to "safeguar[d] the nation's image overseas" as a global leader against communism, in part, led to the desegregation of the US military and education.[86] On the other hand, racial progress stagnated through anticommunist fear during the Cold War. White fundamentalists like Graham played a key role in impeding progress. Accusations that Black civil rights activists were communists were not mere rhetoric, but fundamentally truncated their international human rights vision for racial equality, reducing it to a more localized civil rights frame. Anticommunism set limits on Black civil rights activists' 1950s vision for peacebuilding and decolonization in Asia.[87] Moreover, white fundamentalists and emerging neo-evangelicals further secured a racial wedge through anticommunist theologies that created a false binary between Black freedom and Asian decolonization.

At this time, Koreans like Hyun and Kimm—arrested under the auspices of the McCarran Act—who protested racial injustice in the United States were also cast as communist. The stigma of communism worked to "discredit and make foreign Hyun and Kimm's struggle against racist practices in the United States."[88] Their case "importantly illustrated that anticommunist hysteria of the early Cold War years was entrenched in fear of the foreign."[89] Yet if Hyun and Kimm were representative of "bad" Koreans, then Joon Gon Kim's narrative represented the "good" Koreans from the gaze of Cold War America.

For Joon Gon Kim, facing communism was not a symbolic or abstract spiritual or ideological threat, but a practical and real matter of life and death. He believed that the death of his family was evidence that communism was an evil and godless ideology. His anticommunist conversion narrative positioned South Koreans as "good" allies whose faith commitment to the Great Commission—world evangelization—intertwined with US democratic capitalism, defined against the "red" cause of North Korean communism, which had significant transpacific ripple effects, positioning him against the "red" cause of civil rights. Through Kim's narrative, white fundamentalists witnessed that the world's total evangelization was still possible, even in the aftermath of Mao's communist triumph in 1949, and that America still had the potential to be a "city on a hill," a nonimperial beacon of democratic and Christian hope, in spite of the racial realities that suggested otherwise. And yet such a narrative only further distanced Joon Gon Kim from the North Korean communists for whom he professed sincere love.

Joon Gon Kim and Billy Kim became core to that global evangelization project as they extended nonstate fundamentalist networks across US borders, modernizing these institutions beyond what modernists imagined. The two men confirmed for white fundamentalists and neo-evangelicals that their understanding of a religion of the heart and democracy worked, that they were plausible universal ideals, even for those outside of the United States. Thus, Joon Gon Kim became Campus Crusade's first international and nonwhite partner, and Billy Kim became a spokesperson not only for fundamentalist values but also for US democracy. Yet it came at a significant cost to them, especially as Billy Kim's and Joon Gon Kim's narratives encouraged disavowal of their own racial alienation and the cause for Black freedom.

These two portraits reveal the racial and religious logic undergirding the expansion of white fundamentalist networks across the Pacific, upon which the revival of modern evangelical America depended. Cold War America's alliance with noncommunist Koreans depended on a myth of the United States as a racial democracy, a narrative built upon a foundation of Black segregation, and suppression of Korean students' struggles in Orientalist institutions.

And yet their achievements as Korean leaders were widely acclaimed by white fundamentalists, and by 1973 and 1974, they respectively partnered with Campus Crusade and the BGEA to host the largest revivals in the history of both parachurches, the "most important tools of modern evangelism," which indexed the re-emergence of evangelicalism in the age of Graham.[90] These hidden stories of Cold War alliance reveal the intertwining of revival and racism, via the Pacific, that would transform a niche, white, fundamentalist America into an American evangelical empire.

3

Orphans

The Mirage of Evangelical Diplomacy, 1960–1969

The transpacific networks that Joon Gon Kim and Billy Kim forged through their days as students in the United States continued apace and led to the massive revivals hosted by the BGEA and Campus Crusade in the 1970s. But throughout the 1960s, the racialized networks that had been forged across the Pacific in the 1950s came to have unexpected effects on the lives of Korean children, including orphans like Oh Chiyŏng, who joined the World Vision Korean Orphan Choir. As an eight-year-old, she sang her heart out on the audition stage for the choir.[1] At the time, she was living in a Taejon orphanage, located southeast of Seoul. "I was a baby abandoned on the streets after the war," she recalled.[2] But on August 22, 1960, Oh successfully auditioned to become an inaugural member of the World Vision Korean Orphan Choir.[3]

Upon her admission to this selective choir, Oh could dream of a new future, beginning with the new treats she was promised: a delicious fried egg every day and a piano in her own room. "[In reality], there was an organ in the common room and we had eggs only on Sundays," she recalled. "Of course, our country was so poor, how could they really give us these things?" Despite being misled, she recalled that the choristers walked with an unusually privileged gait: "We were trained to believe that we are 'little ambassadors of Korea' and they said, 'you are ambassadors for God,'" she recalled. "Because we were little ambassadors of Korea, we were trained in manners and etiquette.... We sang in so many languages... and memorized all of the songs." Oh concluded: "At school they would say, 'You choir kids walk differently.' I think it's because we learned how to walk back and forth on stage.... And it's because we had that consciousness: 'I am an ambassador for Korea. I am an ambassador for God.'"[4] Oh's song and multilingual performance on the world stage had the power to elevate her into a "little ambassador" for God and country.

Oh Chiyŏng was chosen from among thirteen thousand orphans and 151 orphanages established in the aftermath of the Korean War. Unlike the bloodless Cold War in Europe, the Cold War in Asia resulted in real wars and the destruction of communities at the grassroots level.[5] As discussed, between three and four million people died in the Korean War, and the nation was divided into two countries, North and South Korea. The orphanages associated with the World Vision Korean Orphan Choir were created in the aftermath of the war as aforementioned Korean Presbyterian minister Kyung Chik Han and US evangelist Bob Pierce sought to connect Seoul's suffering with American evangelical and humanitarian resources. The World Vision Korean Orphan Choir was the next humanitarian venture that Han and Pierce had created to expand their work.

Oh Chiyŏng, along with the other members of the World Vision Korean Orphan Choir, resided in the dormitories at the Musical Institute in Seoul. They trained with Chang Soo Chul, a premier South Korean choir director.[6] Oh and her peers mastered a full repertoire of Korean, American, and European hymns and folk songs, not only in their mother tongue, but, as indicated, also in foreign languages. Alongside the unrivaled musical training, choristers also practiced Christian disciplines: daily early morning prayer, scripture memorization, Wednesday and Sunday worship services, and worship over the radio at bedtime. For ten years, until her high school graduation, Oh toured the world with the choir, including four trips to the United States to perform at large and prominent churches, for political dignitaries, and on the big screen.

No World Vision program was more popular than its Korean Orphan Choir in the 1960s.[7] A musical venture created by Pierce and Han, it was a distinctive choir under Pierce's leadership, from 1960 to 1967. When Pierce left World Vision in 1967 for complicated health and personal reasons, the choir changed its name to the Korean Children's Choir. From 1968 to 1969, the choir made its final tour of the decade without him.[8] Under Pierce's leadership, the choir's purpose had been as diverse as his vast and seemingly endless array of interests. The choir's US public relations firm, McFadden and Associates, attempted to state the choir's aim simply: to "express the appreciation of Korean children to the people of this continent and to illustrate the needs of orphans all over the world."[9] But these orphan choristers were more than grateful singers. When Ted Engstrom took the reins of World Vision in 1969, he declared: "The Korean Children's Choir is one of the greatest PR tools World Vision has and we need to keep constantly aware of this potential."[10] Indeed, no fundraising effort was more lucrative for World Vision in the 1960s than the orphan choristers.

What made the "sober little charmers" not only captivating singers but also such philanthropic gold mines? The World Vision Korean Orphan Choir tapped into an important 1960s racialized Cold War American impulse. Whereas the racial terror of the Jim Crow South globally publicized Black discrimination and revealed America's moral impotence as a global Cold War leader, the nonwhite children of Korea projected a shiny image of global evangelical humanitarianism that underscored the possibilities of US-led global racial uplift and geopolitical peace.[11] This triangulated and transpacific racial logic suggested that the United States was, therefore, the rightful and moral heir to wield global leadership in the age of the global Cold War. At the height of the civil rights movement, these orphan choristers, known as the "happy singing larks," helped white Protestants associated with the "new evangelicalism" to believe that they espoused, and *could* espouse, racial democracy through individual financial donations, sponsorships, and the practice of humanitarianism.[12]

Yet image and reality often did not align. Choristers truly delighted in unforgettable trips to Disneyland, the "happiest place on earth," while on their international tours, but they never shared in the funds they raised. Moreover, the global evangelical humanitarian efforts were, despite best intentions, not necessarily born out of, or conduits for, fostering global racial equality. The chorister's positive image, crafted for racialized Cold War American public consumption, devastated some of the choristers, including one of the most beloved original members, "Peanuts," or Kim Sang Yong, who committed suicide as he protested World Vision's empire of care.

The rebranding of the new evangelicalism in the 1960s was, in part, an outgrowth of US empire-building projects in Korea, mediated through the seemingly innocuous but harsh reality of the South Korean orphan choristers' lives. Scholars have cited Graham's 1957 Madison Square Garden crusade as the hallmark event that divided ultraseparatist fundamentalists like Bob Jones from the "new evangelicals." The new evangelicals would go on to rebrand evangelicalism as mainstream America, with Graham at the helm. World Vision's 1960s history reveals an overlooked transpacific and humanitarian dimension through which the new evangelicals—as exemplified in Pierce's leadership with the World Vision Korean Orphan Choir—reimagined themselves as a mainstream form of evangelicalism. They did so by leveraging transpacific networks devoted to Cold War humanitarian care in South Korea.

The intertwining of religion, race, and diplomacy embedded in the image of the World Vision Korean Orphan Choir facilitated the transformation of the image of a new American evangelicalism, with fundamentalist roots, into a nonliberal but respectable US mainstream movement.

Tracing the history of the World Vision Korean Orphan Choir, this chapter analyzes religion, race, and diplomacy through cultural diplomacy and the myth of the model minority; the "orphan" and Cold War Orientalism; and sentimentalism and a "religion of the heart." This transpacific analysis of religion, race, and diplomacy reveals that the World Vision Korean Orphan Choir was uncritically aligned with Cold War people-to-people diplomacy, smoothing over the dark and tragic history of US-led intervention and militarization in Korea. The choir unwittingly helped to expand whiteness beyond US borders through nonstate networks forged with South Korea, an indispensable factor that helped to rebrand the new evangelicalism.[13] Han's local and indigenous South Korean leadership was foundational for the founding and expansion of World Vision in general and the Korean Orphan Choir in particular. Yet Pierce and Han both underestimated the force of US empire building in Korea, which the "little ambassadors" experienced, in spite of their image as "happy singing larks," and to which they responded, at times with tragic consequences.[14]

The World Vision Korean Orphan Choir's Song

On October 13, 1961, Oh Chiyŏng met South Korean president Park Chung-hee, who greeted the "little ambassadors" before they embarked on a Pan American World Airways plane to the United States. The World Vision Korean Orphan Choir was headed on its first international tour. When they landed in Los Angeles, the Church of the Open Door in Pasadena anchored their experience. The orphan choristers began and ended their tour at the Church of the Open Door to the themes of "Welcome to America" and "Farewell to America."[15] The American-themed beginning and end gestured toward the choir's role as cultural diplomats, of which President Park was fully aware when he greeted them at the airport. Moreover, to begin and end their tour at the Church of the Open Door, founded by the fundamentalist R. A. Torrey, foreshadowed the reconstruction of modern American evangelicalism through global humanitarian activities like caring for orphans.

During the 1960s, as the gaze of the global Cold War in Asia began to shift to Vietnam, the Korean nation waned in significance in the US imagination.[16] In 1961, in the aftermath of the ousting of President Syngman Rhee, General Park Chung-hee seized presidential power in South Korea through a military coup d'état that left the Kennedy administration skeptical of the legitimacy of Park's democratic rule.[17] Chung-Nan Yun notes that during this early period of Park's rule, nonstate actors, including Han and the World Vision Korean Orphan Choir, continued to "spark interest in American government foreign relations" and to develop "a solid Korean-American alliance in the years after the Korean War ceasefire."[18] Yun suggests that when the US government needed nongovernmental actors to support US anti-Soviet and anticommunist efforts, World Vision, and specifically the World Vision Korean Orphan Choir's transpacific networks, facilitated cultural diplomacy between the United States and South Korea.[19]

Park's government "enthusiastically supported" the choir, and while Han mediated connections from the Korean side, Pierce mediated connections to the United States.[20] In supporting the choir, Han forged intimate ties with the South Korean government, which raised his status as a national leader. For helping to bridge gaps with the Kennedy administration, Park granted Han permission to organize the Billy Graham Crusade in 1973, the largest crusade in Graham's career and the topic of the next chapter.[21]

As for the choristers, they enjoyed the "fairy-tale" experience of traveling to the United States, from the joy of riding a Rose Bowl Parade float to heavenly soda pop and ice cream treats. Moon Hyangja recalled: "I almost fainted when I arrived [in Pasadena]. It was a scene out of a fairy tale. I teared up, and I couldn't forget it."[22] Given the poverty of Korea at the time, flying on an airplane to such a prosperous nation was a rare experience that felt almost otherworldly for South Korean children. Just a week into their first international tour, the choristers made US headlines. "Korean Orphans Win City's Hearts," the *Los Angeles Times* declared.[23] "Thirty Korean orphans are falling in love with Los Angeles this week—and it's mutual," the article reported.[24] They were lovable and their voices unforgettable, the *Los Angeles Times* reported. The "songbirds," as the US media called them, were "little" and "joyful." *World Vision Magazine* reported a testimonial: "I knew they would be 'cute,' but I didn't really think their singing would amount to too much. I expected to hear a lot of squeaky little voices.... What a surprise! As they began to sing I could hardly believe my ears. It was the most beautiful, most skillfully executed, most heart-warming music I had ever heard!"[25] The orphan choir's singing could not be overlooked, as they were, first and foremost, musically gifted.

The choir's international tours were also ambitious. During their first three-month tour, from 1961 to 1962, they packed in US performances at Hollywood Presbyterian Church, Carnegie Hall, and "Ed Sullivan's Christmas Program," and sang for Eisenhower.[26] The second tour was by far the most ambitious. Piece expanded the itinerary to twelve countries over seven months. In addition to the United States and Canada, they traveled to Japan and Taiwan, where they performed for President and Madame Chiang Kai-shek. The choristers then hopped through Iran, Israel, France, Germany, the Netherlands, England, and Norway. In India, they performed for Prime Minister Nehru's daughter Indira Nehru Gandhi, who welcomed them warmly. The third tour was again seven months long, but smaller in geographic scope, visiting only North America.[27] During the choir's fourth and final tour, from 1968 to 1969, they sang throughout the United States without Pierce, who had by then left World Vision.

These tours were lucrative. On that last tour alone, the choir earned $264,089 from record sales, advertising, and a special deposit.[28] They raised significant funds through sponsorships, as they garnered 1,942 US sponsors who pledged to give $144 per year as well as $27,226 in cash, totaling $279,588 in potential income.[29] In the 1960s, World Vision ensured its financial security through the choir. The choir had an excellent brand that raised World Vision's fundraising value. Park Jong Sam reflected: "Bob Pierce was a brilliant man.... As the CEO of the organization, he had to handle the responsibilities of fundraising. He didn't know all of the organizations in Korea, but he knew that he could raise funds in the US and send it to Korea." He continued: "He went around to churches and fundraised, but . . . he needed a kind of fundraising tool. A novel idea that he came up with was to create a choir composed of the orphaned children of Korea." Park went on to use a developmentalist paradigm to understand the significance of the orphan choir: "A long time ago, if you considered the Korean War orphan and the country, Korea . . . it was so poor, poorer than countries in Africa. . . . From such a country, orphaned children could sing modernized Western songs and Christian hymns." In so doing, the children came to "represent the thousands of other children. . . . The children of war became a choir. He took this brand and marketed it to the world."[30]

Pierce was an entrepreneurial evangelist. Pierce's "brilliant" global marketing and branding strategy was to captivate global audiences with the fascinating sight of the poor, orphaned Korean children now singing modern Western songs and hymns. So powerful was Pierce's strategy of casting these Korean children as upwardly mobile that as an entrepreneurial evangelist he helped to catapult a parachurch with fundamentalist roots into mainstream American consciousness. As the choristers performed on the *Ed Sullivan Show* and with Julie Andrews, they helped to brand the new evangelicalism as a mainstream American movement.

Entrepreneurial but ever the evangelist, Pierce embedded within his "brilliant" global marketing strategy a multipronged theological mission. Pierce announced that the choir sang "God-inspired music" or "God-given music" that would bring the audience "closer to God." Upon hearing their "inspiring presentation," they would "lift [their audience's] hearts in praise to God," he promised.[31] "Your soul will sing with joy," he declared to Americans, for the children had "God-given voices."[32] They were to "bring to America an understanding of the lives and accomplishments of children in Korea" and "present a spiritual ministry" through the "universal language of music."[33]

Yet Pierce felt that there was "an even deeper reason for the tour," namely Christian faith and service: "The children go everywhere as 'little missionaries' singing on behalf of needy children the world over. They have a great sense of mission, and a precious spirit of Christian dedication."[34] Not only "happy singing larks" and "little ambassadors," the children were also imbued with a moniker of religious significance: "little missionaries." Children perceived as endowed with a God-given talent, they were given the responsibility to spread the gospel through song, even as they were themselves, ironically, children in need. The choir forged bonds across national and racial difference through the shared belief in God, the sacred significance of Christian music, and the theological notion of a global Christian family.

World Vision remade evangelicalism into a respectable mainstream movement in the 1960s through cultural productions like the World Vision Korean Orphan Choir. Orphan choristers may have felt as if they were the lucky stars when they were selected as choristers, but World Vision, as a brand, also needed them. As the orphan choristers sang on world stages like Carnegie Hall, World Vision burgeoned, not only through philanthropic donations, but in terms of optics, rising out of its niche fundamentalist roots and moving more visibly into mainstream American consciousness. The World Vision Korean Orphan Choir displayed the relevance and benevolence of the strain of white Protestantism that emerged out of fundamentalism.

As for the choristers, Yi Hokyun recalled the personal spiritual significance of the tours. While on the 1961–1962 tour, she was baptized in the Jordan River. She recalled, "When we went to Israel, and since [Pierce] is a Baptist pastor, he baptized those who were prepared. In the Jordan River I was baptized on November 2, 1962. He covered us with a towel and then dunked us into the river." She continued: "I felt as though all of my sins were washed away. It felt like my legs couldn't reach the ground and I was walking on air. I was walking but it felt like I was not walking on the ground but floating in the air. That day still seems so fresh to me."[35]

Choristers' fairy-tale-like experiences spanned from Disneyland to the Holy Land. Some, like Yi Hokyun, even experienced existentially transformative life events like the rite of baptism. Such spiritual experiences amplified the dream-like experience of traveling the world as orphans.

The choir was, moreover, a national treasure for South Koreans. At a time when South Korea was still trying to find its economic footing in the global order, they swelled with pride at the sight of the choir. Park Jong Sam recalled:

> Consider how destitute Korea was at that time, but the newspapers reported, "Their sound is as if precious gems were rolling down a silver platter." Even for me, it was when I was in high school.... When I heard that Korean children took a plane to fly to the US to sing... you don't know how much pride I felt. They were the pride of Korea. At that time the only thing the Koreans could be proud of was the World Vision Korean Orphan Choir. There was nothing to be proud of because we were so poor... the work that God did through them received national recognition. They received protection from the government and politics. They received protection from Korean civil society.... They helped the national image and they were used for diplomacy.[36]

Moon Hyangja echoed Park's observations, recalling: "When we left [the choir] we had the Korean flag embossed on our hearts. We had let our country shine and I learned that we were a people indebted to the gospel."[37] By 1963, the choir had become known as a "standard and model," a "top class" choir, the envy of the children in Korea. Moon recalls: "It felt like I received a great privilege to be part of a choir that was so top class.... At that time the choir was more of a focal point than the World Vision organization itself. The choir was a kind of standard and model at that time. People would stop and sit on sheets of newspaper just to hear us."[38] Orphan choristers were, ironically, among the privileged as they brushed shoulders with the global elite. Through Christian musical performance, they raised the image of their nation's status in the world order.

Indeed, the World Vision Korean Orphan Choir's global tours throughout the 1960s were packed with a kaleidoscope of activities. Orphaned children laughed on airplanes and merry-go-rounds. Musically gifted children brought audiences to tears. Children and adults alike were spiritually moved. Two countries strengthened diplomatic ties. War-torn South Korea projected a modern image through Christian song.[39] A forgotten and seemingly backward US religious tradition crafted a new modern face, one song at a time, in the global spotlight. But it was especially their status as "little ambassadors" that made them into the kind of transpacific celebrities who could help catapult the image of a new evangelicalism into mainstream America.

Good "Little Ambassadors": Cultural Diplomacy and the Myth of the Model Minority

The "little ambassadors" densely packed a tripartite connection between crusades, orphanages, and the Cold War, a crucial message for World Vision during this decade, as David King provides.[40] World Vision was focused on Asia in the 1950 and 1960s, and South Korean orphan choristers were exemplars of piety and the promise of triumph over communism and poverty in the region. Their image suggested the goodness of a world ruled by US-led democratic capitalism, and that the Asia-Pacific could become America's lake without the cruelty of empire. The choristers helped to launch World Vision onto the global stage because their image tapped into a racialized Cold War American impulse that cast South Koreans as "good" allies and the United States as benevolent rulers.

As mentioned, beginning with Eisenhower, the US Cold War state had employed people-to-people diplomacy to encourage personal and heartfelt relationships between Americans and the noncommunist world, including in Asia, in order to ameliorate tensions with communist Asia. Communism was concomitantly a domestic and global threat for the United States. Defeating the enemy abroad, then, meant defeating and domesticating the enemy within. As an "ambassador," Pierce helped to shape the World Vision Korean Orphan Choir's image as one closely allied with the US state's Cold War agenda of embracing noncommunist Koreans. Pierce noted: "The meritorious 'diplomatic job' done by the little boys and girls of the choir brings to the fore the importance of people-to-people cultural intercourse."[41] He remarked that the "happy singing larks" were noted for their "completely disarming" presence.[42] The choir helped the United States to mediate diplomatic relations with noncommunist Korea through the innocuous and transformed image of "orphans." Cold War Manichaean logic continued to delineate and discipline "good" and bad" subjects; orphan choristers could be juxtaposed against the "bad" type of Korean, the menacing North Korean communist. The "good" kind of Korean, the orphan chorister, was elevated as desirable in churches, halls of power, and thanks to the power of television, in US homes.[43] World Vision burgeoned in the 1960s by aligning itself with the image of the "good" South Korean Cold War subject, as embodied in the "happy singing larks."

When Pierce reported in the early 1960s on the choir's multiple accomplishments and the wide-ranging media coverage that the choir received from international tours, he excerpted the *Korean Republic*'s reporting on the choir's diplomatic value:

> The enthusiastic support given by Americans to the choir is a clear manifestation of the deep-rooted and solid ties existing between the people of the United States and Korea. It is all the more significant because most of the orphans in the choir are the victims of communist aggression. We further hope that the choir has contributed much toward correcting any wrong impressions of Korea harbored in the minds of some Americans, whether these originate from prejudice or from their association with the wrong type of Koreans while serving or residing in Korea. Diplomacy, or the job of deepening friendships with peoples of other lands, should not be placed under the responsibility of diplomats alone.[44]

The choir depicted the United States and South Korea as having "deep-rooted" and "solid ties," proving South Korea's value as a "good" ally to the United States in the global Cold War. Official diplomats were not the only ones responsible for "deepening friendships" with other nations. Everyday people, including the children of the choir, also proved crucial to advancing diplomacy through culture.

A Manichaean logic of "good" and "bad" Koreans, based on transpacific diplomacy, took further root as it cohered with shifting ideas about race in the United States. Note that the choristers traveled the world, and especially across the Pacific Ocean to the United States, during a moment when "Asians" were being reimagined from the stereotype of the "yellow peril" to the "model minority." Historian Ellen D. Wu argues that by the mid-1960s this racial renegotiation ossified into the new stereotype of Asian Americans as the "model minority," a "racial group distinct from the white majority, but lauded as well assimilated, upwardly mobile, politically nonthreatening, and *definitively not-black*."[45] As transpacific symbols of "good" Koreans, the orphan choristers cohered with the shifting stereotypes about Asians in the United States. The World Vision Korean Orphan Choir's history in the 1960s shows that transpacific evangelical networks were strengthened by the choir's appeal not only to the divisive cultural logics of the Cold War but also to the racial myth of the model minority as it pertained to Koreans in the US imaginary.

By way of background, US geopolitical ambitions in the post–World War II era triggered shifts in notions about nationhood and belonging, and by extension, a reimagination of the racial order. For instance, Japanese Americans, once considered a threat during the Pacific Wars, were reimagined as model racial minorities during the global Cold War as the United States attempted to embrace Japan as an ally. The formation of this new racial myth depended on narrations of Japanese American success as tied to culturally essentialist traits and through triangulation with African Americans. According to the new myth of the "model minority," Japanese Americans apparently "transcended the color line by virtue of their familial habits." The Moynihan Report of 1965 pitted Japanese Americans against African Americans. The report argued that racism against the former had "practically disappeared before our eyes." Moynihan suggested that Japanese Americans had successfully crossed the color line because they had a "close knit family structure," epitomized by the two-parent heterosexual and middle-class family. The report justified African American racial inferiority through a culturally based argument rooted in the family: the "'deterioration of the Negro family'—epitomized first and foremost by matriarchy—was the root cause of the 'deterioration of the fabric of Negro society.'" Japanese American assimilation, then, served as a "model for solving the intractable American Dilemma." However, so-called assimilation did not actually render Japanese Americans equals with whites. The racial logic of the myth of the model minority further "reinscribed ... foreignness." The myth, which attributed Japanese American success to the "practice of an alien culture," served as a culturally based racial strategy for maintaining anti-Black racism and white superiority in the 1960s.[46]

Defined transnationally against the so-called North Korean "menace" and the supposedly racially inferior African American, South Korean orphan choristers were imagined as moldable into white families, especially because of shared evangelical Protestant heritage. South Korea benefited in terms of foreign relations with the United States, as it was cast as the "good" country with the "good" people, as opposed to the North, which was the "bad" country with the "bad" people. Such racialized constructs of the desirable "orphan" and the elevated "model" were transnational extensions of each other. They elevated South Koreans in the white imagination, all the while maintaining the militarized US structures of racial inequality in South Korea. The World Vision Korean Orphan Choir helped to mediate such US-Korean relations of inequality.

Gratitude and Transformation

The narrative that the World Vision Korean Orphan Choir told of US-Korean relations was mediated through theological myths, especially that South Koreans were models of Christian gratitude and transformation. Pierce noted in *The World Vision Korean Orphan Choir* that the choristers were grateful to the United States, in spite of its violent intervention in the Korean War that split the Korean nation in two. As evidence, he publicized the following orphan chorister's remark: "In our concert we sing 'God Bless America' and I love America. I am so happy to be here and say thank you to the people who take care of us."[47] Pierce had argued that the tours were "an opportunity for these little war orphans to express their gratitude to the people of America for their assistance in saving them from starvation and poverty in Korea."[48] From this perspective, it was as if the tragedies of the Korean War could be overcome—nay, were overcome—with US aid, and with ongoing US sponsors for these "happy singing larks." The choir exemplified what a God-centered and a US-led global triumph over communism could achieve: lost orphans were found and now transformed into stars.

Kim Keum Ja exemplified this rags-to-riches narrative of Christian transformation. Pierce testified to the orphan choristers' fairy-tale-like transformations from "forlorn waif" to "songbird."[49] It was as if they had already had this experience, but that the tour itself was enacting this transformation on them. While on tour in 1965, Pierce wrote: "Tragic stories? Yes, but how wonderful when a forlorn waif can become a songbird—bringing joy to the hearts of countless thousands of people."[50] Chorister Kim exemplified this transformation: she had been nicknamed "the Princess" during the choir's first tour in 1961–1962 for her "poise and beauty."

By the choir's second international tour in 1963–1964, Kim Keum Ja had the opportunity to translate her nickname into a reality as she sang for actual royalty, King Olaf V, the king of Norway. As if her transformation from "waif" to "songbird" was now complete, Pierce expressed awe at how "a little orphan girl" was "singing before a king—in the name of the Lord Jesus." Pierce attributed this to "a kind friend in the United States who had become her sponsor," and to God, who "had brought her up from the miry clay and put a new song in her mouth (Psalm 40:2, 3)."[51] Kim Keum Ja represented what was possible when Americans invested in orphans. They could be transformed from orphans into near royalty, bestowing joy to the "hearts of countless thousands of people."[52]

A young girl named Lee In Soon, the "heart-interest of a nation," also showed a transformation. Lee was deaf and mute, but sang with her hands. Yet while the choir was on its second international tour, she began to show signs of progress, reportedly uttering her first words—"I love Jesus"—while in Hong Kong. Mrs. Marlin Jones of Pasadena, who saw Lee In Soon on television, contacted World Vision to provide her with medical care.[53] Lee received a Vicon S-I hearing device through Charles Love, the owner of the Taylor Hearing Center in Pasadena, just in time for a miracle: while at the Rose Parade, for the first time Lee In Soon "heard marching bands with tuba sounds . . . bugles blasting . . . the beat of drums."[54] Afterward, Lee "'sang' with nimble fingers her favorite hymn 'The Lord's Prayer,'" after which "tears of gratitude for being allowed to hear came into her eyes."[55] Alongside a photo spread of Lee In Soon, *Life* magazine testified to her transformation: "Eloquent hands of Lee In Soon, who is mute, speak in sign language the words the others in the choir sing. She was almost totally deaf at tour's start, but has since been fitted with hearing aids that give her 45% hearing."[56] Lee's story in *The Korean Orphan Choir* testifies to evidence of the orphan's transformation from "forlorn waif" to "songbird."[57]

Humanitarian gestures improved Lee In Soon's life, yet not without critique. Father Rutt, an Anglican priest who had come to Korea in 1954 and was a rector at St. Michael's College in Oryu-dong on the outskirts of Seoul, watched Lee's performance and reported in the *Korea Times*: "Recently I was once again ashamed for what is done in the name of my religion."[58] He recalled a news item that featured "the use of a deaf mute child in a money-raising programme in theatres abroad. The item said that she was made to mime during the singing of the Lord's Prayer by an orphan choir." He critiqued:

> The deaf child, like every other unfortunate, deserves sympathy without being turned into an act or a show. Christian charity has respect for the dignity of the individuals who are loved. The sponsor of the show has made a slight bow to consciences by publishing the fact that he is trying to get appropriate medical attention for the child. She could have been given every necessary attention, even given the pleasure of appearing in the show, without having been turned into a spectacle capitalizing on her disability.

Rutt was concerned that such activities would perpetuate stereotypes about Korea, that it was a "pathetic land of disabled people, substandard and to be pitied, the land that soldiers and diplomats hate to be sent to." Unlike the media coverage that hailed the choir as exemplary cultural diplomats, Father Ratt cautioned against its dangers:

> This is the more distressing because of the good that a Korean children's choir can do as an embassy abroad. Indeed this choir does it, with gay and pretty children singing charming songs and singing them very well. The audience has a chance to receive an impression of the charm that Korea really possesses. But when the whole show is advertised as being by orphans, missionary-sponsored, climaxed with a deaf mute, then deep in the subconscious of nearly every viewer will be lodged the basic thought that the poor children come from that miserable land despoiled by war. The war orphans are nearly grown up now, but the image of war orphans can still make sentimental people open their purses.

For Rutt, the image of the "orphan" still cast the children as destitute, even when stories of transformation were highlighted.

Indeed, when Pierce documented the choristers' stories, and especially Kim Keum Ja's and Lee In Soon's, as evidence that orphans could be transformed, he also simultaneously described them in pitiful terms. He narrates that Lee In Soon was "one of the thousands of waifs, hollow-eyed and spindle-legged, who drifted about the streets.... She was stoically oriental about her miserable today and unlikely tomorrow."[59] *Life* magazine testified to Lee's transformation, but also described the choir in culturally essentialist terms, as they innately seemed to embody "diligence, piety" and a "capacity for delight." The captions to photos went into further detail to describe these traits, noting children's diligence in chores and prayer and their foreignness for preferring to sleep on the floor rather than on "soft Western beds."[60]

Moreover, though technically "orphans," they were imagined as having an endless capacity for providing pleasure:

> Wherever they went in the U.S. people gladdened and touched by them outdid themselves to give the youngsters pleasure. . . . But when the children, many of whom had been picked up starving in war-shattered cities, showed their appreciation by raising those temple-bell voices that even professional music critics call angelic, their hearers straightway learned that of pleasure—and love—these children had a vaster store to give than they could ever receive.[61]

The choir had a "vaster store to give than they could ever receive," yet they were also orphans who were "picked up starving in war-shattered cities." Lee In Soon was imagined, on the one hand, as a "waif . . . who drifted about the streets," and on the other hand, as the emblem of the joyful "songbird." The media imagined the choir in polarized and homogenizing categories. Uplifting the World Vision Korean Orphan Choir as the "paragons of piety" did not change their orphan status, but elevated them to an otherworldly status as "other."[62] The choir helped to solidify foreign relations between the United States and Korea, though on unequal terms. They rehearsed how South Koreans could be imagined in the US imaginary with striking positive qualities, especially mediated through Christian ideas of gratitude and transformation, while maintaining South Korea's unequal and "little" status vis-à-vis the United States.

Orphan-Less: "Orphans" and Cold War Orientalism

Though it seemed as if they had an endless capacity for delight, the choristers nevertheless felt the burden of mediating transpacific foreign relations of inequality. While choristers like Oh Chiyŏng, Kim Keum Ja, and Lee In Soon sang brilliantly on the global stage, the incredible weight of their responsibilities dulled their shine. "We were very stressed," Oh remembered. "[We] probably didn't grow very tall because we were on constant alert. . . . Of course we were so good at what we did, but there was also that aspect."[63] The orphan choristers had multiple tasks: to perform at high musical standards, to represent their country and God, to serve as missionaries on behalf of impoverished children around the world, and to engage in people-to-people diplomacy for the sake of the global Cold War. From the first two tours, all donations went toward constructing the World Vision Children's Hospital in Seoul, and Oh lamented that orphan choristers could not retain the funds they raised. She had no resources to tide her over to high school graduation, when she would need to leave the choir.

Oh Chiyŏng also bemoaned that she was one of the only "original orphans." The World Vision Korean Orphan Choir was, ironically, nearly orphan-less, if an "orphan" is defined as a child whose parents are deceased. Moon Hyangja recalled, "My mother was adamant that I join the Sŏnmyŏnghwoe Choir [World Vision Korean Orphan Choir]. You could say that she was a go-getter on my behalf.... I was someone who didn't really have the credentials to join the choir. I wasn't an orphan. But I was somehow accepted."[64] Once she joined in 1963, Moon "realized that a lot of members weren't actually orphans."[65] Consider also chorister Yi Hokyun's story. Her father worked in Japan and her mother could not rear all four daughters alone. Her aunt worked at an orphanage in Pusan, so her mother left her there for care. She recalled, "In fifth grade, I was selected as a member of the World Vision Korean Orphan Choir. I auditioned at the Pusan Young Nak Presbyterian Church."[66] Though Yi Hokyun's family faced significant adversity as a separated family, her stay at the orphanage was temporary. Her parents were alive, and she did eventually reunite with them.

Oh Chiyŏng observed that, from its very origins, the choir was not composed of orphans, though it was advertised as such. She recalled: "Actually, there were children who had families. The criteria was that children of the directors were not allowed to join.... But when I got there, the director's children were there ... and there were kids who had a sister or an uncle—they had relatives." She felt "very lonely" because she was "one of the few who had no family.... Keum Ja, for instance, later found her sisters.... Her sister had a large hair salon.... They lived well.... I found out that so many of them had family.... This is the part that when I reflect on it, it makes me sad." She found that, however, she was "all the more grateful because it gave me an opportunity to meet God and to have a born-again experience."[67] Children had various familial arrangements, reflecting the multiple ways that the Korean War shattered and divided families, including across the 38th parallel, even if it did not always leave children parentless. Perhaps Pierce and Han thought this was a mere technicality, but the lack of accuracy disappointed choristers.

Oh Chiyŏng could not help but feel disenchanted. She commented: "At first I didn't feel good about it. I felt deceived. But it wasn't within my authority... you still had to feel bad for the kids since it wasn't like they all had parents... it was more like they had one or two relatives."[68] As she pointed to a picture of the first choir, she noted:

> She had a mom... who was a widow.... And this girl, she had siblings... She only sang until the second choir and then went back home.... Most of them had at least one familial connection. I was probably the only one who was an "original orphan."... So that's why inside I was lonely even though I looked happy on the outside.... You could only stay at the Music Institute until you graduated high school. For those who left in the middle, they left because they had family. Even if you were let go because you weren't making the cut, it was because you had some place to go.[69]

Oh recalls that being one of the only "original orphans" presented emotional challenges, for she regularly compared her family status with others and worried about her future:

> Where would I go? And, how would I live? Right before I would go to sleep at night, I was lonely. You know, humans are alone in front of God.... I would say to God, are you really there? What's going to happen to me? During the day, though, I was so happy.... Even now, people say that I am photogenic... it became a habit to smile... something that I learned to do ever since I was a child. When it comes time to take a picture, I smile.... Now that I say it, it sounds a bit sad, doesn't it?[70]

She asked challenging existential questions that would ultimately take her on a significant quest that led to a spiritual awakening, her born-again experience, discussed in the next chapter. But the contrast between the image and reality of the choir was reflected in her smile that hid sorrow.

Why was the "orphan" choir nearly orphan-less? First, Pierce's theological understanding of conversion rendered children "orphans" even when those children had parents. Much like the absence of orphans in the World Vision Korean Orphan Choir, five out of the nine narratives in Pierce's 1964 book *Orphans of the Orient: Stories That Will Touch Your Heart* do not represent stories of "orphans," if the term denotes those without biological parents. The lack of correspondence between the title and content in *Orphans of the Orient* reveals that Pierce's evangelical tract is less a journalistic account of orphaned children in Asia than a piece of creative nonfiction, a cultural production like the choir.

The narrative ties together in one frame the children of India, Taiwan, Korea, Japan, and China.[71] Photos accompanying the stories do not correspond to these children's stories. A photo that appears with the story of "Liloo of India" is captioned: "Liloo was a pretty Indian girl *like* this."[72] Liloo is not an orphan. Her parents are in the story. But she does become nearly orphaned for becoming a Christian. Even though she encounters tensions with her Hindu family because of her Christian faith, she is stalwart: "She would not go back to her family and their superstitious worship of angry gods."[73] The book depends on the notion of the "orphaned" Christian convert, resulting from their Asian families' religious opposition. The book suggested that the US Christian parent could step in to care for the newly "orphaned" convert.

Second, the image of the "orphan" was a powerful metaphor for mediating US-Korean relations during the Cold War era; thus, regardless of whether the children had parents or not, the "orphan" image itself was potent for Americans and Koreans. Leaning on the tradition of US sentimentalism, the US Cold War state used the trope of the family to integrate potentially communist nations in Asia into the embrace of US-led democracy, engaging in what Christina Klein calls "Cold War Orientalism." Klein traces the history of the orphan adoption program for the Christian Children's Fund (CCF), which was "an invitation into the Cold War struggle in Asia." The CCF "fine-tuned the equation of political obligation as familial obligation by establishing adoption as a trope through which one could imagine one's relationship with the developing world."[74] Yet far from equalizing Korean and US relations, the demands of Cold War Orientalism exacerbated inequalities.

The CCF was noted for its Korean War adoption work as it described the "'adoptees' as 'tiny ambassadors' for America." Klein concludes: "[The CCF] seared the idea of 'adoption' into millions of Americans' minds as an effective means to fight the Cold War. . . . A typical advertisement from 1952, published in the midst of the Korean War, works by first provoking the reader's anxiety about communism and then offering parenthood as a means to defuse it."[75]

An "orphaned" South Korea would require perpetual American parental care. The World Vision publications, including those pertaining to the World

Vision Korean Orphan Choir, also fell into this narrative. The metaphor of the biological family covered over the militaristic origins of the Korean War and the imperial circumstances under which Korean children became orphans for the United States to save. The metaphor of the "orphan" migrated along transpacific World Vision networks, mediating unequal US-Korean relations through humanitarian care.

Building on Klein's research, Soojin Pate and Susie Woo reveal the racialized Cold War logic that made an eventually nearly orphan-less World Vision Korean Orphan Choir possible and popular. Pate's research locates "Korean adoption within the context of US militarization and empire-building projects during the Cold War in order to illuminate the role that Korean children—both orphans and adoptees—played in facilitating neocolonial relations between the United States and Korea."[76] She argues that, rather than a natural consequence of war, "Korean adoption emerged from the neocolonial relations between the United States and South Korea" established in 1945 with US militarism in South Korea.[77] Pate calls this "militarized humanitarianism," tracing the US militarization of Korea in 1945 as the context out of which the idea of the "orphan" emerged. Pate, moreover, reveals that ideologies of Cold War Orientalism assumed that Koreans would racially assimilate into white families:

> The ideology of Cold War Orientalism constructed Korean adoption as a project of normativity and assimilation, working to integrate Korean children as no different from their white American family members. This project, however, was limited. The nonwhite body of the adoptee, no matter how assimilated he or she may be to white American norms, not only exposes the contradictions of white normativity but also its failure. Although Cold War Orientalism enabled the formation of mixed-race families, it disavowed the mixed-race family at the moment of recognition through assimilative practices and policies.[78]

Narratives of rescue rested on the racial belief that South Korean orphans could be absorbed and assimilated into whiteness, as if they could overcome the color line. Yet, as Pate notes, racial distinctions and inequalities remained, even within the family. As with Klein, Pate argues that the metaphor of the family stood in for US-Korean relations, as if the US state's inclusion and embrace of Korean children as family could smooth over the militarism that instantiated US-Korean inequality.

Even if the choir was nearly orphan-less, the image of the orphan carried powerful Cold War significance, and the choir relied on the diplomatic symbol of the "orphan." In her analysis of the World Vision Korean Children's Choir—which overlapped with the World Vision Korean Orphan Choir, but was distinct from it—Woo suggests that by the time the choir organized its tours, "stories about the choir and adoptees [had] merged, making it difficult to imagine a Korean child who was not orphaned. The homogenization of Korean children as assumed orphans made World Vision's naming of the 'orphan choir' appear to be a foregone conclusion."[79] She notes that the absence of Korean adults reinforced the "fiction that surrounded Korean War adoptions—namely, that all adoptees were parentless." She reflects that, while "many adoptees were indeed orphaned by the war," others "had living biological parents or relatives who could not provide for them given the poverty of postwar Korea."[80] Woo concludes: "What most Americans did not recognize or perhaps not even see was how popular understandings about Korean children that were informed by various cultural productions including that of the choirs were deeply mired in racialized constructs that complicated simplified media narratives touting equal internationalist exchange."[81] The image of the "orphan" rendered Korean children racially desirable as their American audience could imagine stepping into their lives as "parents." Moreover, Americans could save these orphans, and therefore themselves, from the menace of Asian communism.

Caring for the orphaned is a historic Christian value that seems not only harmless but also benevolent and potentially noble. However, the image of the "orphan" was also used to mediate unequal relations between the United States and South Korea. The narrative of American care and rescue was attractive for many Americans, and it was one crucial means through which the new evangelicalism, as mediated through the nearly orphan-less World Vision Korean Orphan Choir, became respectable again in mainstream America.

"Let My Heart Be Broken": Sentimentalism and a Religion of the Heart

The new evangelicalism rebranded itself in the US mainstream through parachurches like World Vision, which, in the 1960s, appealed to America's Cold War Orientalist imagination via global fundraising programs like the

World Vision Korean Orphan Choir. Through the choir, the possibility of racial assimilation into the white family, and therefore, South Korean absorption into US-led Cold War empire, was reinforced by the logic of Christian conversion and inclusion of orphaned Korean children into the family of God. Not only through the metaphor of the biological family, but also through sentimental attachments to God and a global Christian family, US-Korean inequalities were masked and mediated.

No one was better at theologically articulating a sentimental attachment to God than Pierce. Pierce's heart broke for Korea. Out of his broken heart flowed streams of compassion, emotionalism, and sentimentalism that laid a foundation for the renewal of modern American evangelicalism, historically called a "religion of the heart." By way of background, upon witnessing the tragedies of the Korean War in 1951, Pierce traveled to Kojedo, a Korean island, where he famously wrote a legendary prayer on his Bible's flyleaf: "Let my heart be broken with the things that break the heart of God." To this day, this prayer, or "watchword," is a foundational for World Vision, as it is featured in the lobby headquarters in Southern California. In 1964, Pierce wrote a celebration of the World Vision Korean Orphan Choir titled *Orphans of the Orient*, emphasizing the value of the "heart." He wrote that the "*sight* which always *breaks* my *heart* is that of children ... hungry both physically and spiritually." He hoped that the stories and images he shared would "*break* your *heart* as it has mine."[82] He included photos of the children he described so that Americans could see them with their own eyes.

For Pierce, the "heart" was like a divine organ that could mediate sacred connections. By anthropomorphizing God as a being with a "heart," Pierce theologically imagined that humans could connect to God through their own hearts. With less of a focus on the mind or a logic-based means of connecting with the divine, Pierce's prayer prioritized emotion and experience. A "broken" heart, like a tenderized piece of meat, was more malleable, prepared to feel and share in the pain of the divine. If sentimentality is the act of imagining the other's feelings, and acting upon what "feels right," his prayer sacralized sentimental connection with God. Pierce's prayer for divine connection, mediated through shared pain, translated to parallel connections with human suffering. Pierce told Franklin Graham that a key part of his work was to become "a part of the suffering. I literally felt the child's blindness, the mother's grief."[83] Though there was no way for him to feel the child's actual blindness, he believed that he could. A "broken" human heart was all the more sacred as it not only signified solidarity with the divine but also extended to sharing in human pain, especially in cataclysmic conditions like the Korean War.

The heart, and the language of the heart, has carried theological significance for evangelicalism since the eighteenth century when evangelicals were accused of "enthusiasm" for taking their religion of the heart to an extreme. Historians have debated the place of evangelicals between "enlightenment" and "enthusiasm," arguing for evangelicalism's role betwixt and between the two.[84] John Wesley, one of the founders of the evangelical movement in the eighteenth century, has been called the "reasonable enthusiast" for his balanced appeals to mind and heart. Yet recall Wesley's famous heart-centered words upon conversion at Aldersgate: "My heart was strangely warmed."

Pierce's focus on documenting and seeing relied on Enlightenment thinking, which emphasized the use of empirical data and the senses to learn about God's broken heart. At the same time, Pierce mastered the language of a religion of the heart by taking it to its sentimentalist extreme. Todd Brenneman writes: "Instead of solely defining *evangelical* in the context of belief, we should see it as an aesthetic formulated not only on belief but also by affective and experiential concerns."[85] He studies the emotional history of evangelicalism to argue: "Evangelicalism becomes true because it *feels* true. Modern evangelicalism has largely transitioned to a new form of truth, one based not on intellectual assent to propositions but on emotional connections."[86] Though Brenneman primarily focuses on twenty-first-century figures in his analysis, one can see that twentieth-century Pierce was already a master at communicating with emotion, and employed a sentimental theological connection to the divine. When Pierce communicated his visions of Korea to Americans, he did so as an evangelist who desired conversion through heartbreak.[87] The passion that flowed out of his vision was amplified by the emotional demands of a "religion of the heart" with eighteenth-century transatlantic roots.

Tragically, Pierce's vulnerabilities carried a religion of the heart to an extreme, for Pierce's heart was not just broken, but bled for Korea. In *Let My Heart Be Broken*, Richard Gehman wrote that Pierce could not "conceal his true emotions."[88] Richard Halversen, who served on World Vision's board from 1956 to 1983, reported that Pierce "functioned from a broken heart."[89] Pierce's heartfelt identification with suffering was both a strength and weakness as it led to life-altering challenges.[90] Pierce's labor carried a personal cost. There was also a high price for those on the receiving end of Pierce's sentimental care. Pierce saw himself as a conduit between Koreans and

Americans as well as between the heart of God and humanity. But it did not necessarily lead to a humanizing experience for those on the underside of history.

Mercy's Child: Holt Children

Some of the complicated and perhaps unintended consequences of Pierce's heart-centered care can be seen most vividly through his cultural productions, including film, much of which was based on modern Korea. Pierce often translated his broken heart into emotionally evocative images and writings, a reflection of his theological understanding of a heart-centered connection to the divine. According to John Hamilton, Pierce "inaugurated" a genre called the "evangelical social action film," which Hamilton defines as "humanitarian activist films with an underlying emphasis on Christian salvation."[91] Pierce not only was fascinated by the technology of film, but also believed that film was a "God-given tool for educating churchgoers about the miserable conditions of so many in the world, so that they might be moved to do something about it."[92]

Harry and Bertha Holt were among those most affected by Pierce's films, specifically by *Other Sheep* and *Dead Men on Furlough*, which were both meant to serve as a "missionary challenge." As discussed in chapter 1, *Dead Men on Furlough* featured a "thrilling story of a heroic Korean pastor who testifies for Christ before a firing squad" and whose "wife and baby are held as hostages by Communists."[93] The Holts watched these films at a church meeting in Portland, Oregon, and urgently discussed with Pierce the desperate war conditions.[94] As a result, the Holts made the transpacific trip to Korea. In 1956, in an event infamously called "Operation Baby Lift," the Holts traveled with Pierce from Korea to the United States with twelve mixed-race orphans from Korea, eight of whom the Holts adopted. Before the Holts left Korea to return to the states, Pierce made a black-and-white short film with Harry Holt, titled *Mercy's Child: Holt Children*. The Holts saw, their hearts broke, and they were moved to action. And then Pierce used them as an evangelistic example to create another film through which others would see, feel, and then do.

Mercy's Child is a documentary film that opens with Bob Pierce, Harry Holt, seven babies, and their nurse, Kathleen Cowan, sitting on a grass lawn. "This is Mercy's Child, young Suna," announces Pierce as the film begins.

"She's just a little baby, but she has a great big heart full of love for someone," he continues, with a proud grin on his face and sporting his arm badge as a UN correspondent. Pierce notes Suna's "big heart" for her potential American parents. He declares, "This little child is from one of the homes of World Vision for babies here in the capital city of all Korea, the city of Seoul. She's part of a very dramatic and very wonderful story." Holt, who does not speak during the entire film, sits next to Pierce as his example of magnanimous Christian love: "You see, this tiny girl is one of eight little babies about to come to the United States because of the heart and the love of a typical farm family from the western part of the United States." Pierce notes how the babies featured in the film would go on to reside on Holt's Oregon farm.[95]

He narrates the historical reasons as to how these babies were orphaned through the category of "heartbreak":

> The story begins, however, in a very tragic setting. As all of you know, during the past few years, there's been a great deal of death and suffering among the civilian populace of the Korean nation. During the last five or six years there have been almost 300,000 little children like these made motherless and fatherless. And in the midst of all these tragedies there's one very, very special tragedy.... And that is the heartbreak of the little child of mixed blood parentage. Everyone of these little children had a Korean mother and an American, or a British, or an Australian, father. Every single one of these little kiddies have been left alone in the world because of their tragic origin.

As if the war spontaneously occurs as a "special tragedy," without a concrete point of origin, Pierce paints a destitute image of Korean children as motherless and fatherless. Biracial children were mostly born out of wedlock between Korean prostitutes and US personnel in US military camps, but the racialized and gendered history of Korean women's sexual labor under a militarized regime regrettably has no place in Pierce's "tragic" retelling of US-Korean history.[96] Rather than an appeal to empirical history, Pierce persuades by pulling on viewers' heartstrings, repeating terms such as "very tragic," "very, very special tragedy," and "tragic origin."

Pierce's appeals to emotion were also tied to racial imagination. He articulates South Korea's racial tolerance as inferior to that of the United States, casting the United States as a racial democracy where mixed-race children would be welcomed:

And they're living in a nation where people don't understand the different color of the hair and the eyes and the different physical traits of these little children. And therefore, as is often the case, they're not very sympathetic. Now, these little children would have absolutely no future if it were not for one great fact. And that is the fact that someone in America, whose children they were not, actually cared for them. . . . And this moment you'll see on my left a man who is a farmer who has six children of his own in the United States, who came and saw these little youngsters and could not forget them. And in just a few hours he's going to be taking them by plane to his farm in the United States, where they're going to become American citizens. And he's going to bring them up.[97]

At the pinnacle of evangelical humanitarianism stood the Oregon farmer Harry Holt, without whom the orphan children of Korea had no future, according to Pierce. Holt exemplified a white Protestant whose racial tolerance was revealed through his rescue of destitute and nonwhite children from Korea. Pierce reinforced the necessity of US rescue, even overselling US democracy, as he claimed that the mixed-race children would easily become US citizens.

For Pierce, the nation was racially inclusive just as US-led Christianity was racially inclusive. When Pierce penned *Orphans of the Orient*, he imagined white missionaries and "orphaned" children in Asia overcoming racialized differences when they convert to Christianity. When he described people accepting Jesus in India, he wrote, "Up they went—brown hands, white hands, yellow hands," suggesting the universality of Christianity regardless of race.[98] Pierce writes: "'Black or yellow, brown or white, all are precious in His sight,' is a song we often sing. And this story will prove that it is true."[99] Christians could transcend the color line in a global community where all were included regardless of race, ethnicity, and nationality. Yet the "orphan's" integration into a universal Christianity still depended on a hierarchy, in which Glory Light, White Jade, and Precious Girl's absorption into Christianity relied on erasure of past identities, including Asian religious heritages and parents. The universality of the Christian message of salvation cohered with the message of racial, ethnic, and cultural universality that could transcend the boundaries of nation-states—all the while prioritizing the US nation-state over Asian nations and people.

Mercy's Child concludes with Pierce pleading with Americans to express their care and compassion for orphaned Korean children, raising Holt as the pinnacle of moral authority. The Korean children were cast as destitute: "There are as we can tell, hundreds of other little children just like these. In the most bitter and in the realest sense, they are mercy's children. They have no love, no future, no one to care for them at all, unless you and I care for them with the love and mercy of Christ in our hearts." Emphasizing US exceptionalism and responsibility, Pierce pleaded: "I want to say this special word to you today because many of these children have American blood in their veins. They are our special responsibility. And they need special love and care." Holt exemplified that American care: "And there must be some besides Mr. Harry Holt and his lovely Oregon family who will care for these little ones. Now, all of you cannot bring one to your home. We know that. But ... some of you actually could do what Mr. Holt has done. ... You can do something to make one of these lovable little darlings your very own."

As the film concludes, Pierce challenges, "Take one of these youngsters, make this mercy's child through your act of mercy. Help us care for one today." There is a final invitation to support an orphan in Korea financially: "For only ten dollars, support an orphan in Korea. For further information, write to Dr. Frank C. Phillips World Vision, Inc. Portland, Oregon. That's Dr. Frank C. Phillips World Vision, Inc. Portland, Oregon." Pierce appeals to American caretaking, American "hearts," as well as American exceptionalism in caring for the aftermath of war to persuade American Christians to adopt Korean orphans. Pierce asks his American audience to invest in the "orphans" but also in the narrative that he has constructed. This moment marks the launch of the unprecedented transnational and transracial adoption of thousands of children from Korea, which expanded thereafter to other nations.[100]

Pierce's transpacific racial and theological logic is on full display in *Mercy's Child*. Though biracial children are as a result of US and UN troops in Korea, he never argues against the brutality of war. To express Christian "mercy" is to exercise compassion and care for orphans, and to transcend the color line in segregated America. In spite of the global exposure of anti-Black Jim Crow racism in America, whites from the fundamentalist strain of modern Christianity in America were made to feel as if they were less culpable in systemic racism if they could provide individual donations to nonwhite, racially mixed global children whom they could lift out of poverty and the tragedy of war. Pierce suggested America was better suited to do so than Korea, projecting an image of the United States as a racially democratic nation.

Holt was also a white Protestant who emerged from the fundamentalist strain of the fundamentalist-modernist controversy. Along with Pierce, he helped to rebrand his lineage of Christianity through the image of global humanitarian care for nonwhite children, as if to transcend the color line, all the while reinforcing American superiority as his vision painted Korean children as perpetually destitute. As if they carried the world on their shoulders, Pierce and Holt together lobbied for change in Congress to allow Korean "orphans" to enter the United States in an era of Asian exclusion. Out of Pierce's and Holt's bleeding hearts for Korea, they founded a transracial movement, which reinforced the moral superiority of white Protestants, further legitimating the fundamentalist strain of Christianity as mainstream. Through Christian humanitarian care, they legitimated America's moral authority to win the global Cold War and to rule as the unquestionable world superpower. Incorporating Korean orphans into white evangelical families paved a path for "family values" before that became a political platform.

More Than "Waifs" and "Songbirds"

Yet the death of Kim Sang Yong, or "Peanuts," revealed the troubles that haunted the children of the choir. Correspondence between Jim Franks and the new World Vision director Ted Engstrom revealed that the exciting trips abroad, the financial sponsorship, and the gifts were not enough to solve the challenges that choristers faced. Franks wrote to Engstrom with pain, regret, and a desire for correction. Franks's letter began: "Peanuts' death was a shock."[101]

An inaugural member of the choir, "Peanuts" committed suicide at nineteen. He was remembered as the "diminutive performer with the gigantic grin who had to be lifted up to speak into the microphone" and as being the "comedian" of the choir.[102] "Peanuts" participated in the first two international tours with the choir until his "voice changed," at which point he was not brought back for the choir's third tour.[103] The choir chose altos and sopranos, explicitly curating a feminine and childlike sound that a male adolescent going through puberty would disrupt and undermine. Casting South Korea with an effeminate voice was crucial for mediating the Orientalist dynamics of cultural diplomacy. During the choir's fourth international tour of 1968 to 1969, Peanuts helped the choir as a violinist, but by 1970, the teenager was reported dead. The shock revealed latent troubles behind the choir's joyful singing.

Franks's reflections after reporting Peanuts's death to Engstrom suggest that his death was a result of suffering that was widespread among the children. He wrote: "Ted, the choir members are exposed to so much public adoration and attention that they develop deep frustrations. On the choir tours we got to know of their aspirations and ambitions as well as their problems." Franks reported that behind the rosy pictures and the glossy images in American and Korean newspapers and television screens, choristers faced stiff challenges:

> There are those in and out of the Music Institute who at this time have some very severe problems, seemingly unsolvable to them. The choir members' need for love is magnified by their visits to the U.S. and Canada. . . . We had come to the conclusion that something must be done for the children to provide the love they so desperately need and want. . . . We have been praying for and concerned about several children right now associated with the choir who have a crisis in their lives.[104]

Franks did not think the sponsorships from families were adequate in providing the love that many of them desired, and indeed that such attentions only "magnified" their needs. More international tours, he concluded, would not be healthy: "I don't feel another tour of any kind should be undertaken until these psychological and spiritual needs of the children in these special circumstances is known and something done to meet them." Given the extent to which the tone of this letter diverged from the joyful and bright image of the choir, it is not surprising that Franks desired confidentiality.[105]

Franks's concerns reiterated that the "orphan," whether as a result of war or other tragedies, was not a label, image, or representation to be flouted for public relations, fundraising, missionary hopes, entertainment, or diplomatic relations, but a life experience with a much more complex set of challenges and hopes than the choir's adventurous international tours and financial sponsorships could meet. The choristers' experiences, including their misrecognized suffering, exceeded simplistic representation.

Oh Chiyŏng recalled her memories of Peanuts (figure 3.1) and his tragic death:

> For the World Vision Korean Orphan Choir, we were trying to gather sponsors. It was a means for advertising . . . more than sharing the gospel, it was to thank and recruit sponsors. So some people said that they used

Figure 3.1 Oh Chiyŏng and Kim Sang Yong ("Peanuts") meet Billy Graham on their world tour. Peanuts stands to Oh Chiyŏng's right with the Korean flag hanging on his vest.
Source: Photo courtesy of Oh Chiyŏng.

us. This is a painful story, but during the first international tour there was a boy who was my age, and he was a biracial child. He was brilliant but he had trouble adjusting. Instead of thinking of things simply like me, he had a hard time. One day he committed suicide.[106]

She was referring to Peanuts, and she recalled the conversations that she had with him prior to his death:

Before he committed suicide he said, "What do you think of World Vision?" I said, "Well, we should be thankful." He said to me, "Don't you think we just got used?" I said, "Why do you think like that? What would we have done if we didn't have World Vision?" I had a more positive outlook, and he was more negative. Sometimes people were critical that the money that we raised, instead of giving it to us, they gave it to others. He had this perspective, and he told me this and then he died.... He was like, "They call me 'Peanuts, Peanuts,' and they take advantage of me." I was like, "Why do you think they take advantage of you? Why not take that as an endearing nickname? The name is from the *Peanuts* comic."[107]

Peanuts protested the commercialization of his story for philanthropic means. One might even say that through his suicide he expressed a darker form of agency to critique World Vision's empire of care. Though Oh Chiyŏng understood her experience with the choir in a more positive light, she also could not escape a desire for greater advocacy during her time as a chorister:

The days spent with the World Vision Korean Orphan Choir were wonderful, and they took care of us to that point. Honestly, I do think that it would have been nice to have them also take care of what happened to us after the choir—for instance, to help us with employment so that we would have more of a foundation for our lives.[108]

Indeed, Oh Chiyŏng, though touted as a success case, struggled with how to survive and thrive in the days after her international tours with the choir, as she had no family.

Kim Sang Yong's tragic death revealed that the new evangelicalism's humanitarian efforts could have debilitating effects on South Korean children. Though the choir's organizers provided significant financial relief to children, they also smoothed over the tragic history of US militarism in South Korea and imagined the children through racialized stereotypes.

"When I look back at the [images] of the choir, their faces are so bright," recalled Pae Kyungha.[109] Though Pae was a member of the World Vision Korean Orphan Choir during a time when it was no longer called an "Orphan Choir," she knew that those who had gone before her had lived through challenging times. "I asked, if it was such a hard time, how could your face look so bright?" She recalled their responses to her:

> They said . . . we lived in such harsh conditions, but then we'd go abroad and it was like heaven. . . . We were in hotels that could only be seen in our dreams. We ate in places we couldn't even imagine. We met presidents. We ate things we never even heard of. The environment was so good. Their faces could only look so bright because they weren't suffering. In Korea, they lived in such harsh conditions, but then they would go abroad. . . . They couldn't help but look happy because they went from a place where things were hard to a place where things were comfortable. In Korea they didn't even have paved roads.[110]

Pae recalls that for an older generation of choir members, they remembered their tours abroad, especially to America, as if they were visiting "heaven." Indeed, as well as singing in prominent churches and concert halls, they visited the zoo and consumed delightful treats.

Yet the choristers did not necessarily desire to remain in the United States, in spite of how much they enjoyed its adventures. Pierce reported after the second international tour: "Now, they were homesick for the 'Land of the Morning Calm,' and for the sights and sounds of their homeland." World Vision staff Roy Challberg further observed: "On the bus returning from the airport to the Music Institute where they live, the children jabbered and waved, evidently glad to be back on the old, bumpy, congested road filled with kids, ox carts, bikes and more kids."[111] "In one great cheer the children shouted and clapped their hands" when they returned to the Musical Institute. Challberg declared, "It was only an orphanage, but it was home! Tears of joy flowed freely; there were embraces with those who had stayed behind . . . cries of *aboji* [father] to their superintendent. Although these children had slept in fine hotels and tasted the best of accommodations, their happiness proved again: There's no place like home."[112] Their confessions suggested that America was not necessarily the home that the Korean orphans desired, even if they enjoyed the pleasures of airplane rides and fun trips to the United States.

In 1967, Pierce left World Vision. World Vision "outgrew its founder" and went on to become the largest faith-based, humanitarian nonprofit, with increasingly ecumenical and moderately evangelical leanings.[113] For Pierce's part, he went on to create Samaritan's Purse, an evangelical humanitarian nonprofit. In 1973, Pierce found in Franklin Graham—Billy Graham's son—his successor to whom he would bequeath Samaritan's Purse, an organization with parallels to the World Vision of the 1950s and 1960s, which helped to reform the new evangelicalism into mainstream evangelicalism through the image of the "orphan."

The United States saved South Korea, so the narrative goes. Orphans had food to eat and new opportunities as choristers. Widows found financial support from US sponsors. At the same time, such humanitarian and Christian-motivated actions occurred with little critique of the tragic and militaristic origins of the Korean War, the imperial circumstances under which Korean children became orphans for the United States to save. Indeed, World Vision lacked the theological apparatus to critique the imperial presence of the United States in South Korea or the global racial hierarchical order. Upon this racialized bedrock, the "little ambassadors," historically invisible transpacific actors, helped to grow World Vision in the 1960s.

The darker dimensions of this story, however, did not lessen the fervor for evangelical revival in the United States or South Korea, as we will see next. The great paradox of this transpacific history is that, even as South Koreans like Oh Chiyŏng experienced the underside of the emerging US evangelical empire, they also sought to address their personal challenges, and to elevate their status in the world order, through evangelical revival.

4
Revival

Billy's and Billy's Largest "Crusade," 1969–1973

By February 1973, Oh Chiyŏng had graduated from high school, but she had "nowhere to go." One could only stay in the World Vision Korean Orphan Choir dormitory until the end of high school. Serendipitously, however, the director of the Musical Institute hired her on staff, which afforded her the opportunity to live in one of the choir's dressing rooms with two new roommates. Oh Chiyŏng recalled that her new roommates were "born-again Christians." They were part of Joy Mission, an evangelical parachurch founded in South Korea in 1958.[1]

Every Thursday, her roommates would attend a gathering, and "they seemed so full of the spirit and happy." Because Oh was so unhappy, however, she wondered "why they were so happy." Then, one day, her roommate said, "Chiyŏng, I wish one day you could be saved, too." Oh Chiyŏng confessed, "I felt so violated by that. I thought I was saved. 'Do you think I'm not saved?'" She recalled: "I was a faithful Pharisee.... I thought I was the best religiously." Her roommate replied, "You have to become a born-again Christian." Offended, Oh Chiyŏng "told the younger kids at the Musical Institute not to go to Joy Mission." But she was deeply moved by her roommates who "prayed for me."[2]

On Saturday June 2, 1973, Oh Chiyŏng reluctantly attended "Youth Night," the penultimate evening of Billy Graham's five-day crusade hosted at the Yoido Plaza. Youth Night opened with attendees singing the Wesleyan hymn "Love Divine, All Loves Exceling" in English and Korean. Ruth Graham, whose family had been missionaries in North Korea, then welcomed the South Korean youth: "I would urge you young people to bring your sins to Jesus.... Life is not easy for any of us, but when we have the Lord Jesus with us, life has purpose."[3] Oh Chiyŏng had struggled with this same challenge now voiced by Ruth Graham ever since her roommates told her she needed to be "born again."

Yet the 1973 crusade was a stepping stone for her eventual "born again" experience, which occurred through a spiritual vision at a Joy Mission gathering. She reported: "Before I believed with my head, but now I believed with my heart."[4]

Over the course of five days of evangelical revival, three million individuals like Oh Chiyŏng attended Graham's meetings, and seventy-three thousand made "decisions for Christ," the most of any Graham crusade, surpassing his 1957 record-setting, sixteen-week crusade in New York City.[5] The pinnacle of the revival was Sunday June 3, 1973, the day after Youth Night. With the help of Billy Kim, his Korean translator, Graham preached to 1.1 million people, the largest audience of any Graham gathering. Cho Miyŏng, another member of the World Vision Korean Orphan Choir, recalled: "I think that was a special year. . . a year where God had decided that he would pour out his grace on our country. . . . That was also the year that I became a Christian, in 1973. Afterward I looked back, I realized God had planned it."[6]

Billy Graham also understood the crusade in theological terms. He declared to the press: "I have come as a representative of the kingdom of God. I am not here as an American. I represent a higher court than the White House. I am an ambassador of the King of Kings and Lord of Lords. And I have come in that spirit and as his representative."[7] He defined that message to the press: "Christianity is not a system of ethics. Christianity is not just a philosophy. Christianity is a person. That person is Jesus Christ. And your eternal destiny will depend on your response to his offer of love and mercy. That is basically the message we have come to proclaim."[8] His primary purpose as an evangelist was to mediate transactions between heaven and earth, not between countries.

Yet there was no ignoring the temporal significance, the transpacific piety *and* politics, of Graham's visit. When Billy and Ruth Graham disembarked their Korean Airlines flight on May 25, 1973, for instance, a marching band welcomed them to South Korea to the tune of "America, the Beautiful" rather than, say, to a hymn. On the airstrip, Billy met with Ambassador Philip C. Habib, the US ambassador to South Korea, who briefed him privately and hosted a dinner party in his honor, indicating Graham's diplomatic value for US-South Korean relations. Graham next met with South Korean president Park Chung-hee and his wife at the Blue House.[9]

So although Graham arrived in Seoul as a representative of the King of Kings, he also readily engaged with the political kings of South Korea, including Park, who, not unlike a king, legitimated his authoritarian rule in

1972 under the Yusin Constitution. As historian Grant Wacker notes, Graham's "rise as a global religious presence paralleled America's rise as a global political presence in the same postwar decades."[10] Graham was not only an evangelist but also a member of the white religious elite from the United States, South Korea's most important political ally, the more powerful "big brother" in US-South Korean patron-client state relations and the ascendant superpower in the global Cold War order. In 1973 on South Korean soil, Graham represented both God and America. Until now, Graham's largest crusade has been studied largely in national terms even though American evangelicals and South Korean Protestants organized the event transnationally. As Wacker notes, Graham's "international career" has been understudied, even though "it may prove more significant than anything he did at home."[11] At the same time, Timothy Lee has analyzed the 1973 crusade in the context of "South Korea as the site of intensive evangelistic campaigns," though not with an explicitly transnational analysis.[12] But what of the transpacific significance of US–South Korean collaboration in organizing Graham's largest crusade?[13]

Graham and his multiracial, transnational team of American and Korean male evangelists used the crusade not only to strengthen diplomatic relations between the United States and South Korea in the tense Nixon-Park era (1969–1974) of the global Cold War, but also to establish a transpacific evangelical consensus under the canopy of Graham's theology. The crusade encouraged Koreans to believe in both God and America and to imagine their own ascendancy in the world order through evangelical revival.[14] Indeed, not only Billy Kim but also Oh Chiyŏng sought to overcome the legacies of war through revival. But how had the revival come about? And why at that time?

Transnational Religious Requests in a Tense Nixon-Park Era

The 1969–1974 era of South Korean president Park Chung-hee and US president Richard Nixon was an uncertain time for US-South Korean diplomatic relations. The Nixon administration's newly emerging Cold War policy of detente left Park's regime insecure in its diplomatic relations with the United States during a realignment of the Cold War geopolitical order.[15] National security adviser Henry Kissinger's foreign policy realpolitik recognized that the

United States and the Soviet Union no longer held a monopoly in the international order, and instead highlighted China's growth, the Sino-Soviet split, and the limits of US and Soviet power.[16] Rather than pursue a more active foreign policy position—that South Korea should lead in an effort to reunify Korea under the auspices of the United Nations—the Nixon administration pursued a relatively hands-off order of "peaceful coexistence of North and South Korea within a peaceful international order in Northeast Asia."

North Korea, however, still posed a national security threat to South Korea.[17] The Nixon Doctrine of July 29, 1969, the policy that the United States would support allies with economic and military aid but not with ground troops, resulted in both a perceived power vacuum and a reduction of US troops in South Korea. This shocked Park and generated fear that South Korea would face the Soviet, North Korean, and Chinese communist bloc in isolation. Park had worked closely with the Johnson administration to contribute South Korean troops to the Vietnam War, a move he believed would prevent US troops from abandoning South Korea later.[18] Yet the geopolitical gains Park believed he had accrued under the Johnson administration proved to be vacuous under Nixon: the South Korean deployment in Vietnam in 1964 had strengthened the alliance with the United States, but that alliance weakened dramatically after Nixon announced his military pullback in 1969.[19] The six-year, so-called honeymoon period of US-South Korean relations began to unravel.[20] Though South Korea's economic and national standing had grown stronger through the decades since the Korean War, its standing in the world was still indebted to the politics of Washington, DC.

It was in this uncertain geopolitical environment that South Koreans had requested Graham's presence to revive their nation. In 1969, Reverend Chang Suk Young wrote to Graham, inviting him to be the main speaker for a national revival hosted by the Association for a United Church of Korea. When Walter Smyth, writing on behalf of Graham, declined Chang's invitation because Graham had plans in Australia and New Zealand, Chang replied: "I tried to take a chance in prayerful hopes that [Graham] might especially consider [the] urgent needs of our Korean church and also the present sad situation of moral and spiritual aspects of our national life in general."[21] Smyth assured Chang that "Dr. Graham very much wants to come to Korea but we are going to have to see how the Lord directs us so that a suitable time can be decided upon."[22] Not unlike Nixon, Graham had other priorities, and 1969 came and went, but he received more invitations, some of them dramatic in tone. Mrs. Elbert White, a missionary with the Lutheran Church–Missouri

Synod, wrote to him from Ok Soo Dong, a suburb of Seoul: "Yesterday the Lord spoke to me twice . . . [saying] I want you to write Billy Graham and tell him to hold a crusade in OkSooDong."[23] White's divine revelation was the culmination of a series of four visions, with a final one of "an arena packed with people." When she asked how this would be accomplished, she heard an answer to which she replied, "'Oh—through a crusade, Lord?'"[24]

If White was persuaded by the voice of God to invite Graham, Soon Kim was persuaded by Graham's literal voice. Kim, a high school teacher, had been an avid listener to his sermons through radio station 1190 HLKX Seoul. Though he confessed that he could only "understand your message 70%" and desired to "understand English better," he declared himself a steady listener.[25] Kim had gained theological and English language literacy at the same time through Graham's globally circulated media. He asked Graham to listen to the entreaties of people in an "underdeveloped country," appealing not only to Graham's Christian but also his American identity.

The tone of the letters became increasingly urgent, as if without Graham's presence South Korea had no future hope. Reverend Park Ihn Kahk's letter tied religious and national salvation together, asserting that Graham could serve as a "messenger of new life and a spiritual rescuer," ushering in a new phase of "modernization and improvement of new life," which he believed could be "introduced in Korea only through God's words."[26] Wacker notes that by the mid-1960s, Graham "had become what we might call 'The Great Legitimator.'" He "functioned very much as a Protestant saint," and South Koreans desired his sacred legitimating powers for the nation's revival.[27]

Kyung Chik Han wrote the decisive letter on November 20, 1970.

> I am writing a most urgent letter. For years the Korean Churches have been praying for your coming here. We now feel *the appropriate time has come!* If it is at all possible at this time of spiritual hunger in Korea, we want you to come for two weeks. . . . A most interdenominational group met last night and were unanimous that WE MOST URGENTLY ASK you to come.

Han ended his letter with a passionate plea: "In the Spirit of Christ, COME!"[28] Upon receiving this letter, on December 4, 1970, Graham wrote a rare note in response to the flood of letters: "Send a copy of this letter to Walter and tell him that this is very urgent and that I definitely want to accept this invitation."[29] Walter Smyth explained the reason the BGEA would, indeed, prioritize Korea: They hoped to go where people were "ripe for revival and ready for evangelism" as well as places where "the Lord lays upon our hearts. . . . [T]he one from Korea has touched our hearts and we will definitely give it priority."[30]

In the months before Graham's crusade, a US missionary observed that Graham's crusade would be the "great Campaign of the century" for the following reason: "THE WHOLE KOREAN CHURCH IS A MISSIONARY CHURCH ON THE MOVE IN CHRIST'S MISSION TO DISCIPLE THE WORLD!"[31] So it was that the BGEA, located in Montreat, North Carolina, began to work with an executive committee established in Seoul, Korea to organize a crusade in 1973, during the "'zenith of authoritarian government in the history of South Korea, in structure as well as content.'"[32]

Unexpected Revival at the Zenith of South Korean Authoritarianism

Not only Nixon's unilateral decision to withdraw US troops, but also closer relations between the United States and China created an unstable geopolitical environment for South Korea. President Park deemed it necessary to crack down on South Korean domestic politics to protect national security and ensure continued economic progress. A US missionary noted that although "close relations with [the] U.S.A. continue, Nixon's visit to Peking" in 1972 created a "radical shift" in US-South Korean relations. The two nations no longer had a "father-son relationship," but now an "older brother-younger brother relationship" marked by "greater realism and more independence," which for Park posed a threat to South Korean national security.[33] On October 17, 1972, Park declared martial law, outlining a series of amendments to the constitution, which were codified on October 27, 1972, as the Yusin Constitution. Yusin extended Park's presidency for another six years and curtailed the powers of the legislative and judicial branches to secure an unprecedented authoritarian political structure.[34]

Scholars have called the last seven years of his eighteen-year regime (1972–1979) the "dark age of democracy."[35] The Nixon administration tacitly endorsed Park's military regime through its political disengagement.[36] In a document circulated to the BGEA, a US missionary wrote in February, "1972 is fresh in our memories (perhaps a bit nightmarish) as the year of most radical shifts and very exceeding tensions." The missionary noted it was "hard to 'spell' out what really happened in 1972" because of the "almost total Korea censorship" and "surveillance" that "did not overlook the expatriate." He noted that his document was "limited in what it can say," but he let the BGEA know that Park "continues very much in POWER" and that there was an uneasy political climate due to the "trauma of two months of Martial Law and the great changes in democracy in the new Constitution."[37] It is surprising that, in such an oppressive climate, the BGEA did not face more barriers. Graham effectively carried out his largest crusade less than one year after Park's declaration of Yusin.

Under the Park regime, freedom of speech was strictly curtailed, and American expatriates and religious communities were not exempt from surveillance, regulation, and repression, which in some cases made public religious activity challenging. Sociologist Paul Chang's work shows that at the height of political repression in the 1970s, the state suppressed the religious activity of Korean Christians.[38] On April 22, 1973, one month before the Graham revivals, Reverend Pak Hyong-kyu and two other ministers disseminated leaflets titled "Politicians Repent," "The Resurrection of Democracy Is the Liberation of the People," and "Lord, Show Thy Mercy to the Ignorant King."[39] Pak was arrested for attempting to overthrow the government and engaging in "communist" activity.

Transnational connections to the United States offered no protection. As will be further discussed in the next chapter, in 1974, the Methodist minister Cho Wha Soon was imprisoned, and the Methodist missionary George Ogle, an American national, was deported from South Korea for working with the Urban Industrial Mission (UIM).[40] Cho's imprisonment and denunciation as a communist came after she preached a sermon titled "Search for the Kingdom and for Righteousness," in which she said, "Our reality is completely the opposite of the justice of God. In our society, if we say 'white' when we see white or 'black' when we see black, we will be arrested. Now many students and ministers are suffering for this reason. We as workers should not be afraid of arrest, but must fight against the injustices in our working places."[41] Cho implied that the government was preventing people from speaking the truth. Even when workers witnessed injustice, corporations and the Korean Central Intelligence Agency (KCIA) persuaded them or, rather, forced them to "believe" that they were being treated fairly. As for Ogle, he was deported for praying publicly for six Korean men who were unjustly accused of communism.[42] Korean Christians who openly criticized the Park regime faced charges that they were part of a "contentious civil society" in dialectical tension with a "strong state."[43] While a small antiauthoritarian group of Korean and American Christians underwent imprisonment for its religious activity, another group of Korean and American Christians affiliated with the BGEA received permission to organize a Billy Graham crusade in the Yoido Plaza.[44]

How was it possible, and what did it mean, for Korean Christians to organize Graham's largest crusade during this "dark age of democracy"? No one trying to predict the future of Christian missions after World War II could have foreseen the success of American missionaries like Graham in non-Western nations. Idealized images of the American missionary who spread "good news" collapsed before fierce resistance—or thoroughgoing indifference—in both Western and non-Western nations. For many, missions connoted dogmatic claims of Christian superiority and questionable alliances with coercive states.[45]

Christian missionaries were caricaturized as the right arm of colonialism. The dissolution of Western colonies in the East revealed the unsavory collusion of some missionaries with state power.[46] The missionary impulse to spread "good news" too often accompanied a dualistic, hierarchical, "disembodied controlling" view of God. As postcolonial theologian Mayra Rivera Rivera suggests, such a theology of "transcendence has often served to legitimize "decidedly ungodly actions."[47] Historian Dana Robert has shown that not all missionaries colluded with colonial power; some advocated indigenous liberation, and missionaries from some American churches worked to transfer authority to indigenous leaders. But even in some mainline denominations, Christian missions became an "embarrassing remnant of colonial history," a stain requiring removal. Some would have preferred to mute the Matthean Great Commission to spread the good news to the world, or at least to allow indigenous converts to take over the task in their own nations.[48]

In 1973, Graham's good news preaching was not good news for all. In August 1973, Graham held "Spree '73"—"spree" meaning "spiritual re-emphasis"—in London and modeled it after the successful Explo '72 in Dallas, which was hosted with Campus Crusade for Christ. The Church of England's weekly magazine, however, expressed concern about Graham's "hit and run evangelism" and the Reverend Philip Crowe offered his own critique: "'It is wealthy Christians in the West indulging in five days of spiritual luxury. It is the essence of worldliness, and extravagance." In contrast, Spree '73 organizers believed the event could have "astounding long term effects for the Kingdom of God."[49] Yet the very nation that had birthed itinerating transatlantic evangelists like John Wesley and George Whitefield criticized the good news preacher for his extravagance.

Moreover, in June 1973, Graham hosted a series of crusades in Atlanta at which he was criticized for his close ties to the Nixon administration and his ill-fitting individualistic solutions for the social ills facing Black and poor Americans. Reverend James Costlin commented: "It's just a growing awareness of what this man has stood for—the result of many years of Billy Graham's preaching and activities that have not been directed to the needs of the poor and black. He has chosen to take a chaplaincy role to the Establishment rather than relate to the poverty of the people." Graham had called for "'a national and pervasive awakening that includes repentance for our individual sins,' which for Costlin was an "'oblique' approach to social problems."[50] Critics both near and far denounced the evangelist for his lack of class and racial consciousness as well as his subservience to the Nixon administration.

Yet, despite post–World War II critiques of Christian missions, competing theological expressions from dissident Korean Christians, and negative assessments from British and Black Americans ministers and theologians, Graham organized the Korean crusade, one of his largest, in a cross-cultural, cross-racial foreign setting. He spread the "good news" in obedience to the Great Commission, and he proclaimed the gospel of a transcendent God who, through Christ, pronounced both mercy and judgment on sinners, one by one. How did Graham gain such popularity in a non-Western context, considering the criticisms that he represented the interests of colonial powers, the upper classes, and a white Christianity that shied away from demands for justice on behalf of people of color? How did Graham gain so much success among South Koreans given the limitations to freedom of speech under a military dictatorship?

The Political and Diplomatic Value of the Graham Crusade

In a period of intensive governmental surveillance, the 1973 Billy Graham crusade in Korea could not have been organized without the cooperation of Park's authoritarian regime, as Billy Kim himself admitted. It "required the help and interest of the government" as well as the "heads of congress, military leaders, and the press."[51] According to Billy Kim, "[Park] said, if we invite Billy Graham, it's better than one division of US military stationed here in Korea for national security. Because Billy Graham is so well known, he will televise his crusade back to the United States . . . [they] will know we need to save South Korea from North Korean attack."[52] He then arranged for Henry Holley, the BGEA coordinator of the crusade, to "meet the highest leaders of the Korean society." Billy Kim recalled Holley's gratitude for the work he had done to prepare "Graham's meetings with cultural leaders," including an "official meeting with President Chung Hee Park."[53] After the crusade was successfully organized, the BGEA remembered to thank not only the ambassador but also military and government officials, including Prime Minister Kim Jong Pil, who "initiated excellent government support for the crusade," and the director of the Seoul Metropolitan Police, Joh Dong Chul, for "security men and police escort."[54] Graham was "deeply grateful" to a wide variety of national leaders, including "President Park . . . and the hundreds of Christian churches that helped make this Crusade possible."[55] Graham's organization worked hand in hand with a government that had imprisoned dissident Christians and deported missionaries. It worked also, of course, with Korean churches, but critics must have thought that this was the prime example of Christian compromise with dictators.

Graham defended Park's authoritarian rule and denounced his democratic opponents. He said that he admired South Korea for its "schools, colleges and universities" and praised students who engaged in "serious study and discipline," whom he contrasted with the troublemakers who fomented "riots and demonstrations" against the Park regime.[56] Graham commented that he had "never seen such large audiences sit so quietly," "thousands" with Bibles and "thousands" of students "making notes on what was said." Like the promoters of the orphan choir, Graham praised South Koreans as studious, quiet, and passive model citizens.[57]

Graham's views of the protests against Park's authoritarian regime resembled his views of protesters against the Vietnam War. "I'm for change," he said in 1970, "but the Bible teaches us to obey authority. . . . All Americans may not agree with the decisions a president makes, but he is our president.'" After Nixon's speech, Graham reiterated the importance of Christian faith for the nation, a speech that *Time* called "'one of the most effective speeches he has yet delivered.'" Graham's crusades buttressed the Nixon administration.[58] In South Korea in 1973 Graham also strengthened the Park regime by extolling the social order that Park ensured for the crusade. Graham's South Korean collaborators, including Han, the chairman of the Korean executive committee for the crusade, joined Graham in opposing the protesters who demanded democratic rule, freedom of speech, and freedom from fear of their own government.[59] Both the American and the Korean organizers of Graham's crusade praised Park's authoritarian regime and lifted no voice of protest against the repression of dissent.

Underscoring Graham's opposition to protests in both the United States and South Korea was a theological supposition that social change could be best achieved through individual conversions rather than structural or systemic political change. Before Graham arrived in South Korea, he held historic crusades in both Durham and Johannesburg, the first mixed-race meetings in both South African cities. Press reports noted that Graham fearlessly proclaimed "that all races were one in Christ Jesus. In his audience were black and white and brown, sitting side by side. Others were working as volunteers. All of which emphasizes his opposition to apartheid."[60] Yet despite these clear and forthright displays against the assumptions of the apartheid regime in the country, Graham primarily preached a message of individual salvation that called for a change of hearts through Jesus Christ: "'Only Jesus Christ can solve the problems of individual South Africans, of their nation and the world.'" He warned that "no matter how much change is effected by man, Utopia will not come until Jesus Christ returns to earth." He preached that "human nature" carried the stain of original sin and that this sinfulness threatened "life on earth." The "answer" to "controlling crime is not to mount a legal offensive, but to effect a change of heart. This is the miracle produced by faith in Christ."[61] Though Graham's racially integrated crusade in South Africa was a bold declaration against apartheid—a step forward from his more hesitant racial stances in the 1960s—he mistakenly believed that an end to racism would occur only through individual conversions.[62]

As discussed, Graham's beliefs about individual sin and conversion as a prerequisite for social justice had, in the previous decade, caused him to part ways with the civil rights movement.[63] His unresisting individualism put him at odds with the assumptions of Martin Luther King, who believed that racial justice required changes in legal systems, institutional habits, voting restrictions, government regulations, and political behavior. Evangelical "conceptions of sin, social change and personal ethics" were widely used to resist laws that protected the rights of Black people in America, as white evangelicals excoriated religious liberals for preaching a social gospel instead of the real gospel of eternal salvation through belief in the saving death of Jesus Christ.[64] King wanted to alter the habits and institutions of the social order. Graham wanted to transform the habits and perceptions of the heart.⁶⁵ Both visions had political implications.⁶⁶ Graham wanted a just and righteous society, but his message, as well as his unspoken political assumptions, favored conservative solutions in the United States and abroad.⁶⁷

Graham's message of salvation was well received by Christians in Korea who preferred a message that spoke to the heart but avoided any meddling with the structures of Park's regime. Yet this individual and heart-centered approach to the crusade had surprising institutional and structural consequences. It solidified the linkages between South Koreans and Americans through nonstate networks and evangelical parachurches, especially the BGEA itself, but also World Vision and Campus Crusade. Park's authoritarian government encouraged such partnerships because they strengthened diplomatic relations with the United States. Graham's revivals supported corporate and political networks with an international scope. In addition, his individualistic and conversion-oriented theology of the crusade drew South Koreans to a faith in both God and America.⁶⁸

Transpacific Evangelical Parachurch Movements at the Pinnacle of Graham's Success

From May 16 to June 3, 1973, the BGEA and the South Korea–based executive committee organized two weeks of revival in major cities outside of Seoul before the main event—the five-day crusade at which Graham and Kim preached in Seoul itself.⁶⁹ In the days leading up to the Seoul crusade, BGEA associate evangelists partnered with a Korean translator and a choir director to preach their own crusades, at which 1.5 million people gathered.⁷⁰ The five-day crusade itself ended with a worship service on Sunday, June 3, 1973, at which Graham and Billy Kim preached to the largest audience in the history of the BGEA.⁷¹

Attendees made significant sacrifices to attend the crusade, some walking over two hours, carrying their own blankets, and bringing their own rice and dried fish to save money.⁷² Billy Kim recalled the reasons everyday people attended the crusade: "They said, simply, 'We want to receive blessing and mercy and grace.' Our word for grace is ŭnhae. They just say ŭnhae patŭrŏ wassŏhyo. That means they want to receive the grace of God. . . . A lot of them stay all night in the plaza to pray . . . for real genuine revival in this country."[73] When attendees arrived, they sang hymns with a six-thousand-member choir directed by the beloved musical evangelist Cliff Barrows. Behind the choir loomed a massive sign in black and white announcing: "I am the way, and the truth, and the life." While Barrows directed the choir, Bev Shea, equally admired as a musical evangelist for the BGEA, stood at the podium to lead the crowd in the hymn "How Great Thou Art." Shea sang the chorus in Korean, and the next verse in English: "Oh Lord my God when I in awesome wonder..."[74]

Alongside such Americans, South Korean Protestants who had forged transpacific evangelical networks with World Vision, Campus Crusade, and the BGEA came to the fore at the 1973 crusade.[75] The Korean Children's Choir, successors to the World Vision Orphan Choir, performed as special guests. "This Korean Children's Choir was first organized in 1959 by Dr. Bob Pierce, the founder of World Vision International," the announcer declared in Korean. "These joyful and charming young people have won many friends for Korea around the world."[76] The choir had a new name, and it also had new kinds of singers, no longer "orphans" but gifted musical performers carefully chosen through a competitive selection process. When Graham had visited Korea during the Korean War, he had been moved by a blind orphan boy's singing at an orphanage called the Lighthouse. Unlike that boy, who had worn a tattered checkered coat, these children wore colorful *hanboks* and performed professionally on a global stage.[77] The choir, often called the "little ambassadors" or "sweet songbirds," gave a bilingual rendition of "Amazing Grace." The language of spiritual transformation in the lyrics of "Amazing Grace" underscored their development from a choir of "orphans" to a "children's" choir. But these images of renewal and rebirth covered over the afterlives of war, no less exemplified in the stories of Kim Sang Yong, or "Peanuts," and Oh Chiyŏng.[78]

After the choir performed, Bill Bright, the founder of Campus Crusade, walked up to the podium to make an announcement. Campus Crusade's first international site had been established in South Korea through Joon Gon Kim, one of the executive committee members of the Graham crusade. As will be further discussed in the next chapter, in 1972, when Bright's organization sponsored a crusade called Explo '72 in Texas, Joon Gon Kim had announced that he would organize Explo '74 in Seoul and that he expected three hundred thousand people would attend, surpassing the eighty thousand at Explo '72. Bright now recruited the audience to attend Explo '74:

My heart sings with praise to God for what my eyes behold.... In the last four months I've been on four major continents in scores of countries.... But I don't know of any place in the world where he is blessing more than in Korea. Next year in August there will be a great gathering of Explo '74 here in this great country. It is something which you Koreans are launching to invite the rest of the world to participate in. And we're looking forward to what God does here through your leadership as an example to the whole world.... There are four billion people in the world today. Jesus Christ died for every one of them.... And I believe that Korea will play a major role in taking the gospel to all of Asia and much of the world. I thank God for the privilege of being here this week. Thank you.[79]

Bright believed fervently that God could reach the world through Koreans. Graham ascended to the podium to reinforce Bright's announcement: "Now Dr. Bill Bright announced that next August there would be a great training session here. The Koreans have invited thousands from all over America and all over the world to join in a great campaign here next August. Now, that's August of 1974. And we hope that thousands will be trained in evangelism and discipleship to go out and take the gospel to the whole world."[80] Graham and Bright not only collaborated at Explo '72 but also continued to support each other's revivals at this crusade. South Korea was crucially intertwined in Bright's and Graham's 1972, 1973, and 1974 revivals.

Rather than representatives from Presbyterian or Methodist denominations, evangelical parachurches, including the big three, shared the stage at the largest Graham crusade. It was not by chance that these parachurches came to occupy this space. The Korean War led to the birth of World Vision, the internationalization of Campus Crusade, and the transpacific expansion of the BGEA.[81] Graham's revivalistic apex reflected the culmination of a longer Cold War history of the transpacific rise of US evangelical empire. Koreans, however, also sought to use this pivotal moment of evangelical revival to reimagine their place in the world order, as we will see next.

A War at the Heart of a "Religion of the Heart"

When Graham and Kim stepped up to the podium of the revival, it became clear that much had changed over the twenty years since Graham first visited Korea, including the sheer size of the crowd. Yet Graham chose this moment, while preaching on "The Love of God," to awaken memories of the Korean War:

> Twenty-two years ago, I was in Korea. It was during Christmas time, and it was very cold. I've never been so cold in all my life, and I toured along what is now the DMZ. I was at Heartbreak Ridge where there were twelve soldiers huddled together. An enemy sneaked through the line. He threw a hand grenade in the middle of them. It was going to go off in three seconds. A soldier saw it and he jumped. He grabbed it. He held it to his heart. It exploded, but his buddies were saved. They took what was remaining of his body back to America. When they held a memorial service for the soldier, the clergyman took the text I want to take today.[82]

Graham then directed the crowd's attention to John 15:13: "Greater love has no one than this: to lay down one's life for one's friends." The opening military image underscored Christian martyrdom. The self-sacrifice of the US soldier paralleled Jesus's sacrifice on the cross. Graham remembered twelve US soldiers, not unlike the twelve disciples of Christ, in so doing further framing his military anecdote with images familiar to the Christian imagination. The two evangelists, in English and Korean, relied on the salvific power of the US military as the invocation for Graham's largest crusade. They described Americans and South Koreans as bound together through the crucible of war, sacralizing their alliance through the cross.

Stanton Wilson, a Presbyterian missionary, expressed on another occasion the same conviction that the "deep tie" between the United States and South Korea was "one of 'blood,' sacrifice in the Korean Conflict," not unlike the blood of Jesus that reconciled humans to the divine.[83] The theological significance of the Korean War, as well as the blood-based alliance between South Korea and the United States, bubbled to the surface at this height of evangelical success, and served as a symbol, both political and religious, of America's brotherly commitment to South Korea.

Not only for Graham, but also for Billy Kim, memories of the Korean War resurfaced when he mounted the revival podium and talked about his evolution from rags to riches.[84] Once a "shabby" US military houseboy during the war, he now looked "stately on the right side of Billy Graham." On the revival stage, he stood in awe at the thought of such a houseboy, a boy who was "simply useless," standing now on this global stage "as the Lord's holy servant." Billy Kim suggested a religious version of social mobility. He had been "shabby," then "stately," and finally a "preacher."

On this global stage, one man's transformation symbolized what was possible for the nation.[85] South Koreans could find in Billy Kim a model Christian citizen who had evolved from serving as a houseboy under the US military to serving as an ambassador of the majestic God who created the universe, a status that set him alongside Graham, a white American with whom he stood "side by side."[86] An astonishing moment of public piety awakened thoughts of the war and therefore of the geopolitics of the global Cold War.

Billy Kim's evolution signaled the possibilities for more equal diplomatic relations between the United States and South Korea as well as hope for South Korea's ascendancy in the world order. In the shifting climate of detente, during which US and South Korean diplomatic relations were tense, public memories of transnational alliance conjured through revival symbolically knit the two nations tightly together.[87] Not only economic and political actors, but also nonstate actors, including evangelists, became conduits through which diplomatic relations could flow.

The success of Christianity in South Korea that was revealed through the Graham crusade ultimately became a vehicle through which South Koreans like Billy Kim imagined their ascendance—not simply to work with but also to surpass American evangelicals, in a race for revival. One can see these complicated dynamics of power by examining Billy Graham's and Billy Kim's preaching.

Billy and Billy

Unlike the early transatlantic revivalists of the Anglophone world, transpacific revival required linguistic translation from English to Korean. In addition to the rekindling of Korean and American alliance, the translation experience reminded Billy Kim that Graham was an aspirational figure *and* a standard to supersede. When Billy Kim narrated his preaching experience with Graham, the subtitles that he used in chronological succession—"Billy and Billy, Side by Side," "Two Voices as One," and "After the Crusade: Kim in the Spotlight"—showed how he grew from imagining himself, first as a subordinate partner, then as a rival to Graham, and finally to superseding him as an evangelist. Not only Graham, but also South Koreans, wielded the transpacific piety *and* politics of evangelical revival for multiple purposes.

Translating the Message from Fundamentalism to Evangelicalism

Billy Kim and Billy Graham had much in common even before the 1973 crusade.[88] They were both male Baptist ministers married to white women, Ruth Graham and Trudy Kim, and they shared geographical roots in the American South and theological roots in American fundamentalism.[89] As discussed, during the Korean War, Kim Jang Hwan became a houseboy for the US military, whose soldiers gave him the nickname "Billy."[90] An American soldier then arranged for his admission to Bob Jones Academy, a fundamentalist school where he accepted Jesus as his savior. Graham likewise began his theological education at Bob Jones before he transferred to Wheaton College, an evangelical college in Wheaton, Illinois. Graham's departure from Bob Jones was a significant theological watershed for the fundamentalist thread of Christianity. The founder of the school, Bob Jones, denounced Graham's more "liberal" theology, a stance that began to differentiate ultraseparatist fundamentalists at Bob Jones from the neo-evangelicals who ultimately became mainstream evangelicals in the age of Graham. Though Graham and Kim had some theological differences during these early years, even these would collapse when Billy Kim severed his ties to Bob Jones following his translating work with Graham at the 1973 crusade.

Because of Billy Kim's roots in white fundamentalism, the invitation to translate for Graham posed a theological dilemma for him. When he was a student at Bob Jones, he had attended the 1957 Billy Graham crusade in New York. There he had a "vision of wanting to be an evangelist like Billy Graham." When he received the BGEA's invitation to translate for Graham at the crusade, he recalled that "Billy Graham had been like a hero to him. That very evangelist was now asking him to be his interpreter in the Korea Crusade.... It was surely a miracle."[91] Yet to accept the invitation meant severing transnational ties to white fundamentalism, which Billy Kim was reluctant to do, not least because he encountered "a lot of opposition to translate for Billy Graham.... A number of our friends advised us not to do it." If he were to partner with Graham, he was told, his name would be "removed from the Bob Jones alumni records" and he would stop receiving monthly financial contributions from Bob Jones's friends and conservative churches in the United States.[92] Bob Jones University was "the very foundational source of his faith." It was there that he had "met God ... for the first time," "dreamed his visions of faith," and trained to become an evangelist. Because Bob Jones was "like a source river of faith," he thought that without it he would "dry up."[93] Billy Kim was caught between the theological tensions of American fundamentalism and evangelicalism, revealing the powerful influence that the American religious landscape had upon him.

Yet translating for Graham would also bring benefits, and eventually he found the confidence to do the translation. He recalled: "After searching my own heart and praying for some six months with Trudy and a number of close friends, we felt that God wanted me to do the interpreting for Dr. Billy Graham."[94] Billy Kim, therefore, came under Graham's leadership, rescinding his ties to Bob Jones Academy. But Billy Graham also depended on Billy Kim.

At the 1973 crusade, Graham declared his theological position between liberal and fundamentalist Christians and acknowledged his utter dependence as an evangelist in Korea on Billy Kim's able translating skills:

> I believe the Bible to be the inspired word of God. Some people don't believe that. They think it's too orthodox. There are some other people who say that I fellowship with too many people. . . . I proclaim the gospel, and if they come to the banner that I erect, then I say, "Thank the Lord, let them come." We could not do this work here if not for the dedicated ministry and cooperation of hundreds and thousands of people working, praying, and preparing in Korea. And I would be absolutely nothing if it were not for my good voice, Billy Kim.[95]

Graham was referring to liberal Christians who criticized his biblical literalism and to ultrafundamentalists like Bob Jones, who criticized him for associating with Christians in other theological camps. Graham not only helped to carve out an "evangelical" space in the religious landscape of the United States, but also recalibrated theological orthodoxy in South Korea.

The theological shift was costly for Billy Kim. Bob Jones University criticized him severely for his collaboration with Graham. Bob Jones III, the president of Bob Jones University in 1973, wrote to Billy Kim a month after the Graham crusade in South Korea and argued that what he had done was akin to serving as a false prophet of the Antichrist:

> Your life and ministry speak of compromise, ambivalence, a double tongue, pragmatism and Scriptural disobedience. . . . By joining forces with this 20th century Jehoshaphat, a man who could well be the John the Baptist of the Antichrist, you have clearly aligned yourself with New Evangelicalism and all of its evil ramifications.

Jones took Billy Kim's actions personally:Less than a year ago we stood together and talked in the lobby of the Administration Building here on the campus. You assured me that you had been misunderstood by the critics who charged you with compromise and with aiding and abetting New Evangelicalism. . . . I will never be able to believe you again.

He labeled Kim a "religious politician" who associated himself with theological partners at his convenience:

You have been playing the role of the religious politician, getting the best you could get from all segments of the religious spectrum. You are a compromiser. You are also a liar. . . . I hope you will at least have the decency to disavow all connections you have ever had with Bob Jones University. . . . You have turned out to be a disgrace to everything this school stands for. . . . It is certainly no honor to be called the "Billy Graham of Korea."

Jones deemed him a failure not only in the eyes of the university, but also in the eyes of God, taking it upon himself to damn him to hell for disobedience to scripture:

A mind that is disobedient and in conflict with the Word of God will bring no Heavenly reward . . . for the works committed in so doing are wood, hay, and stubble, to be burned in the fire of the Christians' judgment. When you return to the States for your next fundraising effort, please do not include Bob Jones University in your itinerary. We have written you off as a failure because we believe that in God's sight you are exactly that—a failure.[96]

If Graham and Kim had shared common experiences before they mounted the podium in 1973, the crusade moved them even closer together, especially as the two joined in a common repudiation of the white fundamentalism that each had once affirmed.

From Mimicry to Korean Christianity as a Strategy for Ascendance

Translating for Graham compelled Billy Kim quite literally to mimic him. For as Kim prepared to translate, he "took time to practice the accents, gestures, and intonations of Billy Graham."[97] He wanted to emulate his speech patterns and bodily movements and the content of his preaching: "His message was so important that our people needed to hear. I don't want to divert, I don't want to change, I don't want to make his message any different than he preached. And I believe that first night that God certainly put his hand and his blessing upon there [sic]." Billy Kim also desired to "convey the spirit of his message, the content of his message, the love that he has in his message, the charisma he has in his message that not too many people in our world today have." So he prayed: " 'Lord, make me a Korean-speaking Billy Graham.' "[98]

On the heels of civil rights reform, Graham—and later, Ronald Reagan—would espouse a color-blind conservatism that paired well with his understanding of the Christian gospel. Reagan's brand of color-blind conservatism "asserted that the heaviest work of race reform had already been completed by federal civil rights legislation, leaving the last remnants of racial discrimination to be cleaned up by citizens through interpersonal exchange and the workings of a meritocratic capitalist system free of government control."[99] Graham's understanding of the Christian gospel cohered with this political vision because, as mentioned, he tended to put "his trust in individualism," casting doubt on "efficacy of government programs."[100] Graham, as a result, tended to emphasize the universal need for individuals to experience Christian redemption regardless of race or nationality. His commitment to a gospel that went beyond color propelled his desire for global evangelistic efforts to reach individual hearts all over the world.

In both South Africa and South Korea in 1973, Graham preached against theological ideas prevalent in the early 1970s about the racial exclusivity of Christianity. In South Africa, Graham declared that Jesus was not a white man: "Now Jesus was a man. He was human. He was not a white man! He was not a black man. He came from that part of the world that touches Africa and Asia and Europe and he probably had a brown skin."[101] In South Korea, Graham declared that Jesus was not an American or a European: "You know, I have found people here in this part of the world who actually think Jesus was an American. Or they think that Jesus was a European." But they could not have been more wrong: "Jesus was an Asian. He was born and reared in the Middle East." Graham argued that Jesus was racially and culturally closer to South Koreans than to Americans. However, Jesus's Asian background did not mean that Jesus belonged to Asians alone; Jesus belonged to "the whole world." Graham simultaneously articulated Jesus's particularity and universality. He appealed to the universality of the Christian message when he invited his hearers to repent: "Jesus . . . loved you so much. What does he want you to do? First, he wants you to repent of your sins."[102] For Graham, the universal need for repentance made Jesus a savior for all nations.

At the same time, Graham also argued against liberationist approaches to the gospel that emphasized the need for racially particular and contextualized theologies. For instance, Howard O. Jones, the first Black associate evangelist for the BGEA, disliked Graham's individualistic approach to social ills, but his belief in a "colorless" gospel made him a suitable evangelist for Graham's team.[103] Jones argued that "true biblical theology is colorless," and he declared that "the white man does not have an exclusive hold on Christianity.... It is universal in its scope because its founder Jesus Christ is the universal Christ—the Savior for all people regardless of race or color.... I'm glad that when Jesus Christ died on the cross He died for the black man, the white man, the brown man, the yellow man and the red man." At the same time, he denounced the ideas that were emerging in the tradition of a Black theology of liberation:

> Black theology provides no real liberation or redemption for black people ... we must also challenge the exponents of black theology, namely, Rev. Albert B. Cleage, Dr. James H. Cone, and others because their teaching is structured in racism, black separatism and error. They distort the Scriptures to deify blackness, and champion the black man's cause for liberation and the building of a black nation. But even more damaging is the fact that black theology is fundamentally humanism, a materialistic and socialistic philosophy of men. Black theology has no roots in the cross of Jesus Christ ... white theology and black theology must be rejected since both are contrary to the teaching of the Word of God.[104]

Jones believed in preaching a "colorless" theology of redemption through the saving grace of God rather than any theology that emphasized racial particularity. Just as he denounced a Eurocentric imagination Jesus, so too he rejected theologies that seemed to deify blackness. For Billy Kim, to come under Graham's theological banner meant not only a rejection of white fundamentalism and liberationist theologies but also an embrace of a "colorless" gospel. Moreover, if his religious and racial formation at Bob Jones in the 1950s had distanced him from the cause of Black freedom, this crusade aligned him with the vision of the BGEA's first Black evangelist, solidifying the BGEA's multiracial and multinational reach under a "colorless" gospel.

On the revival stage, however, there was no way to overlook racial and national differences. Billy Kim had rued his short height compared to his white classmates at Bob Jones. At the podium with Graham, he stood on a riser that helped him match Graham's height, yet it was a reminder that he was shorter and smaller in stature than a white evangelist like Graham.[105] Yet Graham's commitment to a "colorless," or some might say, color-blind gospel intimated that Billy Kim could, indeed, become Billy Graham. The religious success of the crusade became an aspirational paradigm through which Billy Kim would imagine racial and national ascendancy.

Billy Kim took the opportunity to translate for Graham as a venue to do what he regarded as preaching his own sermon. He surmised that "interpreting for Billy Graham was more like giving a sermon than an interpretation, because people attending were going to be listening to the sermon from the interpreter, and not directly from Billy Graham."[106] As Nicholas Harkness provides, by the end of sermon, it was as if the preaching of "the 'Word' had nearly passed from Graham to Kim." Far from merely mimicking Graham, in these last moments, "within the internal poetic structure of the sermon, the 'Word' was most fully Koreanized" through Billy Kim.[107]

Yet Billy Kim took it one step further. He went so far as to suggest that he was the main preacher: "There were less than 5 percent who understand Billy Graham's English message. They have to depend on a Korean coming in. A lot of people said that it looked like Billy Kim is preaching and Billy Graham is interpreting for the 5% of American soldiers" (figure 4.1).[108]

That was certainly how Cho Miyŏng remembered her experience of hearing the two men as she sat on the podium with the choir:

> I remember just being mesmerized by just watching Rev. Kim Jang Hwan [Billy Kim] because afterward we were talking about it and thought he did a better job than Billy Graham. He translated with so much passion. If Billy Graham's tone would go up, Rev. Kim Jang Hwan's tone would go up a little more.... And when Billy Graham's volume would go up, his volume [would] go up even more. You know, he has such a small stature and he had to stand up at the podium using a booster to match Graham's height.... It felt more like Rev. Kim Jang Hwan was the preacher. We had to listen to it in Korean, so that's why we said Rev. Kim Jang Hwan was a better preacher.[109]

Cho remembered Billy Kim as the leader of the crusade because his linguistic translation helped her understand the message. In the aftermath of

Figure 4.1 Billy Kim towering over Billy Graham in a display at the Billy Kim Memorial Library, Suwon Central Baptist Church, Suwon, Korea. This reconstruction of the 1973 crusade imagines Kim as the main speaker.
Source: Photo by author.

the crusade, for Cho and for Billy Kim himself, the aspiration to become a "Korean-speaking Billy Graham" was a moot point, for it seemed to them and many others that Kim had taken center stage and Graham had served as *his* voice.

Various events reinforced this perception. Kim recalled garnering the attention of the press after the crusades. He was "bewildered when he discovered that an interview was to be with him and not Billy Graham." He thought, "*Billy Graham should have been the one in the spotlight, and more than that, God should be honored most of all, not me.*"[110] He received national attention not only from Korean Christians, but also the wider public, including government and military officials who may not have had a religious interest in the crusade:

> Because of that translation and because such a large number of people attended that Crusade, the daily newspaper, the press and television picked

up the story and overnight you became somebody in the Korean scene. Since the Crusade was over, I have had more invitations, probably [enough] to fill up the next five years, to conduct overseas. Also the secular world was caught up in such a great spirit and the man in the high government places. One of the subjects they want to talk about is the Crusade. They want to talk about the translation and they want to talk about all of it. So it gives me a natural way to witness to some of those men that I would have never had a chance had I not been translator for Dr. Billy Graham. You'd be amazed, you could sit down with the Prime Minister and pray with him, talk to one of the Cabinet members or one of the Congressional leaders, a four-star general. They seek your counsel, seek your advice simply because of what had happened a year ago at that great Crusade.[111]

As a result of his translation work, he became a celebrity overnight and found simultaneous religious and secular success. He found a "natural way to witness," pray with, and influence political and military leaders in South Korea and the United States. Billy Kim's church also grew: "At that time my church was maybe three to four hundred. Since [the] crusade, now we probably have about twenty thousand people."[112] Kim mimicked Graham, but also used him to advance his own vision and aims.

True, Bob Jones lambasted Billy Kim. Yet giving up those ties garnered Billy Kim the spotlight on the national scene as well as on the stage of world Christianity. After the crusade, Graham tellingly observed that the gravitational center of world Christianity was shifting to Asia:

The astonishing growth of the Korean church and the growth of Christianity throughout Asia leads me to feel that perhaps the gravitational center of Christianity is now moving here to the Far East. Christianity began in the Middle East, moved westward to Europe, then to America, and now perhaps to the Far East. I urge church and theological leaders, especially from Europe and America, to come and study the Korean church. I believe the secret of the power and strength of the Korean church is that they believe and proclaim the Bible. They have a strong evangelistic and missionary interest. They couple all of this with great social concern.

Already at this crusade Graham himself felt changed by his experience of evangelical revivalism in South Korea. The whole experience of the crusade made him aware of the bidirectional—albeit, uneven and limited—force of Korean and American evangelicalism: "I seriously doubt if we will ever see meetings quite like this again in my ministry. It has made such a tremendous impact on me personally that I must get away for a few days and evaluate what I have seen and felt. I seriously doubt if my own ministry can ever be the same again."[113]

Moreover, once the crusade aired on US television, Billy Kim received multiple invitations to preach in the United States: "People started asking me to come speak, whether Gideon, whether Lion's Club, Moody, Wheaton . . . a lot of those schools invite[d] me. . . . Southwestern Theological Seminary, Dallas Theological Seminary, a lot of those schools asked me to come to speak, three or four days, for a spiritual emphasis week."[114] Billy Kim wielded the transpacific piety and politics of evangelical revivalism to imagine influencing the world. So did Oh Chiyŏng.

Born Again

For her part, after attending Billy Graham's largest crusade, Oh Chiyŏng began to pray: "Please open my eyes. . . . I was very frustrated. . . . I should have joy, but I didn't yet." Oh recalled that she was "born again," not through the choir, but through a religious experience with Joy Mission, soon after attending the Graham crusade:

> I prayed, "Please let it be the day that my spiritual eyes are open." . . . At the end there was an invitation: "Today there's someone who needs solutions for their life." I raised my hand, and they said that a counselor would take me to the hallway to counsel me. As I went into the hallway and was sitting down, all of a sudden, ever since I was a baby on a dust-ridden road . . . [I could see] the greatness of God's love . . . this is how much God loves me. . . . All of a sudden my eyes were open. . . . I started to pour out my tears. . . . That's how my eyes opened. Inside of me all of a sudden I had so much joy. . . . [After that] I would look up to the stars and say the stars are rejoicing. . . . The motto of the Music Institute was to sing the songs of the mountain, to sing songs that were alive. . . . But every month we said that and we practiced, but those songs weren't alive because we weren't born again. . . . That was that day I was really born again.[115]

Oh had a direct encounter with God, a religious experience that awakened her to a new spiritual reality through which she was "born again."

For Oh's "born again" experience emboldened her to enact significant transformations, including in the World Vision Korean Orphan Choir. She recalled:

> After I was born again I could not just stay idle. . . . Even the [choir] had to become born again. . . . On Thursday we would have a prayer meeting. . . . I told them to go to Joy Mission. . . . In my room we had a secret prayer meeting. . . . Secretly one by one students would come to my room and pray together. . . . That was 1973. . . . About twenty of them had born-again experiences.[116]

Because the choir itself was not providing enlivening spiritual experiences, she sought to ensure that they sang "songs that were alive." She took it upon herself to have "secret prayer meetings" in her room to ensure that choristers were "born again."

In December 1973, she went on to create her own choir, called the Joy Women's Choir, with five other World Vision Korean Orphan Choir alumna:

> We weren't a formal organization, but they told the five of us to go up as the Joy Women's Choir . . . Lee Kyŏnghi, Chung Suryŏng, Moon Hyangja Moon, Park Chŏngshin. . . . We were all World Vision Korean Orphan Choir members. . . . We were born again, we were the best of friends, and we were accomplished singers. . . . Everyone was amazed. . . . So we would sing whenever there was an event . . . especially international guests. . . . We said we might tour the world like when we were part of the World Vision Korean Orphan Choir. . . . But then we ended up traveling even further around the world . . . Europe, Asia . . . Russia, Kenya . . . We performed for twenty-eight years. . . . We have CDs and records. . . . [As children] we performed songs internationally in the language of the nations we traveled, so we had that, we had faith, and we had friendship, something that you cannot purchase with money. . . . We performed for so many missionaries and encouraged them . . . 1973 was such a big year . . . my graduation, my housing, being born again, and starting this choir.[117]

Thus, Oh and four other Korean women not only created a choir, but ultimately traveled further throughout the world, extending the singing they had done as children with the World Vision Korean Orphan Choir, but this time doing so on their own terms. For this reason, nearly twenty years later, when she saw a childhood photo taken of her with Graham, she understood the 1973 crusade in providential terms: "I realized that God had been preparing things for me since then. . . . Sending Billy Graham . . . opened my eyes. . . . If there's one person I need to thank in my life, it's Billy Graham."[118]

Others exhibited the South Korean church's complex view of American Christianity in the aftermath of the crusade. Cho Yonggi Cho, or David Yonggi Cho, now emeritus pastor of Yoido Full Gospel Church, the largest church in the world, suggested the complexity after the Graham crusade had ended. When asked why he prayed for the American church, he said: "They are our parents. They sent the Gospel to us. Now we are grown up. Now we are ready to pray for our parents. That's our obligation."[119] Cho acknowledged the filial, hierarchical relationship the Korean church had with the American church as its "parents." Yet he also subversively noted that "we are grown up" and identified the Korean church as able to use its power as a child to "care" for the elderly—and perhaps he also implied weakening and dying—American church. A race for revival opened a way for Koreans to imagine their own ascendancy in the global order vis-à-vis the more powerful ally and patron-state, the American empire.

Even as Graham's largest crusade marked the height of US evangelical empire, it was also a moment in which South Koreans sought to imagine and achieve their own nationalistic aims and geopolitical aspirations through revival. Koreans helped organize the 1973 crusade, but they did not need help in using it for their own religious and political interests. If some saw it as a Western imposition, far more saw it as a symbol of a Korean church ready to take the gospel to the whole world. The offspring saw no reason why they should not supplant the parent, or at least exercise the same powers. The revival was more than a religious awakening. It was an assertion of South Korea's place among the nations of the world. Where else in the world would more than a million people gather to hear Christian preaching? South Korea was the leader, and in the eyes of some, it was only the beginning.

Moreover, though militarily, economically, and politically South Korea was still indebted to the United States, evangelical revivalism was a vehicle of nonstate power that South Koreans would mobilize to modernize and advance South Korea, engendering aspirations that the client state could influence and even supersede the United States—a means for the new "empire to strike back." That Graham reached his numerical apex in Cold War South Korea not only reveals the transpacific networks that propelled the reconstruction of modern evangelical America into an empire, but also the power that South Koreans saw in an evangelical form Christianity. But the revivalist impulse did not end there. It grew into an "explosion."

5

Explosion

The "New Emerging Christian Kingdom" and the Christian Right, 1972–1980

Graham's largest "crusade" was just one massive revival in a series of transpacific "explosions." Explo '72 and Explo '74—or, Holy Spirit "explosions"—hosted by Campus Crusade were massive revivals respectively in Texas and Seoul. In 1972, Bright gathered eighty thousand people for Explo '72 in the Dallas Cotton Bowl. In 1974, Joon Gon Kim gathered 1.3 million people on opening night of Explo '74 in Seoul, which not only beat Explo '72 numbers but also Graham's largest crusade in 1973.[1] These "explosions" revealed the growing tension between the rise of the US evangelical empire and South Korean Protestants' challenge to it. Indeed, South Korean Protestants made a powerful declaration challenging US exceptionalism, imagining South Korea as the "new emerging Christian kingdom."[2]

On the last day of Explo '72, or "explosion" of the Holy Spirit in Dallas, Joon Gon Kim mounted the revivalistic stage to declare a surprise announcement: "We are planning for an Explo '74 in Korea. We expect it will draw 300,000 people."[3] Joon Gon Kim circumvented the chain of command at Campus Crusade when he announced that he would exceed—even quadruple—the 80,000 people gathered in the Cotton Bowl. Nils Becker, a Campus Crusade staff worker in Korea, recalled: "In the West, we would not declare a number before the event."[4] When Bright expressed his shock at the lack of forewarning—and, the audacity of the claims—Bailey Marks, Kim's immediate superior, assured Bright: "I would have been very happy to have forewarned you if I had known about it myself."[5] "In simple terms, they were befuddled," recalled Oh Chint'ak, a Korea Campus Crusade for Christ staff worker.[6]

Bright and Joon Gon Kim were like "two prongs of a tuning fork," as one biographer put it. That is, "when one was struck with a strategy he believed was of God, it motivated the other, right on pitch."[7] In the heat of the revivals of Explo '72 and '74, their seemingly synchronous pitch had "explosive" effects, however. In expecting Korea to be the next "city on a hill," Joon Gon Kim's understanding of Korean exceptionalism rivaled Bright's of America. Ready for the urgent mission at hand, Kim stated: "Our goal is to fulfill the Great Commission in Korea by 1975."[8] The date is not random; Bright had a vision to fulfill the Great Commission in the United States by 1976 and the world by 1980.[9]

Joon Gon Kim intended to trump him.[10]

Indeed, in the years leading up to Reagan's rise, South Koreans, in a race for revival, challenged US evangelical empire by prompting Americans to recenter Christian power from the West to the East. By the 1980 World Evangelization Crusade, Joon Gon Kim argued for a "Korean-modeled and Korean-led missionary movement," making the "world and all people become our working unit."[11] South Koreans' faith in individual conversions alone as a means for social change, however, led them to forge an unholy alliance with authoritarian Park Chung-hee. If Explo '72, as well as Berkeley Blitz, were sites where US students took an individualistic approach to social change, reinforcing US political conservatism, Explo '74 became a site where South Korean students were discouraged from social protest, in favor of a Christian revolution that buttressed the Park regime.[12] These nonstate networks ultimately connected South Korean authoritarianism with US political conservatism, establishing a transpacific Christian Right.[13]

Explo '72 and the "New Emerging Christian Kingdom"

Explo '72 was a massive event that departed from Campus Crusade's traditional work on college campuses primarily targeting students in Greek campus life and college athletes. Judy Douglass, a longtime staff member, and the wife of Steve Douglass, Bill Bright's successor, recalls, "The ministry staff pretty much objected..., 'That's not what we do. We don't do that.'" Douglass recalls her husband asking Bright, "'Are you sure God told you this?' On this, and several other things, he said, 'This is from the Lord, I know it.'" As a result, they organized Explo '72, but "some left because they said, 'This is not who we are.'"[14] Explo '72 was also unusual for Campus Crusade in that Joon Gon Kim's surprise announcement shifted the organization's focus toward Korea in ways they had not imagined. Douglass, who was then part of the publications department, recalls, "Explo '74 was a crazy thing to try and do because the staff in Korea was small."[15] Campus Crusade "supported him, ultimately, because it wasn't just crazy talk," Oh Chint'ak recalled. Joon Gon Kim had developed a vision for a massive gathering like Explo '74 since 1961 while praying at Samgak Mountain to build Korea as a Christian nation: "Win the Korean campus today, win the Korean nation and the world tomorrow."[16]

The national fame of Graham, the executive director of Explo '72, helped to publicize the event, and he dubbed it the "Christian Woodstock." Johnny Cash and musicians, enthralled by the Jesus Movement culture, entertained the attendees in between their teachings on the Holy Spirit, evangelism, and how to become a Christian.[17] Rather than a representation of a "rigid evangelical conservatism," Explo '72 exemplified a culture of "modern conservatives" who embodied a "dynamic and adaptive evangelicalism that was beginning to attract the attention of secular America."[18] With about eighty thousand attendees, a bit shy of the goal of recruiting one hundred thousand attendees, Explo '72 was, nevertheless, considered a success for the organizers.

Explo '72 attendees made life-changing decisions. Ed Neibling exemplified this life transformation, as he was, reportedly, "just a country boy from Kansas" who then became a global missionary. Neibling was an engineering student at Kansas State University when he heard a pivotal message at the Cotton Bowl: "Dr. Bright challenged everyone to surrender their lives to Christ, to go wherever he would . . . I stood to indicate that kind of decision."[19] Neibling stayed in Dallas for four additional months to attend the Institute for Biblical Studies with Josh McDowell.[20] At the end of the training, he attended a short-term missionary trip: "Bill Bright came in and challenged us for the last month of our summer break to go to Hawaii to work with Japanese students." He recalled that he "went back with almost an Asian heart," echoing Pierce's heart-centered embrace of Korea. In summer 1973, Neibling became a staff member for Campus Crusade: "I felt the Lord's leading to go to Asia. . . . It was obvious that Asia was very much on my heart."[21] He devoted nearly forty years of his life to missionary work in Asia—Joon Gon Kim's surprise declaration at Explo '72, in part, challenged him to do so. Neibling recalls, "That was nice, but quite a big challenge given that night."[22]

When Joon Gon Kim mounted the Explo '72 stage, he employed commanding language. He declared that the spirit of God was "moving fast, deep and big in Korea." Korea, as the "new emerging Christian kingdom," would not only exceed Explo '72 attendees, but also, ultimately, replace the United

States as the center of modern Christian power. He went on to recruit the US crowd to join Korea in this effort: "Join with us for that historic Jesus march." "Pray that Korea will be won for Christ 100%," he challenged the audience, and that Korea would be "a symbolic sample Christian nation" and "uniquely used of God for Christ."[23] Joon Gon Kim declared that he had built up a group of "42,000 hardcore revolutionized Christian students" who were influencing Korea. He conceived of this population of Christian students as a "nucleus of man power" that had been deployed to train others in evangelism and discipleship. Joon Gon Kim even deployed militaristic language that strengthened his command to turn toward Korea, as he declared that, quite literally, "3,500 soldiers received baptism in one day in one division."[24]

Kim's audacious declaration at Explo '72 set off a series of events, redoubling Campus Crusade's energies and pushing its workers toward the Asia-Pacific. Gertrude Phillips, a Campus Crusade staff worker who attended Explo '72, recalled: "I was amazed . . . I hadn't heard about that. It was just the spirit of God that moved him."[25] Douglass recalled the extent to which Campus Crusade in the United States restructured its priorities to support Explo '74. Campus Crusade in the United States provided support in terms of money and people, and she recalls the financial cuts and organizational shifts that Campus Crusade headquarters made for Explo '74. Those "in a nonessential area" were either sent to Korea or replaced hired staff. As they were running a conference center, they replaced hourly workers with headquarter staff to change the sheets and towels in the hotel rooms and to do the landscaping.[26] Douglass's department was considered nonessential, and she found it "challenging" when most of her team went to "fill in where they had let hourlies go, and a number of them went on to Korea to help with administrative duties there." Phillips went to Korea for six months for Explo '74: "I had to have incredible faith to go. It was out of my character to say yes immediately, but I just knew."[27] In part, Phillips could go because of her Cotton Bowl experience when she heard Joon Gon Kim's surprise announcement. "As I look back, that's when the most amazing things happened," she said with tears in her eyes. She continued: "God already knew, before the foundation of the world, that I was going to also be in Korea for Explo '74—that just still amazes me."[28] After six months in South Korea, she devoted nearly twenty years to missionary work in Asia.

Campus Crusade workers primarily characterized the relationship between American and South Korean Christians in terms of the category of faith and cultural differences, which presumed relatively equal relations between the two nations. Oh Chint'ak and Marks characterized their relationship in terms of the category of "faith" as those who motivated each other to exercise one another's "muscles of faith." Joon Gon Kim and Bright "relied on each other's faith to do big things for God," including mass revivals.[29] A shared and idealized Christian identity as "brothers" contributed to this framework. Marks recalled that after Joon Gon Kim's announcement, Bright said: "Well, . . . our brother has made this announcement. Let's get behind him and do everything we can to see how we can make it [happen] from our point . . . from our side."[30] Oh Chint'ak saw their relationship as a balance between East and West that could achieve harmony: "As Bright and Joon Gon Kim's relationship became deeper, their worlds of faith achieved more balance. Bright probably was challenged by the Eastern way of thinking . . . Joon Gon Kim was also challenged by the way Bright worked with his staff. . . . They began to use an approach that transcended the differences between East and West and became God's method of making history."[31] Oh Chint'ak's characterization, however, overlooks the multiple tiers of geopolitical power at work in US-South Korean relations. He commented, "I think, perhaps, that the greatest influence that Rev. Kim Joon Gon gave to Bill Bright was this: 'Faith cannot be calculated.'" Yet Joon Gon Kim employed competitive and militaristic language in his announcement, a strategy that publicly "surprised" executive leadership such that it could not be ignored. Joon Gon Kim forced Campus Crusade to focus on South Korea as a new center of Christian power.

Explo '74: "The New Emerging Christian Kingdom" Spurs a World Vision

Joon Gon Kim's surprise announcement led to Explo '74, which attracted 320,000 Korean delegates, and 2,887 delegates from seventy-eight other countries to South Korea from August 14 to August 18, 1974 (figure 5.1). Explo '74 was organized around the theme "Jesus Revolution, the Holy Spirit's Third Explosion." The primary purpose was to train people to evangelize others.[32] Newspaper headlines announced: "World Christian Leaders Lay a Fuse for Evangelism Explosion." Explo '74 aimed to provide "'a great spiritual fusion whose chain reaction will spread Christ's message.'"[33] Bright declared: "The purpose of Explo '74 is to turn the eyes of Korea, Asia and the world on Jesus Christ."[34] Campus Crusade in the United States had provided

Figure 5.1 Joon Gon Kim and Bill Bright at Explo '74, Seoul, 1974
Source: Until Everyone Has Heard: Campus Crusade for Christ International Helping Fulfill the Great Commission. The First Fifty Years, 1951–2001 (Orlando, FL: Campus Crusade for Christ International, 2007).

financial and human resources for Explo '74 and invested more than a year and a half in planning the gathering.

Campus Crusade burgeoned as a global organization because of Explo '72 and Explo '74. "So many staff went overseas after [Explo '74]," Douglass recalled. In the 1970s, Campus Crusade "began to resemble a foreign missions agency, as its goal shifted from university evangelism to encouraging students to serve as missionaries with Crusade upon graduation."[35] Bright's shift to support the global South was not merely a matter of theology, such as the belief that Korea was a chosen nation, but also a matter of cost: "On the basis of our surveys in Asia, Africa and Latin America, [we] are convinced that, for every dollar we raise, we can expect at least one person to receive Christ."[36] Explo '74 was especially pivotal in Campus Crusade's global shift. "That our ministry could have that kind of impact, and do something that significant in Korea, helped a lot," Douglass recalled. She noted: "The vast majority of our staff went to Asia. A lot went to Europe, but Europe was never as welcoming."[37]

The massive revivals that South Koreans hosted at Explo '74 and their fervent faith influenced Campus Crusade staff to see their faith in global terms, and to even commit their lives to lifelong missionary work. Sharpless learned that the vision of the total evangelization of the world could become a reality in Korea. From his early days as a campus worker at Oregon State, from "day one on campus," Sharpless had taught an introductory Christian series including "the challenge to fulfill the Great Commission, to reach the world for Christ," which was the "most important class." Talking about the evangelization of the world "versus actually seeing the potential fulfillment of the Great Commission" was nothing short of "life-changing." He left Korea "knowing that God could do it." He recalled: "I was able to attend the evening sessions at Yoido Island.... What I saw and witnessed was humanly impossible unless God had done it. The miracle of people of how they got there, the sense of unity and purpose, that was very intense." Sharpless was moved by the visible signs of fervent Korean piety at Explo '74: "The delegates to Explo '74 were not casual Christians. They were committed to see their country reached—you couldn't help but feel that, sense that, be part of that. It was not casual Christianity that week. These were committed people, committed to the Great Commission."[38] He noticed the sacrifices they were willing to make, as many traveled from outside of Seoul and "camped out on hard ground with a thin mat and lived in very basic accommodations and housing and food for over a week." He declared, "You don't do that if you're a casual Christian. This was not a vacation. The people from the city would come by bus in the early afternoon and stay until midnight—it was not convenient, it was not easy." He concluded that "God was doing a special thing in Korea at that time both in the hearts of Korean church leaders and the heart of Dr. Joon Gon Kim."[39] Sharpless could not forget what he had witnessed, and as a result, he committed the rest of his life to Campus Crusade's missionary work: "In 1977, I was reported and released to Asia . . . I went with the understanding that it was a lifetime assignment." As Sharpless articulated, "When you join this movement, you join to see the world reached for Christ."[40]

Phillips, who was similarly recruited to do administrative work for Explo '74, gained a new world vision and met challenges she otherwise would not have faced. She recalled the new lens through which she came to see the world as a result of Explo '74: "Just the experience of being there and seeing that, probably gave me a worldview I wouldn't have had otherwise. Because I had never been to another country.... My world was the continental United States.... I had no experience of anything outside the United States.... It challenged me on a faith level." Had she not had the initial six months in Korea,

"There's no way I would have said yes to twenty years." Philips continues: "I really can say that if I had not had that experience in Korea, I wouldn't have been in place, and I wouldn't have had the faith to keep on going in international ministry. Because seriously, I would not have requested it, I wouldn't have thought of it."[41] She initially refused to go overseas, but while in Korea, she was asked again to consider missionary work in Asia. Now she was much more open. She saw the "fervency of faith of the Korean people," which helped her become "even more serious about my own spiritual faith." She recalled how witnessing Korean piety at Explo '74 changed her life direction: "It was the spiritual that really drew me, the spiritual openness of Asia. . . . I said yes." After Korea, she went to the Philippines, "thinking it would be one term of two, two and half years. I had to have my mother send me more clothes because I just packed for six months." She ultimately stayed for twenty three years: "After that first term I prayed and God showed me I should stay. . . . I stayed for a second term. . . . Then, it was as if God said, stay there until I tell you to leave. . . . I was there twenty-three years. It was just one term into another term." Phillips was inspired not only by Koreans' fervent piety, but also the literal openness of South Korea as a nation. Along routes of empire building in Asia, Phillips experienced a spiritual awakening that shifted her life trajectory in incremental steps.[42]

Like Sharpless and Philips, Neibling recalled the life-changing effect that Explo '74 had upon his life. As much as Bright's staff had resisted him in organizing Explo '72, Joon Gon Kim was met with resistance when he attempted to organize Explo '74. His Korean staff had famously listed one hundred reasons for why they could not execute Explo '74. They went down the list one by one and resolved to have faith in God to overcome each hurdle. Neibling was inspired by the way they overcame all of these seeming obstacles: "During orientation we heard Dr. Kim [speak about] the struggle that it was among the staff to really believe that such a big event could happen. They fasted and prayed." Then they began to go down the list: "They said, 'Can God do this?' They gradually began to answer, 'Yes, God can do it.' The dream became a reality."

Neibling similarly had an experience of overcoming obstacles at Explo '74. He had suddenly been tasked with hosting the overflow site at Ewha University for all sixteen hundred international students. Moreover, the Korean Central Intelligence Agency had grilled him about the details of Explo '74, amid Park Chung-hee's wife's assassination. Neibling recalled his experience of divine assistance: "The week was a supernatural week in my own life . . . I noticed someone else took over. . . . I was there, yes, but someone else was doing it through me." He continued to reflect: "It was a very personal, spiritual, powerful experience, as well as going out to Yoido Island and being a part of so many people who had gathered. . . . The number one lesson I learned is [that if] God calls you to do something, he will enable you to do it." That experience in Korea changed his life: "That prepared me for the rest of forty years of living in Asia. That's why I was able to do many of things that would follow as we were just starting Campus Crusade ministry in many countries." Neibling saw that the reality of challenging circumstances, or even literal facts, could not prevent him from carrying out the work that he believed was ordained by God. Koreans and American missionaries at Explo '74 experienced what they accepted as miracles and the hand of God at work.

Campus Crusade's global influence expanded even further as a result of Explo '74. Sharpless, therefore, emphasized the global character of Campus Crusade and critiqued exceptionalist understandings of the United States as the center of Christianity: "The torch of world missions started [in the] Middle East with Jesus, and then to Europe . . . then down to Africa. . . . It's moved from Europe to America. The American missionary thrust led the world for world missions, and now it's passed over to Asia. . . . So the story is, America is a blip, an important blip." Sharpless eschewed the image of Campus Crusade as "American": "With the number of long-term American missionaries that have stabilized or decreased, the number of Asian missionaries has greatly increased. So the story is not an American story. For many, many years the vast majority of our impact has been outside of America. It's a global organization." He insisted: "America is one of those countries. . . . Have we done a good job telling that story? Well, most people in America think we're a campus ministry in the United States."[43] Sharpless critiqued the towering image of the United States and intimated that Campus Crusade was a decentered organization composed of independent national chapters: "The fact is the DNA that Dr. Bright always had is that we're not a US-based ministry with overseas branches but a global ministry of unique independent countries committed to see their countries reached for Christ."[44] The story of Explo '74 itself reveals the pivotal influence that South Koreans had influencing Americans toward missionary work, and the global trajectory of Campus Crusade itself.

In that regard, South Korea was unique in its contributions toward Campus Crusade's global growth. Douglass recalled: "[South Korea] is still probably the most significant partnership that we have because, well, it was the first, so we learned how to do it as a whole with Dr. Kim and his team." The Korean partnership was unique in terms of the number of Korean who have traveled to other nations as missionaries from Korea, a missionary-sending nation: "The majority of the countries at first are receiving; Korea, immediately, was sending." She noted: "Korea is the first country that was sending, and they set a model for other countries that they have aspired to.... I think that model of growing your own ministry yourself, and then sending, is maybe one of the best contributions to the partnership."[45] South Korea's revivalistic prowess set a new standard for Campus Crusade's global expansion.

Yet the tensions between the global and national character of Campus Crusade and the events at Explo '74 still cracked through, revealing the heightened priority of the nation-state even as the evangelistic revival was a transnational event that spurred a global vision. Tensions about who "owned" the revival also pervaded correspondence. Bright had been criticized for overestimating the 1974 revival numbers to the American press and felt the heat to provide concrete evidence, something that only Joon Gon Kim could provide as the one closer to the roots of the movement. At the same time Bright expressed his "love and encouragement," he also insisted that Kim provide "documentation" for the revival statistics to "give further credibility" to his claims.[46] Bright could pose as the overseer of the revival, but Joon Gon Kim held the real evidence of its success, which put pressure on Bright to get the facts straight.

Moreover, Joon Gon Kim's reflections on Explo '74 grounded its success in Korean roots. "Explo '74 was not only an international Christian conference," he reported, but a movement "from the grassroots of Korean Christianity."[47] He went on to assert that the statistics garnered at Explo '74 accounted for the largest of several categories, including the largest Christian gathering in recorded history.[48] He pronounced these data points as evidence of a new moment in Christian history: "Many sincere Christians have questioned my own confidence in setting a 1975 target date for the total Christianization of Korea. I dare to commit my life and energies toward that goal because I am convinced that Explo '74 has helped to usher in another reformation in Christian history."[49] However, even as South Korea's revivalistic fervor became a global model for white evangelicals, the politics of the Cold War continued to undermine the South Korean desire for global ascendancy. While Joon Gon Kim challenged a Bright- and US-centered Christian kingdom, he was still transnationally tied to the politics undergirding Explo '72 and Explo

'74 as these events became entangled in South Korean authoritarianism and US conservatism, forging a transpacific Christian Right.

Forging a Transpacific Christian Right: Explo '72 and Explo '74

The year of Explo '72 was the height of the Vietnam War student protests in the United States. By way of background, the Students for Democratic Society turned its focus to ending the Vietnam War between 1965 and 1967. In 1965 alone, 120 teach-ins took place at university campuses, generating new antiwar student groups such as the National Student Association. The peak of the antiwar student movement was in 1970 and 1972, in response to new US attacks on North Vietnam and Cambodia.[50] In the 1971–1972 academic year, there were 350 university protests nationwide. Nixon came under heavy critique when two hundred thousand anti–Vietnam War protesters gathered at his second inauguration. In the spring of 1972, at some campuses, including the University of Minnesota, "antiwar activism exploded."[51] Within this broader context of student activism, the Third World Liberation Front's protests gave way to the nation's first School of Ethnic Studies in 1968 at San Francisco State University. These activists aligned themselves with national liberation movements in Third World countries, protesting US involvement in the Vietnam War. These movements for liberation had particular significance for Asian Americans who saw an extension of a US imperialist agenda in Vietnam in their own experience of racism and class oppression. They understood their experience in the United States as people of color living in an "internal colony" from which they "needed to be liberated."[52]

Campus Crusade and Student Activism in the United States

Campus Crusade aggressively engaged the left-wing activism of college campuses during the late 1960s and early 1970s.[53] Indeed, Campus Crusade "grew alongside New Left movements" as it "responded vigorously to the New Left, antiwar protests, and the counter culture."[54] Berkeley Blitz, a massive evangelistic event hosted in January 1967, is a key example of Campus Crusade's evangelical activism that engaged the Left. When Reagan, then governor of California, fired Clark Kerr, president of the University of

California, left-wing students protested at Berkeley's Sproul Hall. Campus Crusade students had already occupied Sproul Hall to evangelize leftist students and to stage their own protest "against the secular age." Campus Crusade speaker Jon Braun called students to seek "God's love as the only solution for the world's problems."[55] Bright used rhetoric tailored to an activist generation: "Jesus Christ was history's greatest revolutionist."[56] Not only did Campus Crusade workers seek Christian conversions, they also mitigated leftist radicalism: "Campus Crusade workers disrupted protest rallies by seizing free speech platforms and carrying signs and chanting slots of their own: 'Prince of Peace,' 'Students Denouncing Sin,' 'Boycott Hell! Accept Jesus.'"[57] American evangelical political agitation at this time was not limited to electoral politics, but also included grassroots activism at evangelical revivals. If leftist movements reached their peak in the early 1970s, Explo '72 was a space where conservative evangelical activism thrived, serving as a foil to these war protests.

Indeed, as John Turner highlights, Explo '72 exemplifies the conservative evangelical activism typically overlooked in historical accounts of the 1960s and early 1970s.[58] Explo '72 delegates favored Nixon over McGovern for president by a margin of more than five to one. Nixon, moreover, had been interested in campaigning at Explo '72 for re-election. Graham had encouraged the visit, but Bright decided against it because of disagreements among his staff. Yet the Explo '72 crowd listened to a Nixon telegram that "echoed the Explo '72 theme reminding delegates that 'the way to change the world for the better is to change ourselves for the better.'"[59] Bright declared, "Explo '72 can do more to bring peace to the world than all of the antiwar activity combined."[60] At Explo '72, Nixon and Bright "foreshadowed the courtship between evangelicals and conservative politicians that accelerated in the mid-1970s."[61] Students at Explo '72 voiced their pro–Vietnam War attitudes. In a procession of international flags, the "banner of South Vietnam produced a 'sustained ovation' from the crowd."[62] US evangelicals would become swept up in the culture wars, with abortion taking center stage in the wake of *Roe v. Wade* in 1973. But, as seen here, anticommunist and pro–Vietnam War attitudes also undergirded US evangelical conservative activism. At Explo '72, political conservatism held personal and ultimate stakes that looked like grassroots activism.

But evangelical, conservative activism did not remain within US borders. Joon Gon Kim played a crucial role at Explo '72. Explo '72 and Explo '74 not only became a high watermark of evangelistic activity in both nations, but also served as a transpacific means for connecting the politics of South Korean authoritarianism with US conservative evangelical activism. If the Berkeley Blitz as well as Explo '72 became sites where US students took an individualistic approach to social change, then Explo '74 became a site where South Korean students were discouraged from social protest—they were encouraged to take an individual and conversion-centered approach to social change, effectively endorsing Park's military regime. The two revivalistic events helped to forge a transpacific Christian Right, reinforcing not only soul saving but also authoritarian and evangelical conservative politics on both sides of the Pacific.

South Korean Authoritarianism and US Evangelical Conservatism

During the 1960s and 1970s, Christian missionaries were implicated in the US imperialist agenda in non-Western nations, which "reaped huge profits for the United States while wreaking havoc in Asia."[63] Out of these struggles emerged liberation theologies, such as *minjung* theology, born in the 1970s as a response from South Koreans against the military dictatorships of the time. *Minjung* literally signified "the people," and *minjung* theology sought liberation for the people, the oppressed. One of the key leaders in this movement was Kim Jae Jun, who had stood in opposition to Joon Gon Kim since the mid-twentieth century. Recall that in the 1940s, Joon Gon Kim was enrolled at Chosun Theological Seminary, a seminary founded by Kim Jae Jun, who rejected biblical literalism and sought to establish a theologically liberal alternative to the historic Pyongyang Theological Seminary, a fundamentalist institution. In 1947, Joon Gon Kim helped to lead a group of fifty-one seminary students to denounce the Chosun Theological Seminary's theological liberalism and to found, in 1952, a Korean chapter of the National Association of Evangelicals (NAE).[64] In the early 1970s, with the rise of Park Chung-hee's military dictatorship, Kim Jae Jun's and Joon Gon Kim's theological differences emerged more sharply in the public sphere as Kim Jae Jun vehemently protested the Park regime and Joon Gon Kim actively collaborated with it through Explo '74.

While American students were protesting the Vietnam War en masse, South Korean students protested Park's military regime. Continuing a longer Korean tradition of student protests, including the student revolution on

April 19, 1960, that ousted Syngman Rhee, students were reignited in 1971 with the sensational suicide of Chon Tae'il, a student who self-immolated in protest of the unjust labor conditions under Park's regime. Chon was a poor garment worker in the textile factors who self-immolated on November 13, 1970, as his final protest against a government that sacrificed the human rights of workers for the sake of national economic progress.[65] In the summer of 1971, students protested labor rights, compulsory military training, and the most recent presidential election as a general critique of Park's regime.[66]

In 1972, Park instantiated Yusin rule and passed a series of emergency decrees (EDs), systematically repressing antigovernment activity, which only increased student protest. ED 4, declared in 1974, repressed student activism in the "Minch'ong incident," which resulted in 1,024 students in custody, 253 sent to the Emergency Martial Court, and 180 convicted and sentenced. The government accused these students of engaging in a communist revolution associated with the People's Revolutionary Party (PRP). In July 1974, a group of intellectuals and Christian pastors, including Catholic Bishop Chi Haksun and Reverend Pak Hyong-Gyu, were imprisoned and interrogated for their alleged support of the PRP.[67] By 1975, especially after the Minch'ong incident and the PRP case, student activism was quelled by the state, and public protests dropped off significantly.[68] Because of the repression of dissident student groups, from 1975 to 1979, a small group of dissident Christians protested the Park regime.[69] At this time, just as Campus Crusade's activities in the United States actively opposed leftist student activism, the organization's activities in South Korea served as a foil to these dissident Christians. Campus Crusade's transpacific networks mitigated leftist activism in the United States and South Korea, in favor of a Christian revolution in which changed individual lives would change the world.

Changed Lives Change the World

The transpacific Christian Right that Bright and Joon Gon Kim forged depended on soul-winning, which was inextricably tied to a vision to establish Korea as a Christian nation, an impulse Bright shared for his own country. Bright and Joon Gon Kim believed that individual salvation through evangelical conversions would transform the world. They believed in the revolution that would come when their nations were Christianized one person at a time. Campus Crusade called Americans and South Koreans to choose Jesus, one person at a time, and thereby to hold individuals accountable for the transformation of society. Joon Gon Kim declared: "There is the internal human revolution and social revolution . . . [W]e believe that social revolution is possible [only] through human revolution. . . . This one thing is clear: social action does not constitute evangelism." He continued: "No matter how important it is, how urgent it is, and how pleasing it is to God, it cannot constitute evangelism; that is my viewpoint, my way of interpreting the Bible on this matter."[70] Like Joon Gon Kim, Bright believed that social change came through saving individual souls, as opposed to bringing institutions to justice. He suggested that the message of Explo '72 was "Changed people in sufficient numbers make a changed world."[71] During his "Here's Life, America" campaign, Bright also often articulated the idea that social reform, in terms of decreases in divorce rates, alcoholism, and racism, would take place through the evangelization of America.[72] This was a view that those in the NAE also shared. Instead of advocating for the United Nations, as many in mainline Christianity did, those who were part of the NAE wanted Congress to pass a resolution to "support and strengthen missionary endeavors throughout the world," which they felt would "raise the moral responsibility of all citizens to the point where they will obey world law."[73]

To be sure, Bright maintained that he was politically neutral. Hoping to preserve Campus Crusade's nonprofit status, he discouraged his staff's political engagement, including during the civil rights movement. When his closest associates made him aware that his nonpolitical stances represented conservative politics, he was alarmed.[74] Souls mattered to him, not politics, he insisted. Joon Gon Kim similarly prioritized souls. He acknowledged the difficulty in drawing the line between religious and political action, but he defined himself against so-called liberation Christians in Korea who lived out their faith through social protest, and prioritized a gospel for the oppressed under Korean military dictatorship.[75] He declared that most Christians believed the "church should stay out of politics."[76] Kim and Bright prioritized individual conversions, evangelism, discipleship, and the Christianization of their nations, not politics.

Yet Bright and Kim were active participants in the political machinery of their nations. As Jim Wallis's April 1976 exposé in *Sojourners* detailed, Bright held close right-wing associations with conservative politicians, advocated for the decentralization of government, and held unwavering anticommunist commitments.[77] Campus Crusade's funding in the late 1960s came from "right-wing Republican financial sources" who supported Bright's vision of "less government, more money, more ministry." As committed as Bright was to political neutrality, he was "equally serious about channeling youthful devotion into a conservative, Christian, Republican politics."[78] Kim, like Bright, was entrenched in the conservative politics of his nation. He evangelized the military dictator Park Chung-hee, curried favor with him to secure land for Campus Crusade, and organized the Presidential Prayer breakfast series in 1968. As Nami Kim observes, the Presidential Prayer Breakfast series, later named the National Prayer Breakfast, became a religious foothold for the Korean Protestant Right: "Since its establishment, the National Prayer Breakfast in South Korea has justified and even praised US-backed military dictatorships, and the majority of Protestant pastors who have participated in the National Prayer Breakfast for decades are the leading figures of the Protestant Right."[79] Much like Bright, Joon Gon Kim's work had high political stakes and engaged some of the most important political figures of their day. Yet they both perceived and articulated their work in soul-saving terms, which was a core feature of the transpacific Christian Right that they established through Explo '72 and '74.[80]

The Authoritarian Politics of Explo '74

At Explo '74, Joon Gon Kim actively addressed clergy's and students' political agitation from the left. In a context of political repression, Explo '74 was made possible because it served Park's regime by supporting Christians who opposed dissident Christians. At Explo '74, Joon Gon Kim offered an alternative understanding of "revolution" and "freedom" that actively countered leftist or liberal notions of freedom. Kim declared: "There have been industrial revolutions, cultural revolutions, political revolutions. Let us enter the Holy Spirit revolution to love our enemies and pray for those who persecute us."[81] Bright reminded South Koreans that "atheism was only one step away from communism," and that the "only nation strong against communism is a nation with a vital faith in Jesus Christ." Campus Crusade became a transpacific movement that actively used evangelical revival not only to convert souls, but also to actively oppose leftist politics. The media asked Joon Gon Kim about the political climate in Korea and whether he would "make any effort to help the clergy that was recently imprisoned for 15 years." He declared that he had the "authority to teach Jesus Christ" and that, "as long as churches preach the gospel of Jesus Christ, we have no problem." He argued that "in the name of freedom some suffer" (likely referring to the imprisoned pastors), but that there was a "difference between suffering in the name of freedom or in the name of Jesus Christ."[82] He preferred the latter.

The article went on to recount Joon Gon Kim's encounter with communists. Though communists had killed his wife and father, the article reported that he had learned to love as a result of the freedom he experienced through Christ. Indeed, when he actually met the very leader responsible for his family's death, he "explained to him that [he] had come in the name of Jesus to express God's love for him." He recalls, "One night I called on a Communist leader, at the risk of my life. Strange to say, he accepted me with welcome.... We prayed together, though enemies." He found that "my Lord created a mind in me to love my enemy." As a result, he evangelized the communist leader, who "became a new man that night." That man went onto be "a faithful witness for Christ among the Communists and is taking care of 30 converts from Communism, having prayer meetings in his house. This was the turning point in my soul-winning ministry."[83] For Joon Gon Kim, evangelism effected not only spiritual change, but also political change, as the communist leader had experienced both through his conversion. Through Explo '74, an "'explosion' of brotherly love, prayer, and other teachings of Jesus is expected to do more than any other single event to spread peace, joy and unity among the nations of this decade."[84] He saw this as the path to national change.

Explo '72 and Explo '74, however, were interlaced with scandalous political events, indicating how close these evangelistic revivals were to the hard politics in both nations. The Watergate break-in occurred on the night of Explo 72's Jesus Music Festival. An assassination attempt on the South Korean military dictator Park Chung-hee resulted in the death of South Korea's first lady on the second day of Explo '74. Sharpless recalled that there were "significant political challenges that week with the president's wife being assassinated.... We're not sure [about] the stability of the country, but we're here to help change this country and lead people to Christ. That intensified the sense of purpose and focus." He recalled the fear that this "country may go into anarchy. That overlaid the intensity of the feeling of the people who were there, including me."[85] Yet Neibling rather blithely remembered his years under military dictatorship in South Korea and later the Philippines. He recalled, "I personally believe that those years, as we look back on them, actually being there during it and in the Philippines under Marcos, one thing they did was bring a lot of order out of a lot of potential chaos and to bring peace." "Now the rule was a bit strong, no question. Certain rights may be violated, but it brought relatively a lot of peace and it enabled it to lay the foundation for economic progress, which later became very impressive in Korea," he concluded.[86] He lent support to a South Korean regime that executed people without due process. One year after the declaration of ED 4 and Explo '74, for instance, a martial court convicted twenty-three people considered members of the PRP. Most received fifteen-year sentences, and eight were unjustly executed, as will be further discussed. Neibling justified the state's actions against its citizens not only through spiritual reasoning but also economic reasoning: "The economic transformation is almost as amazing as the spiritual transformation. I think they go hand in hand. I personally would not say that that was such an evil thing." As for the role of Campus Crusade, he saw Explo '74 as benefiting the South Korean state politically and economically: "We were not against the rulers of the country and the politicians and all that they want. . . . Why else would the ROK [Republic of Korea] army want . . . all of the millions of men to hear the gospel as they were serving their time in the military? . . . That was not done in secret. It had to be endorsed as something that would be done to benefit the country."[87] Neibling had few qualms about the Park regime's active support for Explo '74.

Yet Americans and Koreans critiqued Joon Gon Kim's and Bright's vision for social change and the evangelistic activities at Explo '74. Liberal Korean Protestants, for instance, criticized the strategy of evangelism that Explo '74 endorsed, especially at a time when Park's regime was gravely violating human rights.[88] Korean theologian Kim Chongnyŏl provided the following critique: "I do not wish to think of evangelization and humanization separately. . . . Christ came to the world (i.e. he became humanized, a true human) in order to enable each individual and all of humanity to live in a manner worthy of human beings."[89] For a liberal like Kim Chongnyŏl, "to evangelize was to change society, to eliminate the structures that created and perpetuated social and economic justice." Americans also criticized Bright for declaring so boldly that there was religious freedom in Seoul. At a time when Koreans were under the rule of a military dictatorship, Bright naively reported to the *Chicago Tribune*, "There is more religious freedom in South Korea than in the United States."[90] Even Graham critiqued him for this insensitive statement.[91] Rather than evaluating Explo '74 through the political conditions of South Korea itself, he saw the evangelical revival through the lens of the debates for religious freedom in public schools in the United States: "Dr. Bright [then] admitted that he had not discussed political activity by religious leaders in South Korea with Christian leaders. But he contended that the openness of discussions on Christianity in South Korea's public school campuses exceeds that permitted in American public schools."[92]

Ultimately, Park Chung-hee thanked Bright for hosting Explo '74 in South Korea. Bright had helped to prove that the state had not engaged in religious repression, essentially quelling leftist arguments against Park that came from dissident Christians against his authoritarian rule:

> I would like to share your satisfaction that Explo '74 had been a great success and marked a great milestone in the propagation of Christianity in Korea. It is gratifying to note that this event has proved to the world that "Christians had more religious freedom in South Korea than in any other country..." despite some Christian activists who have create a false impression as if there were religious repression in Korea.[93]

Park used Explo '74 and Bright's statements to prove to other South Koreans, and the world, that dissident Christians were not being repressed for unnecessary reasons.

Park had in mind Methodist minister Cho Wha Soon and American Methodist missionary George Ogle, who exemplified the kind of dissident Christians he aimed to repress, and that Explo '74 transnationally silenced. On May 15, 1974, the police broke into Cho's home and arrested her for violating Emergency Decree No. 4. Cho had preached a sermon on April 28, 1974, titled "Search for the Kingdom and for Righteousness," a sermon written on the heels of the Bando Company struggle, in which the company owners had promised young women workers their rights, only to rescind their offer and employ the KCIA to spy on labor union activity. As previously discussed, the government had also detained eight men, convicting them as communists; there was little evidence to suggest that they were, in fact, communists, but it was believed that the government wanted to make an example out of the men to crack down on government rebellion.

Ogle had little knowledge of this event, but the wives of these men pleaded with him to use his position as a westerner and clergyman to help them. He used public prayer as a means for protest. On Thursday October 9, 1974, Ogle provided the prayer for the gathering at the Christian Building in Seoul:

> Christ is often mediated to us through the most humble and weakest of our brothers and sisters. Among those now in prison are eight men who have

received the harshest of punishments. They have been sentenced to die, even though there is little evidence against them. They are not Christians, but as the poorest among us they become the brothers of Christ. Therefore let us pray for their lives and souls. Probably they have committed no crime worthy of death.[94]

Ogle did not explicitly state the innocence of the men or oppose the government, but he implied just enough to get him a visit from the KCIA the next day. He used his position as a clergy person to pray for the men, a seemingly neutral public act, but under Yusin rule, it was seen as a procommunist move and an antiauthoritarian attack. He was interrogated and charged for violating the anticommunism laws.

By December 14, 1974, Ogle was deported to the United States. On April 9, 1975, the eight men were executed.[95] As sociologist Paul Chang notes, "While progressive Christian leaders were being arrested and interrogated by the Yusin regime, the much larger conservative Christian community was enjoying tremendous growth." Joon Gon Kim claimed: "When church and government are harmonious through assistance and cooperation, the church will be holy and the state will prosper."[96] Kim worked with the Park regime to organize Explo '74, preserving harmony between the state and church. Explo '72 and Explo '74 forged a transpacific Christian Right, based in revivalistic and anticommunist politics, which ultimately reinforced South Korean authoritarianism and the grassroots activism of US evangelical conservatism.

Koreans led Campus Crusade in globalizing its efforts. The evangelistic fervor and piety displayed at Explo '74, in particular, persuaded white evangelicals like Neibling, Phillips, and Sharpless to change the direction of their lives, especially toward lifelong missionary work. As a result, Koreans saw themselves as increasingly holding the mantle for revival, as they influenced white evangelicals toward mission work. Yet these enchanted transpacific networks of revival were entangled in the authoritarian and conservative politics of nation-states. They forged a transpacific Christian Right that foreshadowed the rise of the Christian/Protestant Right respectively in the United States and South Korea. The authoritarian and conservative politics that undergirded this transpacific network of revival not only lifted Koreans in the eyes of white evangelicals, but would also go on to undermine their vision for national ascendancy.

Sharing the World Stage: World Evangelization Crusade '80

Korean Christianity expanded into a global force, a "regional Protestant superpower," as a result of the 1970s revivals.[97] As for Joon Gon Kim, in the same year he was promoted to the position of director of East Asia Area of Affairs for Campus Crusade, he served as the executive chairman of the organizing committee for the 1980 World Evangelization Crusade (WEC), one of the world's largest evangelistic crusades.[98] For WEC '80, the organizing committee adapted slogans from Campus Crusade's American campaign: "I Found It!" "New Life in Jesus!" and "You Too Can Find It!"[99] Korean and American speakers spoke at the event: John Wright, head of the Southern Baptists' home ministries, Bill Bright, Donald McGavran, and Carl Henry, to name a few. Joon Gon Kim also preached a sermon titled "A Nation without a Vision Will Perish." To achieve democracy and unification, the nation had to be evangelized, he asserted. A grand total of 17.25 million attended the four-day crusade, the largest evangelistic revival in Korean history at that time, yet again exceeding the size of prior revivals.[100] An estimated 700,000 people committed their lives to Christ for the first time, two million experienced the fullness of the Holy Spirit, and 100,000 volunteered to serve in foreign missions.[101]

The 1980 World Evangelization Crusade was meant for world evangelism, and it was the decisive step for Korea to assume leadership of the world's evangelization.[102] Joon Gon Kim, as the chairman of the planning committee, asserted in his usual urgent fashion: "Our first goal in the campaign is to achieve, most speedily and efficiently, the supreme goal of carrying out evangelism." He declared that they were "mobilizing" all of the necessary resources and "intensively organizing" people. This revival would help energize the Korean nation for the sake of "earnestly star[ting]" a "Korean-modeled and Korean-led missionary movement," which would make the "world and all people become our working unit."[103] The evangelization of the world belonged to Koreans, he argued. Kim was ready to set the stage for the Christian revolution in the world, with even Bright and his nation as a "working unit." As a continuation of his declaration at Explo '72, Kim's announcement for WEC '80 challenged the United States as the center of world Christianity, and was a means to critique the US evangelical empire itself. Yet he sought not to argue for demilitarization of the peninsula or an end to the

US Cold War in Asia, but to replace American Christian triumphalism with Korean Christian triumphalism.

Koreans believed that they had surpassed the religiosity of the secularizing West. One of the Korean preachers at the revival declared: "The period of Euro-American missions is over. Now Korea must assume the responsibility of evangelizing the Third World—this kind of mission is increasingly demanded of us these days; what can we the believers do to take part in missionary work?"[104] *Christianity Today* reported that the South Korean church "has deliberately moved from being a missionary receiving church to a missionary sending one."[105] This exceptionalist and even supercessionist rhetoric echoed not only the language of American exceptionalism, but also the language of a new chosen people, hearkening back to the Israelites. Oh Chint'ak recalls the significance of WEC '80 in terms of providing South Koreans with a sense that they could be global missionaries: "It started because we had the help of the US, but it was also the case that it was through Explo '74 that we saw the growth that we had collected at that point, and we could see the possibility for the national evangelization that Rev. Kim had declared. No other country in the world declared that through Campus Crusade it would evangelize the whole nation or that it would as an entire nation send out global missionaries." The '80 WEC crusade was a decisive moment: "[W]e promised that ten thousand would be sent out as missionaries. I stood up that day too, and ten thousand others stood up that day." The Christian battalion that Joon Gon Kim had imagined raising up was coming alive through not only at Explo '74 but even more decisively at WEC '80. Bright believed they "inaugurate[d] a post-Western missionary era in which missionaries from countries like Korea took their faith around the world." He reflected after the 1980 revival: "I have been involved in evangelism and discipleship programs for over 30 years . . . but I can assure you that there has never been anything in the history of the world that would compare with what our eyes saw and our ears heard during that incredible, phenomenal, unprecedented week of meetings in Seoul, Korea."[106]

Bright compared Korean faith to that of European Christian patriarchs. He stated: "Korean Christians as a whole have the unusual commitment which Martin Luther and John Wesley had before they were converted."[107] The success of Korean faith served as an example for Americans: "I believe that what God has done spiritually in Korea is a message from Him saying, 'If you trust Me and obey Me, I can do the same thing in your home, in your church, in your community, in your nation.'" He continued: "Let us believe God to this end and not view the phenomenal experience of Korea as just something that they (the Koreans) have done, but as something that God has done as an example for all of us, that we might believe Him and trust Him for the great and mighty things which He promises to those who walk in faith and obedience."[108] If Joon Gon Kim had once learned the pragmatics of evangelistic success from Americans, Koreans now inspired white evangelicals like Bright to believe in the power of world evangelization.

Yet note that, as with Explo '74, WEC '80 was organized as a form of revolution, a spiritual revolution that opposed leftist movements. The evangelistic success, led by Joon Gon Kim, at WEC '80 only strengthened the transpacific Christian Right that prioritized the politics of individual conversion as the only means for social change. In the wake of Park Chunghee's assassination on October 26, 1979, a new military regime led by Chun Doo-hwan took over the nation. Students revolted against the martial law of the new authoritarian rule, which led to a bloody massacre in spring 1980, the Gwangju Uprising.

Oh Chint'ak initially protested the new government, but over time he moved into an evangelistic movement that he called a spiritual movement. He recalled that in South Korea, "evangelicals" believed in a spiritual revolution, while "activists" believed in a social revolution:

> [Activists] continued to say that we needed to change institutions in order to change society and that we needed to resist authority. We said that we couldn't change the nation like that. People needed to change. We shifted our movement toward the direction of prayer and the Bible. We were engaged in a spiritual movement, and they were engaged in a social movement. That was the perspective of evangelicals at that time. We evangelicals maintained our distance from social engagement.[109]

Oh Chint'ak reflects on how the identity "evangelical" came to signify "Christian." He shows that the term "evangelical," moreover, defined itself against social engagement as well as protest as a means for social change. He suggested that the division between North and South Korea was akin to the division between activists and evangelicals during this time.

In this sense, "activists" were aligned with communist North Korea and "evangelicals" coded as South Korean and therefore aligned with the United States. He recalled:

> Those who continued to protest, they were what we called *undong-gwŏn*, or "activist"—that's where that term came from. . . . Much like the nation was divided after the Korean War, with the North leaning toward the left and the South leaning toward the right, college students were also divided. . . . Among the college students there was something called the Korean National Youth Union, and those who sided with them were on the left, and desired to change society by generating a social revolution. But those who thought this was too extreme and witnessed merciless casualties realized this was not right. So as people who saw things from a Christian perspective, we dropped our stones and desired to change souls. So the direction of our movements shifted.[110]

The primary reason that Oh Chint'ak stopped using protest as a means for social change was because he believed that he was harming his friends:

> For about three to four months we really protested hard. We wore towels around our heads, put toothpaste on our faces and hid from gas bombs in every alleyway, but if a military police car suddenly exploded, then the police would die. . . . What we realized, ultimately, was that it was people like our friends . . . who got hurt and that we could not change the military government. . . . We began to wonder why we had to sacrifice our own friends and why we had to get hit by gas bombs thrown by our very own friends. . . . There was a student named Yi Hanyŏl from Yonsei University who died after being hit by a gas bomb. That event ignited . . . into a national demonstration.[111]

Oh Chint'ak disagreed with the violent tactics of the student protest movement and, moreover, believed social engagement was futile because it did not enact the desired change.

Like Joon Gon Kim, he believed that real change came through changing people: "We believed that people had to change in order for systems to change. . . . Ultimately, we believed that people could not be changed without God. The thing we were supposed to do, then, was to pray that God would work." He believed that through Campus Crusade's evangelistic activities they had discovered a more long-term solution to address political and national instability:

> Ultimately for us, more than our immediate circumstances, we hoped for the reality that goes beyond our circumstances, and even if things did

not move in the direction of our wishes, we held onto the hope that God would change things at some point. Because of this, even if things did not change immediately, we didn't get influenced this way and that by our circumstances, but believed that it was something that God would do. So we weren't easily shaken by our circumstances. And we didn't expect to see the results we had hoped for in this life. In other words, we saw things a bit more long term.[112]

He perceived that the government permitting WEC '80 was a means through which God intervened in the world: "In the midst of the political instability, you can see that the new government made the decision from their perspective, but from God's perspective you could say that God did it." Like Neibling, Oh Chint'ak found justification for his approach to social change through evangelism in the evidence of economic development, or South Korea's economic "miracle": "If you look back, it was while this government held power that the nation had its greatest economic success—ironically." Oh believed that WEC '80, therefore, had a "butterfly effect" in that the revivalistic activity helped to stabilize the nation and facilitate its economic uplift.

Oh Chint'ak found justification for the authoritarian state as he imagined God intervening and using the state in spite of itself, especially given the evidence of economic development. By extension, the signification of the term "evangelical" as against "activist" was justified as the means through which Christian orthodoxy could be defined. Thus, not only in the United States but also in South Korea, an allied nation, "evangelical" was solidified as mainstream orthodoxy by 1980 through effective use of the state. The transpacific Christian Right continued to grow through Campus Crusade's network as their vision of evangelical revival, grounded in individual conversions, flourished with the support of US conservatism and South Korean authoritarianism.

By 1980, with the election of Reagan, and then the successful execution of WEC '80 in South Korea, evangelicals secured mainstream positions in both the United States and South Korea. They did so not only by lobbying but also by evangelizing. Evangelism signified a political alternative to leftist protest that could use the state as a means for carrying out a primarily Christian vision for the evangelization of the world. Massive evangelistic rallies like Explo '72, Explo '74, and WEC '80 came to signify a means to carry out and sustain a Christian vision that many predicted would wane in a modern era, but instead expanded by following the routes of US Cold War expansionism in Asia and most pointedly in South Korea. Campus Crusade's transpacific networks in South Korea fueled the global growth of the organization, not only as a means to convert souls, but also as a bulwark against communism in Asia, in which both American evangelicals and South Korean Protestants were invested. Moreover, South Koreans critiqued American exceptionalism, as the Christian headquarters, not to call for decolonization but to replace Americans as the heads of Christian triumphalism—to create their own Korean-led Christian kingdom.

They could do so by quelling leftist movements and leveraging their relationships with a South Korean authoritarian regime that was similarly interested in denouncing leftist protests. Campus Crusade, one of the most influential evangelical parachurches in the late twentieth century, grew in global power and influence because of the US Cold War state's investments in combating global communism. In so doing, Campus Crusade's system of belief gained the power to define Christian orthodoxy in the United States and globally, deeming other definitions of belief as heterodox or communist. The religious Cold War continued, not only empowering the Great Commission but also fueling the politics of the transpacific Christian Right, which would give way to the Christian and Protestant Right in both the United States and South Korea. The ethos established at these massive revivals had embedded in them the religious ideas that would also fuel a political movement. The Christian Right was not just a political phenomenon but also a movement tied to the existential politics of revival—not only in the United States but also in South Korea. That religiopolitical ethos, however, would undermine Joon Gon Kim's vision of Korea as the "new emerging Christian kingdom."

Conclusion

In 1981, Joon Gon Kim continued to share with Bright his vision of Korea as the "new emerging Christian kingdom." However, he now added the role of Korean America, for he started to observe a sea change in the United States. Whereas the "US churches" held Sunday service at the coveted 11:00 a.m. hour and the ethnic churches in the afternoon, they were now changing time slots, taking over prime time: "This is a sign that the Korean church is making the greater impact and needs to have an impact on the American church itself. The Lord gave us the idea that Korean citizens can be a great manpower source in the United States itself." Korean immigrant congregations in the United States had originally rented church space from "U.S. churches," but he observed they were now outgrowing them.[1]

He visited Los Angeles, San Jose, New York, and Washington, DC, where he held Campus Crusade Leadership Training Institutes and pastoral seminars. In the aftermath of Explo '72, Explo '74, and WEC '80, he saw hundreds attend his trainings, and contended this was a fruitful time for Korean American churches.[2] "We desire to have a second Puritan impact, spiritually speaking, in the United States. The first Puritans landed on the East Coast. The second Puritans will be from the ripe, alive church of Korea," he declared.[3] Channeling his excitement from the transpacific revivals, he announced Korean Americans would mimic South Korea's revivalistic "explosion" by leading Madison Square Garden into a "Jesus '82" revival.

Yet his excitement for Koreans to venture into their own errand into the wilderness, as the "second Puritans," was dampened with mourning the underside of that triumphant past.

The "second and third generation," he noticed, "are not well adjusted as Koreans living in America." He worried: "They are lonely and looking for reality." He continued: "I have noticed that the majority of Koreans have struggled for identity and purpose in the U.S. for several years."[4] South Korean revivalistic success mismatched racialized immigrant realities.

In Bright's response, he praised him as usual. He wrote: "My heart continues to sing praises to our Lord . . . as you went from city to city." He was also eager to have Joon Gon Kim send "10,000 missionaries to Europe, the United States and other countries." But perhaps Bright had read the memo incorrectly: for he cited ten thousand missionaries as opposed to the one hundred thousand that Joon Gon Kim had projected to send.[5] He also made no mention of the struggles of the second and third generation that burdened Joon Gon Kim.

Campus Crusade, an organization at the center of the US evangelical empire, was built by the hands and feet of Koreans, and its very global direction shaped by Cold War South Korea, as discussed in the previous chapter. Koreans, therefore, should have had a rightful place at the center of the organization. Joon Gon Kim had been working with the organization since 1958, when he met Bright at Fuller, and became Campus Crusade's first nonwhite and international partner. Yet Bright's lack of response mirrored Campus Crusade's historic misunderstanding of immigrant and nonwhite realities. Campus Crusade had invested heavily in overseas work, as in South Korea, when those evangelistic and revivalistic activities prioritized world evangelization through individual salvation—saving people, one by one, for the sake of Jesus Christ. When it turned toward the social and structural needs of "the least of these," including the role and needs of nonwhite staff and students in the United States, that multicultural world vision melted away.

As discussed, primarily devoted to individual conversions as the means for social change, Bright cautioned his staff against participating in the civil rights movement. In 1981, only sixty of the organization's four thousand staff members were Black. In 1986, staff training featured a film *America, You're Too Young to Die*, glorifying US history with little commentary on the history of slavery, alienating Black staff members. In the 1990s Tom Fritz, a Black staff member, would forge a new path for racial/ethnic minority ministry by creating Impact Movement, geared toward Black students. Yet Campus Crusade would have difficulties integrating Black students and staff in particular, and nonwhite students and staff in general, into its white-dominant institution.[6]

For his part, Joon Gon Kim had been masterful in passing down a Korean tradition centered on individual salvation and personal holiness, but what vision of social salvation and social justice did he offer South Korea and Korean America? While at Fuller, and in his later years at the height of the 1970s revivals, he preached the power of individual salvation for the sake of social transformation. He envisioned world evangelization as the primary route to national salvation for the Korean peninsula. But that vision came at the cost of holding hands with an anticommunist organization that, since the 1950s, positioned Joon Gon Kim against the "red" North Koreans and the "red" cause of civil rights. His vision for world evangelization led to massive gatherings that swayed white evangelicals to devote their lives to lifelong missionary work, but at the cost of linking arms with an authoritarian South Korean regime, backed by US conservatives. The legacy of the transpacific Christian Right that had formed through those massive revivals now undermined the possibilities for Korean America—that is, Joon Gon Kim's religious vision had focused on the power of individual conversion, lacking a robust social vision that would account for the limits of race and immigration, which continued to undermine US democracy.

When the people of Kim's nation—those with whom Bright had so closely partnered across the Pacific—immigrated to Bright's home country, the limits of Joon Gon Kim and Bright's synchronous network, were readily revealed. Bright's and Joon Gon Kim's transpacific network flagged in the face of race and immigration. South Korean Protestants had their own responses to the US evangelical empire and even sought to supersede its global power. Yet, even as their local agency was powerful, the structures of power with which Korean Protestants contended, and continue to contend—the history of Koreans' racial erasure, integration, and model minoritization, which gave rise to the US evangelical empire—dampened that potential.

The anticommunist politics of the global Cold War shaped the formation of a transpacific Christian Right that not only impinged upon the human rights of Koreans in the peninsula, but also placed significant limits on nonwhite people in the United States. Joon Gon Kim could pass down a powerful Korean tradition focused on individual conversion and personal holiness, but not one that could overcome the social and structural barriers that prevented racial uplift. *Race for Revival* shows that the modern Korean Christian tradition of pursuing individual conversions, without attention to social justice and social holiness—sometimes even actively supporting unjust political regimes—was forged through the crucible of the global Cold War. It is a movement reinforced by a cognate political and theological ethos forged in modern evangelical America, which South Koreans helped to build, but from which they were also marginalized. Revival is not a race, but Joon Gon Kim envisioned outpacing the US evangelical empire into the 1980s. And yet his vision could not dismantle whites' evangelical faith that they were the race that held the mantle for revival. Indeed, even as world

Christianity "exploded" in the Third World, with polycentric nodes of activity, the US evangelical empire remained intact.

Joon Gon Kim's Korean Campus Crusade, therefore, extended its own branch to serve the needs of the 1.5 and second generation. In 1982, just one year after Kim wrote Bright with his concerns, Korea Campus Crusade for Christ in America was founded.[7] In 1996, a Korea Campus Crusade staff member, Dong Whan Kim, opened up a Great Commission Training Center in Los Angeles that fueled the increase of KCCC in America chapters on campuses in Southern California. Here was the hallmark characteristic that revealed how much of an empire Campus Crusade had become, as it marginalized the very people who had constructed it, from its foundation to its global reach. Epic Movement was also a ministry focused specifically on outreach to Asian Americans, though it had not been available when Kim wrote to Bright in 1981. In the late 1980s under the leadership of Henry Tan, Metamorphosis (based out of Singapore, with staff focused on Asian American ministry) worked on the University of California–Irvine and Cal Poly Pomona campuses. Leaders like Margaret Yu, Brent and Leila Wong, and Eric Kaneshiro were raised up from Metamorphosis.

In the 1980s and beyond, the presence of Korean American evangelicals in particular and Asian American evangelicals in general expanded at record rates in evangelical American institutions. As mentioned, scholars dubbed them "God's whiz kids" and "model moral minorities," especially as they made their presence known on college campus ministries like Campus Crusade. But these surprising contemporary statistics of Korean American evangelicals in particular and Asian American evangelicals in general have a longer transpacific history, which shows that they, in fact, helped to build the very institutions that make up the core of modern evangelical America. Thus, the Asian American presence in these evangelical institutions has as much to do with a paradoxical sense of a transpacific heritage of faith as it does with a desire for American belonging. Yet the legacy of that faith, at least in the Korean Christian tradition, is rooted in the power of individual conversion alone as the path toward social transformation, a legacy that could not adequately pave a way for US evangelicals of Asian descent to claim the very spaces they built.

In the early twentieth century, evangelicals were unlikely to regain their dominance in American society, and few predicted that an evangelical form of Christianity would "explode" in South Korea. Yet, in the Cold War era, evangelicalism burgeoned in both modern nation-states. Franklin Graham is a prominent figure whose rise is indebted to the Cold War history featured in this book, as he is the head of two parachurches—the BGEA and Samaritan's Purse—bequeathed to him by Billy Graham and Pierce. Franklin Graham was one of six clergy who prayed or read scriptures at the inauguration of the forty-fifth US president.[8]

Some have wondered how white evangelicals like Franklin Graham came to engage in "compassionate" missions across US borders while also supporting white supremacist views domestically. But we do not have to look far to see that the new evangelicalism in the 1960s set the stage for a humanitarianism that sought global compassion without global equality.

From 1980 to 2020, the US Republican Party stamped "evangelical" onto its public face. So did Donald Trump, further branding the term with the hot iron of white Christian nationalism, which exploded on January 6, 2021, when insurrectionists sieged the US Capitol. The 2016 presidential election revealed for some, and confirmed for others, that nonwhite evangelicals were vulnerable to the whims of white evangelical voters, who largely opposed the political views of their coreligionists of color. The 2020 presidential election did not show a seismic shift in white evangelical votes. While 81 percent of white evangelicals voted for Trump in 2016, 76 percent voted for him in 2020.[9]

These votes indicate that, though nonwhite evangelicals may represent the future for some, they still live in the borderlands of a white-led US evangelical empire. Evangelicals of color experienced a betrayal at the polls in 2016 and 2020, but what this book shows is that their struggle did not begin in the twenty-first century, or even within the borders of the US nation-state, or even with the Reagan era. Rather, the roots date at least as far back as the Truman and Eisenhower era, with the Cold War, and across the Pacific. For evangelicals, #exvangelicals and non-evangelicals, who seek to reform the movement, or dismantle the hierarchical forms of power embedded within it, this book shows that they must contend with the history and legacies of the Cold War in Asia that helped to make modern evangelical America into an empire.

Race for Revival shows that, rather than parallel and disconnected phenomena, the late twentieth-century rise of the US evangelical empire as well as the "explosion" of South Korean Christianity were interconnected movements. The Korean War, the first "hot" war of the Cold War, linked a new generation of white fundamentalists and South Korean Protestants who forged networks that helped to reinvent white fundamentalism into mainstream evangelical America. In spite of the decolonization movements that critiqued the Western missionary enterprise, white fundamentalists followed Cold War expansionist routes into South Korea, which led to the founding of World Vision, the internationalization of Campus Crusade, and the transpacific expansion of the BGEA. South Koreans were incorporated into these parachurches with a Cold War Orientalist logic that portrayed the US democratic state as one that espoused racial equality even while it reinforced white supremacy.

At the same time, South Koreans also used these parachurches to reimagine their place in the global Cold War order. South Koreans' contributions in founding, internationalizing, and globalizing these organizations led them to believe that they could become the next leaders of Christian empire. Such South Korean Protestant nationalist ambitions intimated critiques of US Cold War expansionism, but were caught up in forging a transpacific Christian Right. The three parachurches featured in this history—the BGEA, Campus Crusade for Christ, and World Vision—have transformed since their mid-twentieth-century origins.[10] Yet they remain powerful institutions in contemporary America, Korea, and the world.

The history featured in this book has several implications. *First, American religion is connected to the world.* US religious movements do not grow in isolation but through their deep connections to people and movements around the world. South Korean evangelicalism burgeoned into a powerful tradition, in part because of ongoing American interests in the peninsula. At the same time, evangelicalism in America became a viable and powerful tradition because of American interests in the peninsula. That is, US Cold War expansionism in South Korea animated the reinvention of US evangelicalism. Because US exceptionalist narratives of history tend to obscure the global and transnational forces through which American religious movements are started, grow, and transform, the narration of America's religious past needs to be pushed and set in a global context.

As shown, the growth and legitimation of American evangelicalism, a beleaguered movement in the early twentieth century, was indebted to its linkages to non-Western nations. A movement popularly known today for its defense of America, including its intense xenophobia, ironically could not have regained its dominance in American society without the contributions of non-Western peoples. But is it possible for the evangelical movement to be global without being imperial? In the aftermath of the forty-fifth American president's "travel ban," Franklin Graham expressed his views on immigration, declaring that refugee care is not a biblical value.[11] Recall that Graham's organization hosted its largest crusade, not within the borders of the United States, but across the Pacific in South Korea. The BGEA is indebted to non-Western nations and the American privilege of crossing borders into other nations. Yet Graham exercises willful ignorance in rejecting the very categories of people—"foreigners"—upon whom the BGEA depends.[12] Insofar as transnational evangelical networks depend on racial inequalities or support for authoritarian regimes in non-Western countries, it is not possible for the movement to be global without being imperial.

Second, religious ideas have political ramifications. Indeed, even religious ideas that seem to have no overt political agenda can have political ramifications. Worldviews like Billy Graham's and Billy Kim's, in which personal salvation is of utmost value, nonetheless had political effects. Their revival could not have been organized without accommodating an authoritarian regime. We also saw that South Koreans used the politics of evangelical revival to reimagine their own place in the global Cold War order. The stories of the two Billys, World Vision, and Campus Crusade show that it is not possible to separate piety from politics. Thus, rather than eschewing politics, it is necessary for American and global Christians to steward the inevitable commingling of piety and politics.

As it pertains to Christians in Korea, and throughout the diaspora, the politics of their piety is especially necessary to examine, given the fervor and power of their faith. By 2006, the United States and South Korea were respectively ranked as the number one and number two missionary-sending countries in the world.[13] On a per capita basis, South Koreans send out the most missionaries in the world, an astonishing statistic given the size of the country and the historical presence of shamanism, Buddhism, and Confucianism as the nation's primary religious traditions.[14] Not only do the United States and South Korea send out the most missionaries in the twenty-first century, but evangelicalism is also a dominant movement in both nations. The "Korean Protestant Right" wields significant influence in contemporary Korean politics and as a "regional Protestant superpower" in Asia.[15] This explosive contemporary phenomenon was, in part, due to the transpacific Cold War. As part of that legacy, Ju Hui Judy Han argues that some contemporary Korean/American missionaries ride the coattails of US empire, replicating developmentalist racist arguments about Africans and others in Third World nations.[16] They carry with them white supremacist ideas learned from the legacies of racial hierarchy embedded within the US military and culture in Korea, which includes Korean Christianity.[17] How have they, and how will they, consider the political—including, racial implications—of their missional piety? There is a hunger for ascendancy fueling contemporary South Korean missionaries to claim their own place in the world order. As Han concludes, even as they are "following the trail of American footsteps," they "have their eyes set beyond the empire's horizon."[18] But they may run the risk of replicating harmful political ideologies in these transnational and interracial encounters if they do not have a robust vision for mitigating these social ills.

Third, religious and racial possibilities are shaped by geopolitical realities. Though white evangelicals, South Korean Protestants and the Korean diaspora may not protest atheistic communism as explicitly today, some segments of these communities wage holy wars against "others," whether their targets are immigrants, queer people, feminists, liberals, Muslims or proponents of more socialist forms of Christianity, including liberation theologies. A binary theological paradigm pits them against a world they believe is under siege, which dates back to the years of a religious Cold War between good and evil.[19] Indeed, many of evangelical America's holy wars are undergirded by a longer transpacific history of racialized anticommunism forged through US Cold War empire building in Asia.

Consider that, alongside the Confederate and "Jesus Saves" flags, the South Vietnam flag was flying high at the Capitol siege in early 2021. As Viet Thanh Nguyen argues, white nationalists in the United States and the South Vietnamese diaspora share a nostalgia for a "lost cause."[20] But these politics have been rehearsed before—Explo '72 was a site where the South Vietnam flag was celebrated and pro–Vietnam War Christians rallied in massive crowds, in a race for revival against what they perceived as the atheistic communist world. The South Vietnamese flag inspired a standing ovation at Explo '72, an event transnationally intertwined with Explo '74 in Seoul. The fear of socialism and communism continues to animate white nationalist-inspired evangelical politics as well as that of the anticommunist Vietnamese diaspora in the United States. South Korean Protestants and the Korean diaspora are intertwined within this geopolitical context insofar as they helped to sustain a transnational religious context that nurtured pro–Vietnam War politics for the sake of the global and religious Cold War, a war that has not ended. When we "de-cold war" these very religious expressions, including evangelical Protestantism, new religious, racial and political possibilities may emerge.

Race for Revival argues that the "forgotten war" has led to a forgotten peace. To retrieve that peace, we must call for an end to the unending Korean War, including the cessation of US empire building as well as the use of race to govern others. Otherwise, we are in a never-ending war, constantly rehearsing a past that continues to haunt, with no resolution.

Revival is not a race, and one race does not have a monopoly on revival.

Notes

Preface

1. They attended Changhyun Methodist Church in South Korea.
2. Charles Kim, Jungwon Kim, Hwasook Kim, and Serk-Bae Suh, eds., *Beyond Death: The Politics of Suicide and Martyrdom in Korea* (Seattle: University of Washington Press, 2019), 172.
3. For a brief historical overview of *minjung* theology, see Sebastian Kim and Kirsteen Kim, *A History of Korean Christianity* (Cambridge: Cambridge University Press), 229–255; for a discussion on the sociopolitical context from which *minjung* theology emerged, see Paul Y. Chang, "Carrying the Torch in the Darkest Hours: the Socio-Political Origins of Minjung Protestant Movements," in *Christianity in Korea*, ed. Robert Buswell Jr. and Timothy S. Lee (Honolulu: University of Hawai'i Press, 2006), 195–220; for an introduction to liberation theology more generally, see Gustavo Gutierrez, *A Theology of Liberation*, trans. and ed. Sister Caridad Inda and John Eagleson (New York: Orbis Books, 1971).
4. Wha Soon Cho, *Let the Weak Be Strong: A Woman's Struggle for Justice* (Oak Park: Meyer Stone & Co, 1988).
5. Liberationist and evangelical traditions cannot be simplistically divided, as there is significant gray area, but the former does tend to lean liberal and the latter more conservative, especially theologically if not also politically.
6. See Paul Freston's use of the term "regional Protestant superpower" in reference to South Korea. Most Asian nations do not have sizable Christians populations, with the exception of the Philippines, which is mostly Catholic. Paul Freston, *Evangelicals and Politics in Asia, Africa and Latin America* (New York: Cambridge University Press, 2001), 61.
7. As Timothy Tseng notes in his assessment of the "changing face" of US evangelicalism, evangelicals of Korean descent are a significant demographic in the Asian American evangelical population. Koreans make up the largest percentage of Asian American evangelicals: 34 percent Korean, 25 percent Chinese, 14 percent Filipino, 11 percent Indian, 10 percent Japanese, 2 percent Vietnamese and 5 percent other (Pew Research Center 2011 Asian American Survey). Timothy Tseng, "The Changing Face of Evangelicalism," in *The Future of Evangelicalism in America*, ed. Candy Gunther Brown and Mark Silk (New York: Columbia University Press, 2016), 172–173.
8. Rudy Busto, "The Gospel according to the Model Minority? Hazarding an Interpretation of Asian American Evangelical College Students," in *New Spiritual Homes: Religion and Asian Americans*, ed. David Yoo (Honolulu: University of Hawaii Press, 1999), 178–179; Rebecca Kim, *God's New Whiz Kids? Korean American Evangelicals on Campus* (New York: New York University Press, 2006).

Acknowledgments

1. Helen Jin Kim, "Reconstructing Asian America's Religious Past: A Historiography," in *Envisioning Religion, Race and Asian Americans*, ed. Khyati Joshi and David Yoo (Honolulu: University of Hawaii Press and UCLA Center for Asian American Studies, 2020), 13–41.

Introduction

1. A few notes about terminology: I use quotation marks for the term "crusade" to underscore the term's historically problematic connections to military medieval expeditions. But for ease of reading, I will not place the word in quotation marks going forward.
2. "Korea Crusade—'73 TV Film." Archives of the Billy Graham Center, Wheaton, IL.
3. Grace M. Cho, *Haunting the Korean Diaspora: Shame, Secrecy and the Forgotten War* (Minneapolis: University of Minnesota Press, 2008), 54.
4. Newspaper coverage following the 1973 Billy Graham crusade in Korea noted that Graham "preached to more than three million people altogether—breaking the record total of his 16-week crusade in New York City in 1957, which was 2.1 million. Associate[d] crusades held at the same time by members of the Graham team in other parts of the country drew an additional 1.5 million people." "Billy Graham's Korean Crusade: Million Heard Him Preach," Religious News Service, Seoul, June 5, 1973. "Korea-News 1972–1974," Folder 140–146, Box 140, Collection 17, BGEA–Crusade Activities, Archives of the Billy Graham Center, Wheaton, IL.
5. "Korea Crusade—'73 TV Film." As will be discussed in chapter 3, the choir was previously called the World Vision Korean Orphan Choir.
6. The language of "explosion" was commonly used to describe the exponential increase in Christianity in South Korea in the late twentieth century. See Bong-Rin Ro and Marlin Nelson, eds., *Korean Church Growth Explosion* (Seoul: World of Life Press, 1983).
7. Charles Armstrong, *The North Korean Revolution, 1945–1950* (Ithaca, NY: Cornell University Press, 2003), 6.
8. As Chung Shin Park notes, by contrast North Korea, the original hub of Christianity in Korea, had approximately ten thousand Protestants and four thousand Catholics by the mid-1980s. Chung-Shin Park, *Korean Protestantism and Politics* (Seattle: University of Washington Press, 2003). Moreover, prior to the growth of Christianity in Korea between 1907 and 1988, Confucianism, Buddhism, and shamanism predominated the religious landscape of Korea. Timothy Lee notes that approximately 483,366 South Koreans, or about 1 percent of the population, claimed Confucianism as their religion in 1985. This figure contrasted with 8,059,624 (20 percent) for Buddhism and 8,354,679 (21 percent) for Christianity (combining Catholics and Protestants). Minister of Economic Planning Board, 13th Population

and Housing Census of the Republic of Korea 153 (Seoul: Ministry of Economic Planning Board, 1985), 288, table 6. Timothy Lee, *Born Again: Evangelicalism in Korea* (Honolulu: University of Hawai'i Press, 2010), 155. See also fn 52 for statistics on South Korea's religious landscape.
9. Freston, *Evangelicals and Politics*, 61.
10. Rebecca Kim, *The Spirit Moves West: Korean Missionaries in America* (Oxford: Oxford University Press, 2015).
11. The Yoido Full Gospel Church's offices mentioned here are located at the Kookmin Ilbo building in Seoul.
12. For the rise of evangelical conservativism in late twentieth-century US history, and especially the connection to the Sunbelt, see Darren Dochuk, *From Bible Belt to Sunbelt: Plain-Folk Religion, Grassroots Politics and the Rise of Evangelical Conservativism* (New York: Norton, 2011); Lisa McGirr, *Suburban Warriors: The Origins of the New American Right* (Princeton, NJ: Princeton University Press, 2001). Joyce Mao extends this geographic turn to Asia, showing how, for instance, the John Birch Society's fundamentalist Christian focus on "freeing" China from communism solidified the making of the modern right. *Race for Revival* extends this argument as it focuses on Cold War South Korea, and moves beyond organizations like the JBC to those that became a part of mainstream evangelical America. See Joyce Mao, *Asia First: China and the Making of Modern American Conservatism* (Chicago: University of Chicago Press, 2015).
13. Dochuk, *Bible Belt to Sunbelt*, 227.
14. On the "religious Cold War," see Andrew Preston, "Introduction: The Religious Cold War," in *Religion and the Cold War: A Global Perspective*, ed. Philip Muehlenbeck (Nashville, TN: Vanderbilt University Press, 2012), xi–xxii; see also Dianne Kirby, *Religion and the Cold War* (New York: Palgrave Macmillan, 2003); Angela Lahr, *Millennial Dreams and Apocalyptic Nightmares: The Cold War Origins of Political Evangelicalism* (New York: Oxford University Press, 2007).
15. William Inboden, *Religion and American Foreign Policy, 1945–1960: The Soul of Containment* (New York: Cambridge University Press, 2008), 261–262. For Inboden's discussion of the Cold War as a religious Cold War, see 1–25; for specific attention to Truman's and Eisenhower's religious vision of the Cold War see 105–157, 257–311. Inboden shows the crucial role that liberal Protestants especially played during the Cold War era in forging an alliance of religious leaders united against communism. *Race for Revival* shows that, when focusing on the Cold War in Asia especially, the role that fundamentalists and emerging evangelicals played in transnational and religious alliance building is central.
16. For religion as it pertains to the Cold War in Asia, see Seth Jacobs, *America's Miracle Man in Vietnam: Ngo Dinh Diem, Religion, Race and US Intervention in Southeast Asia* (Durham, NC: Duke University Press, 2005). For discussion on Korea in particular, see Kai Yin Allison Haga, "An Overlooked Dimension of the Korean War: The Role of Christianity and American Missionaries in the Rise of Korean Nationalism, Anticolonialism, and Eventual Civil War, 1884–1953" (doctoral dissertation, College of William and Mary, 2007).

17. See, for example, Melani McAlister, *The Kingdom of God Has No Borders: A Global History of American Evangelicals* (New York: Oxford University Press, 2018); Heather Curtis, *Holy Humanitarians: American Evangelicals and Global Aid* (Cambridge: Harvard University Press, 2018); David King, *God's Internationalists: World Vision and the Age of Evangelical Humanitarianism* (Philadelphia: University of Pennsylvania Press, 2019); David Kirkpatrick, *A Gospel for the Poor: Global Social Christianity and the Latin American Evangelical Left* (Philadelphia: University of Pennsylvania Press, 2019); David Swartz's *Facing West: American Evangelicals in an Age of World Christianity* (New York: Oxford University Press, 2020); see also the following—while it does not focus on evangelicals, it provides a helpful global contextualization of American religion: David Hollinger, *Protestants Abroad: How Missionaries Tried to Change the World but Changed America* (Princeton: Princeton University Press, 2017).
18. Robert Wuthnow, *The Restructuring of American Religion: Society and Faith since World War II* (Princeton, NJ: Princeton University Press, 1988), 133–173.
19. George Marsden, *Reforming Fundamentalism: Fuller Seminary and the New Evangelicalism* (Grand Rapids, MI: Eerdmans, 1987), 84.
20. Joel Carpenter, *Revive Us Again: The Reawakening of American Fundamentalism* (New York: Oxford University Press, 1997), 177.
21. Indians, for instance, developed a strong aversion to "conversion" itself at this time because of their experiences as part of the British Empire. Thanks to Arun Jones for highlighting this point.
22. Carpenter, *Revive Us Again*, 185. While the mainline Protestant missionary force decreased from seven thousand to three thousand from 1945 to 1980, evangelical missionaries grew from about five thousand to thirty-two thousand.
23. Christina Klein, *Cold War Orientalism: Asia in the Middlebrow Imagination, 1945–1961* (Berkeley: University of California Press, 2003), 19–20.
24. Nathan O. Hatch with Michael S. Hamilton, "Epilogue," in *Reckoning with the Past: Historical Essays on American Evangelicalism from the Institute for the Study of American Evangelicals*, ed. D. G. Hart (Grand Rapids, MI: Baker Books, 1995), 398.
25. See the use of the term in Marla Frederick McGlathery and Traci Griffin, "'Becoming Conservative, Becoming White?': Black Evangelicals and the Para-church Movement," in *This Side of Heaven: Race, Ethnicity, and Christian Faith*, ed. Robert J. Priest and Alvaro L. Nieves (New York: Oxford University Press, 2007). See also historian John G. Turner's use of the term in his introduction: John G. Turner, *Bill Bright and Campus Crusade for Christ: The Renewal of Evangelicalism in Postwar America* (Chapel Hill: University of North Carolina Press, 2008).
26. Dochuk, *Bible Belt to Sunbelt*, 226. See also fn 20 for reference to Robert Wuthnow's work *Restructuring of American Religion* which contextualizes this shift in the US religious landscape.
27. See the works listed in fn. 19 for the many ways that scholars are exploring the global dimensions of evangelical parachurhces; see especially David King's study of World Vision as he focuses almost singularly on globally contextualizing one evangelical parachurch. King, *God's Internationalists*.

28. See, for instance, John G. Turner's study of the role of Campus Crusade in the renewal of evangelicalism, which has an important chapter on the role of South Korea: Turner, John, *Bill Bright and Campus Crusade for Christ: The Renewal of Evangelicalism in Postwar America* (Chapel Hill: University of North Carolina Press, 2008). Timothy Lee studies the longer history of Korean Christianity as an evangelical movement and includes US actors though primarily considers religious developments in a national framework. See Lee, *Born Again*. The transpacific focus of this book extends these works in both geographical directions.
29. Early Methodist societies, for example, were first voluntary societies, not unlike parachurches. David Hempton has emphasized the transnational and global reach of these early evangelical networks based in voluntarism. See Hempton, *Methodism: Empire of the Spirit* (New Haven, CT: Yale University Press, 2005); see also David Hempton, *The Church in the Long Eighteenth Century* (London: I.B. Tauris, 2011). Consider also the work of W. R. Ward, who shows the significance of an earlier time period and international spread in the origins of evangelicalism. W. R. Ward, *The Protestant Evangelical Awakening* (New York: Cambridge University Press, 1992). For a closer look at how eighteenth-century evangelistic networks were also intertwined with empire, see Peter Choi, *George Whitefield: Evangelist for God and Empire* (Grand Rapids, MI: Eerdmans, 2018).
30. The literature that engages Cold War Orientalism and US empire building in Asia usually does not foreground religion as the central analytical lens even as religious actors or themes are core to the narrative. See, for example, Catherine Ceniza Choy, *Global American Families: A History of Asian International Adoption in America* (New York: New York University Press, 2013); Susie Woo, "A New American Comes Home: Race, Nation, and the Immigration of Korean War Adoptees, 'GI Babies,' and Brides" (doctoral dissertation, Yale University, 2010); Arissa Oh, *To Save the Children of Korea: The Cold War Origins of International Adoption* (Stanford, CA: Stanford University Press, 2015); Soojin Pate, *From Orphan to Adoptee: US Empire and Genealogies of Adoption* (Minneapolis: University of Minnesota Press, 2015).
31. Nami Kim, "A Mission to the 'Graveyard of Empires'? Neocolonialism and the Contemporary Evangelical Missions of the Global South," *Mission Studies 27* (2010): 20.
32. David Bebbington, *Evangelicalism in Modern Britain: A History from the 1730s to the 1980s* (London: Unwin Hyman, 1989). The National Association of Evangelicals also uses this four-pronged rule alongside its "NAE Statement of Faith" for self-definition: "What Is an Evangelical?" https://www.nae.net/what-is-an-evangelical.
33. Randall Balmer, *Mine Eyes Have Seen the Glory: A Journey into the Subculture of Evangelical America* (Oxford: Oxford University Press, 2006).
34. For the distinction between "political" and "religious" evangelicalism, see Wes Markofski, "Return of the Monolith? Understanding the White Evangelical Trump Vote," in "Forum: Studying Religion in the Age of Trump," *Religion and American Culture 27.1* (2017): 2–56.
35. Janelle Wong, *Immigrants, Evangelicals and Politics in an Era of Demographic Change* (New York: Russell Sage Foundation, 2018).

36. Anthea Butler, *White Evangelical Racism: The Politics of Morality in America* (Chapel Hill: University of North Carolina Press, 2021), 2.
37. See, for example, Todne Thomas, *Kincraft: The Making of Black Evangelical Sociality* (Durham, NC: Duke University Press, 2021).
38. Wong, *Immigrants, Evangelicals and Politics*.
39. See Anthea Butler's discussion of the term as political and Matthew Avery Sutton's discussion of the term's demise. "Forum: Studying Religion in the Age of Trump," *Religion and American Culture* 27.1 (2017): 2–56. doi:10.1525/rac.2017.27.1.2. On evangelical militant masculinity, see Kristin Du Mez, *Jesus and John Wayne: How White Evangelicals Corrupted a Faith and Fractured a Nation* (New York: Liveright, 2020).
40. My description of a "shape-shifting network" draws on Catherine Brekus's description of evangelicalism as a "loose coalition" and Melani McAlister's as a "network-in-motion." See Catherine Brekus, *Sarah Osborn's World: The Rise of Evangelicalism in Early America* (New Haven, CT: Yale University Press, 2013), 11; McAlister, *Kingdom of God*, 69.
41. Bruce Cumings, *The Korean War: A History* (New York: Modern Library, 2010), 188–201, as quoted in Yuan Shu and Donald Pease, eds., *American Studies as Transnational Practice: Turning toward the Transpacific* (Hanover, NH: Dartmouth College Press, 2016), 4.
42. Kuan-Hsing Chen, *Asia as Method: Toward Deimperialization* (Durham, NC: University of North Carolina Press, 2010), 8.
43. Chen, *Asia as Method*, 8.
44. Klein, *Cold War Orientalism*, 18.
45. Paul Kramer argues that among the many nations whose otherwise disparate histories became "permanently inseparable" in the twentieth century, the United States and the Philippines are a prime example. The United States and South Korea serve as another example of two nations that now, due to the ongoing legacies of war, are inseparable—not just at the political and the economic levels, but also the religious. Paul Kramer, *Blood of Government: Race, Empire, the United States and the Philippines* (Chapel Hill: University North Carolina Press, 2006).
46. Heonik Kwon, *The Other Cold War* (New York: Columbia University Press, 2010), 1.
47. In this book, these historical figures will be referred as "Kyung Chik Han," "Billy Jang Hwan Kim," (or "Billy Kim") and "Joon Gon Kim," according to the widely used spelling of their names. Note that, in other references, they may be called "Han Kyŏngjik" "Kim Changhwan" and "Kim Chungon," according to the McCune-Reischauer system.
48. Kwon, *The Other Cold War*, 1.
49. Kevin Kruse, *One Nation under God: How Corporate America Invented Christian America* (New York: Basic Books, 2015).
50. Butler, *White Evangelical Racism*. See also Carolyn Renee Dupont, *Mississippi Praying: Southern White Evangelicals and the Civil Rights Movement, 1945–75* (New York: New York University Press, 2013).
51. Robert E. Buswell Jr., ed., *Religions of Korea in Practice* (Princeton, NJ: Princeton University Press, 2007), 3.

52. Lee, *Born Again*; Park, *Korean Protestantism and Politics*; David Yoo, *Contentious Spirits: Religion in Korean American History, 1903-1945* (Stanford, CA; Stanford University Press, 2010).
53. Sung-Deuk Oak, *The Making of Korean Christianity: Protestant Encounters with Korean Religions, 1876-1915* (Waco, TX: Baylor University Press, 2013), 271-305.
54. Helen Hardacre, *Shinto: A History* (New York: Oxford University Press, 2016), 431-434. Note Thomas's caution against stereotyping Japan as a Shinto state, reinforcing incorrect perceptions of modern Japan as religiously intolerant. Jolyon Thomas, *Faking Liberties: Religious Freedom in America-Occupied Japan* (Chicago: University of Chicago Press, 2019).
55. The others were adherents of Chungdokyo and Buddhism.
56. Mark Mullins, "Japanese Christianity," in *Nanznan Guide to Japanese Religions*, ed. Paul Swanson (Honolulu: University of Hawaii Press, 2006), 116-118.
57. See Oak's introduction for an extensive literature review on the debate: Oak, *Making of Korean Christianity*, 1-33.
58. Scholars have long debated the role of US missionaries in the non-Western world and in the birth, growth, and success of Korean Christianity, engaging the excoriating interventions against the marriage between US empire and Christian missions. The critique of "cultural imperialism" not only provided a clear paradigm by which the previously colonized could express their discontent, but also put historians of Christian missions on the defensive; moreover, it has engendered work that understands the agency of indigenous Christians and Christianity as a global religion. Why was there a shift in the center of Christianity from the "global North" to the "global South" in the twentieth century, in spite of the critiques of cultural imperialism? Scholars such as Dana Robert and Lamin Sanneh study the rise of Christianity in the global South and document the unexpected and rapid expansion of Christianity in spite of the critiques of cultural imperialism. See Dana Robert, *Christian Mission: How Christianity Became a World Religion* (Malden, MA: Wiley-Blackwell, 2009); Lamin Sanneh, *Translating the Message: The Missionary Impact on Culture* (Maryknoll, NY: Orbis Books, 2009).
59. Oak, *Making of Korean Christianity*, 305; see Deok-Joo Rhie, *A Study on the Formation of the Indigenous Church in Korea, 1903-1907* (Seoul: History of Christianity in Korea Research Institute, 2000), 34 (translation mine).
60. Here, the phrase "race for revival" refers to the competitive spirit—especially with Cold War America—embedded in Cold War South Korean Protestants' impulse to fulfill the Great Commission. We will also see how the phrase refers to the racialized tensions and dynamics that vexed the transpacific networks forged between these two groups.
61. See Lee, *Born Again*.
62. Kim, *The Spirit Moves West*.
63. Through her close study of University Bible Fellowship (UBF), she discovered the enduring influence of "American global Christianity" and found that though UBF prizes evangelizing white college students, their work ultimately "clashes with the dominant white American culture and racial hierarchy." Kim, *The Spirit Moves West*.

64. Jehu Hanciles, *Beyond Christendom: Globalization, African Migration and the Transformation of the West* (Maryknoll, NY: Orbis Books, 2008), 385.
65. Nami Kim, *The Gendered Politics of the Korean Protestant Right: Hegemonic Masculinity* (Cham, Switzerland: Palgrave MacMillan, 2016), 6. Pro-American, anticommunist Protestant Christians came to occupy high positions in the US military government (1945–1948) and the Syngman Rhee cabinet. Kim suggests that the "theological rationalization of anticommunism" in South Korea "mirrors anticommunist propaganda in the post-World War II US context" when, as Jonathan Herzog notes, a "spiritual-industrial complex" in the United States associated communism with theological evil. Jonathan Herzog, *The Spiritual-Industrial Complex: America's Religious Battle against Communism in the Early Cold War* (New York: Oxford University Press, 2011).
66. Kim, *Gendered Politics*, 3. Kim draws parallels between the US Christian Right and the Korean Protestant Right. In the same year that the Christian Council of Korea was founded, 1989, the Christian Coalition of America was founded by Pat Robertson. The CCK defined itself in distinction from the Korean National Council of Churches.
67. Kim, "Graveyard of Empires," 9.
68. Mae M. Ngai, "Transnationalism and the Transformation of the 'Other,'" *American Quarterly* 57.1 (2005): 60.
69. Several fields and subfields have taken heed of the transnational and global turn. In his speech to the American Historical Association, for instance, Eric Foner acknowledged the contribution of Asian American historians in writing American history from a "Pacific world perspective." Eric Foner, "American Freedom in a Global Age," *American Historical Review* 106.1 (February 2001): 1–16. Several notable works mark this transpacific approach to US history. See, for example, Eiichiro Azuma, *Between Two Empires: Race, History, and Transnationalism in Japanese America* (New York: Oxford University Press, 2005); Augusto Espiritu, *Five Faces of Exile: The Nation and Filipino-American Intellectuals* (Stanford, CA: Stanford University Press, 2005); Jane H. Hong, *Opening the Gates to Asia: A Transpacific History of How America Repealed Asian Exclusion* (Chapel Hill: University of North Carolina Press, 2019); Madeline Hsu, *Dreaming of Gold, Dreaming of Home: Transnationalism and Migration between the U.S. and South China, 1882–1943* (Stanford, CA: Stanford University Press, 2000).
70. As discussed, I intervene in the literature on the rise of American evangelicalism to set it in a global context. Note that from the eighteenth century to the twentieth century, evangelical history will often mention Koreans or the Pacific context, but may not explore it in depth. David Hempton in *Methodism* studies the eighteenth-century rise of evangelicalism as a global movement, including among African Americans and Koreans. His book has been translated into Korean as well, revealing the significant interest in the rise of evangelicalism among Korean academics and students. Grant Wacker's most recent work on Billy Graham also mentions Graham's global influence, and at the center of his book is the image of Graham's largest crusade, the very image that this introduction opens with, as evidence of the global influence of the "Protestant Pope." Grant Wacker, *America's Pastor: Billy Graham and the Shaping of a Nation* (Cambridge, MA: Belknap Press of Harvard University Press, 2014).

71. Thomas Bender, *Rethinking American History in a Global Age* (Berkeley: University of California Press, 2002), 6. See also Bender's's *A Nation among Nations: America's Place in World History* (New York: Hill and Wang, 2006).
72. To be sure, this book draws significantly from concepts within the literature of US-Korean relations, including the work of historian Tae Gyun Park and political scientist Katherine Moon, but then extends these works into a transpacific frame.
73. Archival sources and interviews are listed in the bibliography.
74. Lon Kurashige, Madeline Y. Hsu, and Yujin Yaguchi, "Introduction: Conversations on Transpacific History," *Pacific Historical Review* 83.2 (May 2014): 183–188. The purpose of this special issue, according to the guest editors, was to bring greater coherence to the "emerging research area of 'transpacific history,'" which tends to bridge "two or more conventional fields, including histories of the American West, U.S. immigration and ethnicity, U.S. diplomatic and international relations, Asian American Studies, East Asian Studies and Pacific Islander studies" (183).
75. Gary Okihiro, "Toward a Pacific Civilization," *Japanese Journal of American Studies* 18 (2007): 73–85.
76. Okihiro, "Toward a Pacific Civilization," 77.
77. Epeli Hauʻofa, "Our Sea of Islands," in *A New Oceania: Rediscovering Our Sea of Islands*, ed. Eric Waddell, Vijay Naidu, and Epeli Hauʻofa (Suva: School of Social and Economic Development, University of the South Pacific in association with Beake House, 1993).
78. Kim, "Reconstructing," 20.
79. Henry May's 1964 essay "The Recovery of American Religious History" is thought to be one of the key essays in recovering the direction of the field in the late twentieth century; Perry Miller's intellectual history work was also a key framework upon which the field built itself. Building upon May's essay is Jon Butler, "The Future of American Religious History: Prospectus, Agenda, Transatlantic Problematique," *William and Mary Quarterly*, 3rd series, 42.2 (April 1985): 167–183. He proposes directions that are not "clerically dominated institutional histories" or "continued concentration on the Puritan origins of American culture." Yet in all of these conceptualizations of American religious history, there is no call to look toward the Pacific for a usable past.
80. Laurie Maffly-Kipp, "Eastward Ho! American Religion from the Perspective of the Pacific Rim," in *Retelling U.S. Religious History*, ed. Thomas Tweed (Berkeley: University of California Press, 1997), 130.
81. Maffly-Kipp, "Eastward Ho!," 130.
82. Consider that Ann Braude's seminal essay "Women's History *Is* American Religious History" was published in the same volume as Maffly-Kipp's essay in 1997, Tweed, *Retelling U.S. Religious History*. On the heels of Braude's intervention, a significant body of scholarship on American women's religious history emerged. To be sure, the religious history of American women burgeoned for other reasons, including the maturation of women's history in American history in general. For a historiographical assessment see especially the volume on women's religious history edited by Catherine Brekus, *The Religious History of American Women: Reimagining the Past* (Chapel Hill: University of North Carolina Press, 2007).

83. David Yoo and Rudy Busto, respectively, make these observations. See Yoo's introduction in Yoo, *New Spiritual Homes*; see Busto's essay "DisOrienting Subjects: Reclaiming Pacific Islander/Asian American Religions," in *Revealing the Sacred in Asian and Pacific America*, ed. Jane Naomi Iwamura and Paul Spickard (New York: New York University Press, 2004). As a result, the Asian American religious subject was essentialized and rendered invisible, resulting in reductive and binary conceptualizations; see Timothy Tseng, "Beyond Orientalism and Assimilation: The Asian American as Historical Subject," in *Realizing the America of Our Hearts: Theological Voices of Asian Americans*, ed. Fumitaka Matsuoka and Eleazar S. Fernandez (St. Louis, MO: Chalice, 2003), 69.
84. Scholars of Asian American religions have innovated theories and pioneered methods to produce content that made visible otherwise invisible Asian American religious subjects, resulting in the subfield of Asian American religions. Much literature has been devoted to studying this heterogeneous Asian American religious landscape. See Kim, "Reconstructing."
85. As Yuan Shu and Donald Pease state: "The Cold War may have ended in Europe, but its colonial and imperialist dynamic continues to mediate colonial and postcolonial history throughout the Asia Pacific." Shu and Pease, *American Studies*, 5.
86. Rachel Cohrs, "North Korea's Secret Christians," *The Atlantic*, April 28, 2018.

Chapter 1

1. Note that the global reach of World Vision expanded considerably after Pierce's departure. Please see David King's comprehensive study on the origins and historical development of World Vision: King, *God's Internationalists*.
2. William Yoo, American Missionaries, *Korean Protestants, and the Changing Shape of World Christianity, 1884–1965* (New York: Routledge, 2017), 182. Yoo notes especially Pierce's admiration for Han as an example of someone who confirmed his own orientation toward faith.
3. Please consult David Swartz's helpful reconstruction of World Vision's Korean origins; David Swartz, *Facing West: American Evangelicals in an Age of World Christianity* (New York: Oxford University Press, 2020), 35–65; see also my reconstruction of the Korean and Korean War origins of World Vision: Helen Jin Kim, "Gospel of the 'Orient': Koreans, Race and the Rise of American Evangelicalism in the Cold War Era, 1950–1980" (PhD dissertation, Harvard University, 2017).
4. "Docu Movie—Kyung Chik Han," in *The Complete Collection of Rev. Kyungchik Han, Visual Materials, No. 5 Docu 2* (DVD collection in Korean) (Kyungchik Han Foundation, Seoul).
5. Kathryn Moon, *Sex among Allies: Military Prostitution in U.S.-Korea Relations* (New York: Columbia University Press, 1997); Ji-Yeon Yuh, *Beyond the Shadow of Camptown: Korean Military Brides in America* (New York: New York University Press, 2002); Choy, *Global American Families*; Oh, *Save the Children*; Susie Woo,

Framed by War: Korean Children and Women at the Crossroads of US Empire (New York: New York University Press, 2019).
6. This chapter treats religion as an independent category of analysis, highlighting the role of transnational religious actors in the Korean War.
7. "3. Kyung Chik Han, the Volunteer," in *Complete Collection of Rev. Kyungchik Han, No. 5 Docu 2.*
8. "Docu Movie."
9. "Case History of Lee-Kim Duck Hei (widow in Tabitha Home). H#6 A#411." Korea Projects 1956–1978. World Vision Inc., Central Records, Monrovia, CA.
10. Kyung-Chik Han, *Kyung-Chik Han Collection*, ed. Eun-seop Kim, vol. 1 (Seoul: Kyung-Chik Han Foundation, 2010), 455–456.
11. "Docu Movie."
12. "Docu Movie."
13. Bob Pierce, *The Untold Korea Story* (Grand Rapids: Zondervan Publishing House, 1951), 45–46.
14. Yoo, *American Missionaries*.
15. For further discussion on Korean Protestantism and early nationalist politics, see chapter 4 "The Protestant Church and Early Nationalist Politics, 1880–1919," in Chung-shin Park, *Protestantism and Politics in Korea* (Seattle: University of Washington Press, 2009), 117–138.
16. "Docu Movie."
17. "Docu Movie."
18. "8. World Vision and Pastor Kyung Chik Han," in *Complete Collection of Rev. Kyungchik Han, No. 4 Docu 1.*
19. Hardacre, *Shinto*, 434.
20. Bruce Cumings, *The Origins of the Korean War*, 2 vols. (Princeton: Princeton University Press, 1990).
21. Gi-Wook Shin, *Ethnic Nationalism in Korea: Genealogy, Politics and Legacy* (Stanford, CA: Stanford University Press, 2007), 161–165.
22. Shin, *Ethnic Nationalism in Korea*, 162.
23. Susan Choi, *The Foreign Student: A Novel* (New York: HarperCollins Publishers, 1998) 64.
24. The Taft-Katsura Agreement was established in the aftermath of Japan's victory in the Russo-Japanese War (1904–1905).
25. Sheila Miyoshi Jager, *Brothers at War: The Unending Conflict in Korea* (New York: Norton, 2013). See also Cumings, *Origins of the Korean War*, vol. 1; Cumings, *Korean War: A History*.
26. Jager, *Brothers at War*, 73.
27. Juche, literally "self-reliance," is a combination of Marxist and neo-Confucian thought, which has over time become a national North Korean "religion." See Kim Il Sung, *On Juche in Our Revolution* (Pyongyang: Foreign Languages Publishing House, 1975); for further study, see Jae Jung Suh ed., *Origins of North Korea's Juche: Colonialism, War and Development* (Lanham: Lexington Books, 2013).

28. Established in September 1945, it was the first political party in the country since liberation, established to promote democracy and reform the nation according to Christian ideals. Haga, "Overlooked Dimension." See also Kai Yin Allison Haga, "Rising to the Occasion: The Role of American Missionaries and Korean Pastors in Resisting Communism throughout the Korean War," in Muehlenbeck, *Religion and the Cold War*.
29. Han, *Kyung-Chik Han Collection*, 285.
30. Haga, "Overlooked Dimension," 148–151.
31. As indicated, Pyongyang was historically the center of Korean Christianity.
32. J. Herbert Kane, *A Global View of Christian Missions from Pentecost to the Present* (Grand Rapids: Baker Book House, 1971), 261–272. Kane writes: "Following WWII there was a large influx of new missions from the United States [to Korea]. According to the 1968 edition of the *North American Protestant Ministries Overseas Directory*, there are almost fifty mission organizations in Korea. Thirty-seven of these entered Korea since 1945. . . . No other mission field, not even Taiwan, is so completely dominated by American Missions. Only three missionary societies out of a total of forty-seven are completely non-American. Two other missions, being international, include non-American personnel" (272). Though Kane's understanding of Korean exceptionalism here needs to be evaluated and critiqued, his reference to the post-1945 missionary presence in Korea is empirically grounded. See *North American Protestant Ministries Overseas Directory* (Waco: Missionary Research Library in cooperation with Missions Advanced Research and Communication Center, 1970).
33. Kane, *A Global View of Christian Missions*, 272.
34. The title of this section is a reference to Darren Dochuk's book *From Bible Belt to Sun Belt*.
35. Dochuk, *Bible Belt to Sunbelt*, 188–189.
36. Patrick Allitt, *Religion in America since 1945: A History* (New York: Columbia University Press, 2003), 22.
37. Inboden, *Religion and American Foreign Policy*, 64. He warned other American intellectuals against allowing communism to infiltrate their minds at the cost of rejecting the American values of democracy. See also Herzog, *Spiritual-Industrial Complex*.
38. Inboden, *Religion and American Foreign Policy*, 69. Dulles served as secretary of state under President Dwight D. Eisenhower from 1953 to 1959 and was an aggressive anticommunist whose religious discourse, Inboden argues, strongly shaped the course of the Cold War between the Christian United States and the atheistic Soviet Union; Dulles, he provides, was not a fundamentalist, but his religiopolitical worldview created a moralistic discourse of good and evil between the United States and Soviet Union.
39. For further discussion on neo-evangelicals and anticommunist rhetoric during the Cold War, see Elizabeth Barstow, "'These Teen-agers Are Not Delinquent': The Rhetoric of Maturity for Evangelical Young Adults, 1945–1965" (PhD dissertation, Harvard University, 2010).

40. William Hutchison, *Errand to the World: American Protestant Thought and Foreign Missions* (Chicago: University of Chicago Press, 1987).
41. Marilee Pierce Dunker, *Man of Vision: The Candid and Compelling Story of Bob and Lorraine Pierce, Founders of World Vision and Samaritan's Purse* (Waynesboro: Authentic Media, 2005). See also Marilee Pierce Dunker, "Korea Is Transformed into a Nation That Blesses Others," April 21, 2015, https://www.worldvis ion.org/christian-faith-news-stories/korea-transformed-nation-blesses-others.
42. By comparison, the liberal Protestant corollary to YFC, the Student Christian Movement, tended to place missionaries in university or healthcare settings with a focus on socially engaged ministries.
43. It was first called Bethany Church when it was founded in December 1945.
44. Han, *Kyung-Chik Han Collection*, 414.
45. Gwen Wong, Inter-Varsity Christian Fellowship Archives, Oral History. Provided courtesy of Inter Varsity USA archivist Ned Hale. Inter-Varsity began as a British movement among evangelical students in Cambridge and London in the late nineteenth century; it was a conservative evangelical alternative to the Student Christian Movement. The US branch of Inter-Varsity, however, did not begin until 1939. Keith Hunt, *For Christ and the University: The Story of InterVarsity Christian Fellowship, 1940–1990* (Downers Grove, IL: Intervarsity Press, 1991). YFC was an evangelistic organization that came out of the fundamentalist strand of the fundamentalist-modernist controversy in the early twentieth century. Billy Graham and Bob Pierce met each other through YFC.
46. Phone conversation with Bob Pierce's daughter, Marilee Pierce Dunker, August 2015.
47. See the introduction for a historical overview.
48. See fn 58 in Introduction for reference to Sung Deuk Oak's discussion on how these became indigenous Korean Christian practices.
49. Pierce, *The Untold Korea Story*, 10–11.
50. Pierce, *The Untold Korea Story*, 66–67.
51. Kyung Bae Min, World Vision 50 Year History, *1950–2000* (Seoul: World Vision Korea, Hong Ik Jae Publishers, 2001), 178–179.
52. For an overview of Kim Ch'anghwa and Paek Okhyŏn's story, see "Our Daddy Died for Truth: A Radio Show by Bob Pierce." World Vision Inc., Central Records, Monrovia, CA; Min, *World Vision 50 Year History*, 178–181; "Christmas in Korea," in *World Vision Pictorial*, 68 (the publication year of the *World Vision Pictorial* is not recorded on the publication, but it was most likely 1953); "My Daddy Died for Truth," *World Vision Magazine*, June 1959, 12.
53. "Our Daddy Died for Truth." Kim Ch'anghwa ("Chang Hwa Kim" in source) was a high school math teacher, a father of four, and a North Korean refugee school. He taught at Seoul National University Attached Middle School.
54. As a result of his spring 1950 travels to Korea, when he met Kim Ch'anghwa and Kyung Chik Han, and in response to the outbreak of the Korean War in 1950, Pierce hastily prepared to return to Korea.
55. Kim Ok Hyun, "God Leads Me," 2. Testimony of the First Sponsorship: Widow Ok Hyun Kim and Her Four Daughters Were the First to Be Sponsored by World Vision,

1951. World Vision Inc., Central Records, Monrovia, CA. (Note that this source incorrectly gives Paek Okhyŏn her husband's last name—Kim Ok Hyun.)
56. War widows often had to abandon their children at orphanages and could not afford to return for them. As historian Arissa Oh reports, war widows were especially vulnerable, sometimes by coercion, to recruitment into sex work: "In 1952, the U.S. State Department reported that 2,658 'UN Aunties'—one of the many terms used to describe prostitutes who served foreigners—had been arrested in a five-month period in Seoul alone; of this number, half were widows." Oh, *Save the Children*, 49. When the US military first entered the southern region of Korea in 1945, camptowns, or *kijich'on*, providing sexual services for troops emerged nearly simultaneously. The number of Korean women working at camptowns increased to about two thousand during the war. See Yuh, *Beyond the Shadow*, 19–23.
57. Her favorite verses were from John 14:1–4. Kim, "God Leads Me." This source cites the King James version of John 14:1–4: "Let not your heart be troubled: ye believe in God, believe also in me. In my Father's house are many mansions: if it were not so, I would have told you. I go to prepare a place for you. And if I go and prepare a place for you, I will come again, and receive you unto myself; that where I am, there ye may be also. And whither I go ye know, and the way ye know."
58. Case History of Lee-Kim Duck Hei (widow in Tabitha Home).
59. There is some discrepancy in the amounts Bob Pierce gave to Paek Okhyŏn. Kim, "God Leads Me," says that after Paek met Pierce with Han in 1951 at the Tabitha Widow's Home in Pusan, she and her four daughters received twenty-five dollars per month and then fifty dollars every other month from World Vision. Also note that World Vision began its official child sponsorship program in 1953, historically the organization's main program, but before that, it sponsored a war widow—Paek Okhyŏn—whose husband died because of his collaboration with Pierce.
60. Bob Pierce and Dorothy Clark Haskin, *Orphans of the Orient: Stories That Will Touch Your Heart* (Grand Rapids: Zondervan Publishing House, 1964), 86.
61. Kim, "God Leads Me."
62. Billy Graham, *I Saw Your Sons at War: The Korean Diary of Billy Graham* (Minneapolis: Billy Graham Evangelistic Association, 1953), 11.
63. BGEA Korea 1952 Visit Photo File, Image 101. Archives of the Billy Graham Center, Wheaton, IL.
64. BGEA Korea 1952 Visit Photo File, Images 191 and 200. Archives of the Billy Graham Center, Wheaton, IL.
65. This exemplified, in some senses, the way in which leadership in Korea at this time was really looking not only to Koreans like Han but also to Americans—both to provide military and government guidance and to provide religious guidance. The jointly translated and preached gospel was a powerful platform upon which to stand. They needed each other to get the message across to the Koreans for it to persuade as much as it did.
66. Nadia Kim, *Imperial Citizens: Koreans and Race from Seoul to LA* (Stanford, CA: Stanford University Press, 2008).
67. Graham, *I Saw Your Sons*, 49.

68. Du Mez, *Jesus and John Wayne*, 48.
69. See Du Mez, *Jesus and John Wayne*, 35; and Kruse's discussion of Eisenhower and Graham in *One Nation Under God*.
70. The publication year of the *World Vision Pictorial* is not recorded on the publication, but it was most likely 1953. Ray Provost, a Presbyterian missionary, took many of the photos. Grady Wilson was also on this trip, as was Dave Morken, the director of YFC in Japan.
71. Billy Graham, *Talking Pictures: The Hour of Decision in History / Let Freedom Ring*, 1953. BGEA Phonograph Records Collection 102. Archives of the Billy Graham Center, Wheaton, IL. The cover of *Talking Pictures* has an image of Syngman Rhee's meeting with Billy Graham taken during "Christmas in Korea" in December 1952.
72. Susan O'Brien, "A Transatlantic Community of Saints: The Great Awakening and the First Evangelical Network, 1735–1755," *American Historical Review* 91.4 (October 1, 1986): 811–832.
73. See images of Bob Pierce in BGEA Korea 1952 Visit Photo File, Images 52, 68, 182, 179, 202, 319, 328, and 457. Archives of the Billy Graham Center, Wheaton, IL. Pierce's video camera had at least three lenses—for short, medium, and long shots—through which to record footage. See also John Hamilton, "An Historical Study of Bob Pierce and World Vision's Development of the Evangelical Social Action Film" (PhD dissertation, University of Southern California, 1980), 19–22. Hamilton notes that Pierce's first camera, a 16 mm, was purchased in 1941. On it, he filmed home videos of his daughters. He filmed two movies before he went to China for China Challenge—Miracle Miles in the Orient, in China in 1947, and in 1948 he filmed significant amounts of 16 mm Kodachrome silent film. *38th Parallel* was his first film of Korea. Dick Ross produced or directed the first nine of the Bob Pierce films for World Vision from 1948 to 1956, under the name Great Commission Films, which eventually became World Wide Pictures under the BGEA in 1956.
74. Hamilton, "Historical Study of Bob Pierce," 71–73. Great Commission Films spent nearly $200,000 to film, significantly more than later films, which cost $30,000–40,000. Great Commission Films' first film, *The Flame*, which cost about $200,000, was also about Korea, as was *Of Such Is the Kingdom*, Great Commission's last film with Pierce. Hamilton also notes that Dick Ross believed that they could script the films in advance, "particularly the dramatic stories."
75. Hamilton, "Historical Study of Bob Pierce," 83. Note that "Chang Hwa Kim" is Romanized in this text as "Kim Ch'anghwa," according to the McCune-Reischauer system.
76. Historian Catherine Ceniza Choy, *Global American Families*, might categorize a 1950s film as such.
77. Hamilton, "Historical Study of Bob Pierce," 81.
78. "Communism in Korea Portrayed by Film," *Torrance Press*, November 22, 1954, 11.
79. Choy, *Global Families*, 31.
80. "Our Daddy Died for Truth."
81. See footnote 78; Lee, Keye, and Wong are Chinese American actors who played relatively prominent roles in films throughout their careers. See the following IMDB profiles to follow their careers:

Richard Loo, http://www.imdb.com/name/nm0519618/?ref_=nm_mv_close; Keye Luke, http://www.imdb.com/name/nm0525601/bio?ref_=nm_ov_bio_sm; Jean Wong, http://www.imdb.com/name/nm0939134/bio?ref_=nm_ov_bio_sm.

82. Hamilton, "Historical Study of Bob Pierce," 83.
83. Ellen Wu, *The Color of Success: Asian Americans and the Origins of the Model Minority* (Princeton: Princeton University Press, 2014), 112.
84. Yoo, *American Missionaries*, 196, 199.
85. Josephine Park, *Cold War Friendships: Korea, Vietnam and Asian American Literature* (Oxford: Oxford University Press, 2016), 6.
86. Park, *Cold War Friendships*, 10–11.
87. "World Vision Inc. Missionary Disbursements 1951–1959." World Vision Inc., Central Records, Monrovia, CA.
88. "Docu Movie."
89. Park Jong Sam (Sam Park) was Korea World Vision's president from 1995 to 2006. Park Jong Sam (Sam Park), Oral History Interview. Seoul, Korea. April 27, 2016.
90. "World Vision Inc. Missionary Disbursements 1951–1959," 5.
91. "World Vision Inc. Missionary Disbursements 1951–1959," 7.
92. Young-Gi Hong, "Encounter with Modernity: The 'McDonaldization' and 'Charismatization' of Korean Churches," *International Review of Mission* 92.365 (April 2003): 239–255.
93. Jane Iwamura, *Virtual Orientalism: Asian Religions and American Popular Culture* (New York: Oxford University Press, 2011). This notion of Korean War martyrdom parallels Jane Iwamura's concept of the "Oriental Monk," which pinpoints the importance of Asian religions in American religious formation, all the while erasing the Asian people's contributions. The concept of the Korean War martyr operates, however, with a different theological assumption since it is connected to the Christian concept of martyrdom as it mimics the death and sacrifice of the first martyr in Christian history, Jesus Christ.
94. Gary Vanderpol, "The Least of These: American Evangelical Parachurch Missions to the Poor, 1947–2005" (doctoral dissertation, Boston University School of Theology, 2010); King, *God's Internationalists*; see also David King, "Seeing a Global Vision: The Evolution of World Vision and American Evangelicalism" (Unpublished Emory University Doctoral Dissertation, 2012);
95. See Pierce and Haskin, *Orphans of the Orient*, 60.
96. Dean R. Hirsch, "World Vision Began in Korea," in Min, *World Vision 50 Year History*, 87.
97. Hirsch, "World Vision Began in Korea," 87.
98. Thereafter, he paved a path that set into motion not only international adoption but also the formation of a new religious institution. Bob Pierce introduced the story of Korean War orphans to Harry Holt, who is largely responsible for beginning the international adoption movement in the United States. See Oh, *Save the Children*; see also their video together about sponsoring and adopting Korean babies: *Mercy's Child*. BGEA. Archives of the Billy Graham, Wheaton, IL.

99. Lee Hokyun, Oral History Interview.
100. Lee Hokyun, Oral History Interview.
101. Park Jong Sam (Sam Park), Oral History Interview.
102. "Docu Movie."
103. See footnote 7. In both David King's and Gary Vanderpol's religious histories on the global and social justice orientation of World Vision, Paek Okhyŏn, Kim Ch'anghwa, Kyung Chik Han, and Tabitha Widow's Home are not named. Moreover, in Arissa Oh, Catherine Ceniza Choy, and Susie Woo's transnational histories of Korea and World Vision, these names and stories do not appear either.
104. See also Dunker, "Korea Is Transformed."

Chapter 2

1. Susan Choi, *The Foreign Student: A Novel* (New York: HarperCollins Publishers, 1998). For further discussion on race and the Korean War in Choi's novel, see Daniel Kim, *Intimacies of Conflict: A Cultural Memory and the Korean War* (New York: New York University Press, 2020).
2. Leslie Bow, *Partly Colored: Asian Americans and Racial Anomaly in the Segregated South* (New York: New York University Press, 2010), 8.
3. For a helpful history of Korean Protestant students in the Jim Crow South during the Progressive era, see the example of Yun Ch'i-ho Chris Suh, "What Yun Ch'i-ho Knew: US-Japan Relations and Imperial Race Making in Korea and the American South, 1904–1919," *Journal of American History* 104.1 (June 2017): 68–96.
4. Billy Kim, *The Life of Billy Kim: From Houseboy to World Evangelist* (Chicago: Moody Publishers, 2015), 29. Note that Kim writes about himself in the third person; his justification is that the third-person perspective provides an omniscient point of view and, therefore, the perspective of God.
5. Historian of Korean Christianity Rhie Deok-Joo categorizes Billy Kim and Joon Gon Kim as leaders who represent the "second generation" of Korean Protestantism. The "first generation" of Korean Protestantism constitutes the first wave of converts in the early twentieth century. See Rhie, *Study on the Formation*, 34 (translation mine).
6. Cindy I-Fen Cheng, *Citizens of Asian America: Democracy and Race during the Cold War* (New York: New York University Press, 2013), 117–148.
7. Joon Gon Kim and Billy Kim were part of a longer history of Korean students immigrating to the United States for higher education, and specifically, connected to, or for the purposes of, Christian education, including Yun Ch'iho and Kim Hwallan (Helen Kim), and as discussed in the previous chapter, Kyung Chik Han. Joon Gon Kim's and Billy Kim's presence in the United States can be seen as an extension of the education that figures like Yun received in the United States. What remains distinct is that Joon Gon Kim and Billy Kim helped to extend these white fundamentalist networks to South Korea and the United States through Bob Jones, Fuller, and Campus Crusade. For a discussion of Korean immigrant history and the Methodist

church, specifically, see Hong Ki Kim, *A History of One Hundred Years of the Korean-American Methodism I, Part I* (Upland: The Committee on Publicaion of 100 Year History of the Korean-American Methodist Church, 2003).
8. Bow, *Partly Colored*, 14. Here I incorporate Bow's theorization of racial interstitiality, as she argues: "Thinking interstitially is a matter of turning one's gaze toward the space of the in-between to envision alternative connections and affiliations that complicate black and white" (5).
9. Klein, *Cold War Orientalism*, 23.
10. Klein, *Cold War Orientalism*, 19. As mentioned, Klein draws on Raymond Williams's understanding of cultural hegemony as generating "structures of feeling" through which "ideological principles that support a given arrangement of power are translated into regularized patterns of emotion and sentiment."
11. Klein, *Cold War Orientalism*, 19.
12. Klein, *Cold War Orientalism*, 58 and 27.
13. Klein, *Cold War Orientalism*, 16.
14. Klein, *Cold War Orientalism*, 30.
15. Marsden, *Reforming Fundamentalism*, 84.
16. Graham transferred to Trinity Institute in Florida and then Wheaton College. Cliff Barrows, one of Graham's closest friends and among the first members on his evangelistic team, was also a graduate of Bob Jones.
17. When Graham invited liberal theologians from Union Theological Seminary to join his New York crusade, Bob Jones University critiqued him for associating with the Antichrist. Graham was much more willing to overcome theological differences with liberals for the sake of expanding his influence, whereas ultraseparatists like those at Bob Jones desired a more separatist approach and distanced themselves from other subcultures.
18. Marsden, *Reforming Fundamentalism*, 3; Wuthnow, *Restructuring American Religion*, 174; Carpenter, *Revive Us Again*. Harold Ockenga, Wilbur Smith, Everett Harrison, Carl F. H. Henry, and Harold Lindsell were the first recruits to the seminary's faculty. The establishment of the National Association of Evangelicals and later the National Religious Broadcasting Association, the National Sunday School Association, the Evangelical Foreign Missions Association, the Commission for Church Schools, and the Commission on War Relief gave evangelicalism a national identity in the postwar years. While these institutions would firm up the network of evangelicalism, it is important to note that the standard categories of "evangelical" and "fundamental" were not formed yet in the late 1940s.
19. The 1908 Gentleman's Agreement between the United States and Japan curtailed the entry of Korean laborers to the United States since Korea was a Japanese protectorate. The Immigration Act of 1924 further restricted Korean (and other Asian) flows to the United States.
20. See, for example, Mary Paik Lee, *Quiet Odyssey: A Pioneer Korean Woman in America*, ed. Sucheng Chan (Seattle: University of Washington Press, 1990).
21. Ian Haney-Lopez, *White by Law: The Legal Construction of Race* (New York: New York University Press, 2006), 56–77.

22. Shelley Lee, *A New History of Asian America* (New York: Routledge, 2014), 5–26; Erika Lee, *At America's Gates: Chinese Immigration during the Exclusion Era, 1882–1943* (Chapel Hill: University of North Carolina Press, 2003).
23. Jane Jangeun Cho, "Immigration through Education: The Interwoven History of Korean International Students, US Foreign Assistance, and Korean Nation-State Building" (PhD dissertation, University of California, Berkeley, 2010).
24. Klein, *Cold War Cosmopolitanism*, 30–31.
25. Bob Jones University, *The Vintage* (yearbook), 1954. Archives Research Center–Mack Library, 48, Greenville, SC. An Asian, French, and Spanish Fellowship also existed; see "Doodah" under the section "Special Days," *The Vintage*, 1954.
26. Nonwhite students hailed from Hawaii, South Korea, China, Taiwan, the Philippines, India, Indonesia, Japan, Singapore, Guam, Thailand, Guatemala, Greece, Cyprus, Syria, Lebanon, Haiti, Mexico, Israel, Honduras, and Panama. They also came from Indiana, Texas, Virginia, California, Florida, Illinois, North Carolina, New Jersey, and South Carolina. Bob Jones University, *The Vintage* (yearbook), 1950–1959. Archives Research Center–Mack Library, 48, Greenville, SC.
27. See image with quotatation: "Glenn Anderson proves there are still a few rebels who have not joined the union. Dr. and Mrs. Woodbridge and Ray Kusumoto seem ready to join." Fuller Theological Seminary, 1952 Yearbook. Fuller Theological Seminary Archives and Special Collections, 31, Pasadena, CA.
28. Billy Kim, CBMCI Chairman Waldo Yeager, "I Was a House Boy for GI's," February 1966, 13. Far East Broadcasting Company, Seoul.
29. Jang Hwan (Billy) Kim biographical details: Kyung (Isaac) Kyu Kim, "The Education and Cultivation of Intercultural Leaders: A Study of Twelve Prominent Native Born Koreans" (PhD dissertation, School of Intercultural Studies, Biola University, 2009), 83.
30. For a discussion on Korean student immigration to the United States during the Japanese colonial era, see Yoo, *Contentious Spirits*.
31. Kim, *Life of Billy Kim*, 36.
32. Kim, *Life of Billy Kim*, 37, 39.
33. The history of Chinese "coolie" labor is also relevant. Moon-Ho Jung, *Coolies and Cane: Race, Labor and Sugar in an Age of Emancipation* (Baltimore: John Hopkins University Press, 2006).
34. David W. Wills, "The Central Themes of American Religious History: Pluralism, Puritanism, and the Encounter of Black and White," in *African American Religion: Interpretive Essays in History and Culture*, ed. Timothy E. Fulop and Albert J. Raboteau (New York: Routledge, 1997), 7–20.
35. Stephanie Hinnershitz, *A Different Shade of Justice: Asian American Civil Rights in the South* (Chapel Hill: University of North Carolina Press, 2017), 73.
36. Kim, *Imperial Citizens*, 6.
37. Kim, *Life of Billy Kim*, 40.
38. Angelo Ancheta, *Race, Rights and the Asian American Experience* (New Brunswick, NJ: Rutgers University Press, 1998), 29.
39. Hinnershitz, *Different Shade of Justice*, 80.

40. Hinnershitz, *Different Shade of Justice*, 81.
41. On June 30, 1971, the district court for the District of Columbia handed down a ruling in a case called *Green v. Connally*. In light of the Civil Rights Act of 1964, religious, segregated schools in Mississippi would lose their tax-exempt status. As the IRS enforced this ruling, one of the schools it targeted was Bob Jones. Bob Jones did not admit African Americans until 1971 and then, out of fear of racial mixing, did not admit unmarried African Americans until 1975. Randall Balmer, *Evangelicalism in America* (Waco, TX: Baylor University Press, 2016).
42. Bob Jones University, *The Vintage* (yearbook), 1954. Archives Research Center–Mack Library, 5, Greenville, SC.
43. "Billy Kim Needs Funds to Continue in School." Billy Kim Personal Papers, Binder 1, Far East Broadcasting Company, Seoul.
44. Kim, *Life of Billy Kim*, 41.
45. Kim, *Life of Billy Kim*, 41.
46. Billy Kim's narratives mirror theologian Sang Hyun Lee's concept of Asian immigrant conversion as pilgrimage. Lee provides a theological orientation toward the categories of pilgrimage, exile, and stranger for the liminal/in-between space that Asian Americans inhabit. The idea of political estrangement aligns well with the theological concept of exile. Sang Hyun Lee, "Pilgrimage and Home in the Wilderness of Marginality." In Special Issue "Racial Spirits," *Amerasia Journal*, 22 (1), (1996): 149–160.
47. Kim, *Life of Billy Kim*, 41.
48. Kim, *Life of Billy Kim*, 43.
49. Kim, *Life of Billy Kim*, 43.
50. Kim, *Life of Billy Kim*, 43.
51. March 4, 1955, "SC Winner at Democracy Workshop," Columbia, South Carolina. Billy Kim Personal Papers, Binder 1, Far East Broadcasting Company, Seoul.
52. Billy Kim, "I Speak for Democracy." Billy Paper Personal Papers, Binder 1, Far East Broadcasting Company, Seoul.
53. Vernon Rieck, "My Chum: Stories of Real People. Billy Kim's Biggest Adventure. Part I" (adapted from an article by Carl L. Powers in *Power* magazine, Scripture Press, 1957), August 1960.
54. Rieck, "My Chum."
55. Bailey Marks, *Awakening in Asia* (San Bernardino, CA: Here's Life Publishers, 1981), 21.
56. As will be discussed later, Chosun Seminary was started by Kim Jae Jun, who led a liberal Korean theological movement against biblical literalism. Note that, as George Marsden points out, Fuller Theological Seminary was founded by American fundamentalists who subsequently became neo-evangelicals; as he shows, the founding of Fuller Theological Seminary was a part of that theological transformation. Marsden, *Reforming Fundamentalism*.
57. Michael Lewis Richardson, *Amazing Faith: The Authorized Biography of Bill Bright* (Colorado Springs, CO: WaterBrook Press, 2000), 158.
58. Oh Chint'ak, Oral History Interview.

59. Clarence Roddy, a professor of homiletics at Fuller Seminary, declared that "Henrietta Mears was the best preacher in Southern California." Note her Presbyterian denominational affiliation would have prevented her from being eligible for ordination, but she was considered the "power behind the throne" of many influential male religious leaders. Though not ordained, Mears was widely recognized as a successful preacher and religious educator who influenced many to go into the ministry. It was, for instance, during a stay at Mears's retreat center, Forest Home, that Graham had a reawakening experience right before launching into his crusade ministry. Mears created Forest Home in 1937. Turner, *Bill Bright*, 20.
60. Turner, *Bill Bright*, 8.
61. Turner, *Bill Bright*, 37.
62. Turner, *Bill Bright*, 38.
63. Joon Gon Kim, Campus Crusade for Christ, Inc. Campus Crusade for Christ International Archives, Orlando, FL. The date and particular purpose of this writing are unclear. I would estimate, though, that this is a document written shortly after Kim decided to partner with Bright to start the Korean Campus Crusade for Christ; the document was clearly written after they met at Fuller and before the 1972 and 1974 revivals.
64. Kim Jae Jun's leadership led to the creation of a new Korean Presbyterian denomination. Hapdong aligned with the NAE and Tong Hap aligned with the World Council of Churches. Joon Gon Kim was the education committee leader for the Korean chapter of the NAE. The NAE's statement of faith was as follows: "We believe the Bible to be the inspired, the only infallible, authoritative Word of God. We believe that there is one God, eternally existent in three persons: Father, Son and Holy Spirit. We believe in the deity of our Lord Jesus Christ, in His virgin birth, in His sinless life, in His miracles, in His vicarious and atoning death through His shed blood, in His bodily resurrection, in His ascension to the right hand of the Father, and in His personal return in power and glory. We believe that for the salvation of lost and sinful people, regeneration by the Holy Spirit is absolutely essential. We believe in the present ministry of the Holy Spirit by whose indwelling the Christian is enabled to live a godly life. We believe in the resurrection of both the saved and the lost; they that are saved unto the resurrection of life and they that are lost unto the resurrection of damnation. We believe in the spiritual unity of believers in our Lord Jesus Christ."
65. Woo Suk Kang, "The Evangelical Movement as Revealed in the Life and Thought of Joon Gon Kim" (master's thesis, Chongshin University, 2015), 8. Korea Campus Crusade for Christ Headquarters, Seoul (translation mine).
66. Joon Gon Kim, Campus Crusade for Christ, Inc. Campus Crusade for Christ International Archives, Orlando, FL. The date and particular purpose of this writing is unclear. I would estimate, though, that this is a document that was written shortly after Kim decided to partner with Bright to start the Korean Campus Crusade for Christ: the document is clearly from after they met at Fuller and before the 1972 and 1974 revivals.

67. Nils Becker, *Fireseeds from Korea to the World: Tribute to Dr. Joon Gon Kim, Founder of Campus Crusade for Christ* (Orlando, FL: Campus Crusade for Christ International, 2007), 59.
68. Joon Gon Kim, Campus Crusade for Christ, Inc. Campus Crusade for Christ International Archives, Orlando, FL.
69. The *Four Spiritual Laws* was solidified in 1959 by Bright as the following: (1) God loves you and has a wonderful plan for your life, (2) man is sinful and separated from God, thus he cannot know and explain God's plan for his life, (3) Jesus Christ is God's provision for man's sin through whom man can know God's love and plan for his life, (4) we must receive Jesus Christ as Savior and Lord by personal invitation. The *Four Spiritual Laws* is one of the most widely distributed religious pamphlets ever, with approximately 2.5 billion printed to date. "History," Campus Crusade for Christ Online, accessed November 1, 2011. http://campuscrusadeforchrist.com/about-us/history.
70. Joon Gon Kim, Campus Crusade for Christ, Inc. Campus Crusade for Christ International Archives, Orlando, FL.
71. Turner, *Bill Bright*, 151. Bright had also met a Pakistani student named Kundan Massey at Fuller shortly after he met Joon Gon Kim. Massey founded the Pakistan chapter of Campus Crusade. Ray Nethery was the first Campus Crusade director for Asia and then resigned in 1968, handing off the job to Bailey Marks. Marks began to streamline the nine Asian chapters of Campus Crusade, which had been otherwise acting rather independently of each other.
72. Klein, *Cold War Orientalism*, 37.
73. Henrietta Mears shared this sentiment when she warned her parishioners at the Forest Home in 1947; Bill Bright and Billy Graham were both frequenters of the retreat site Forest Home. Turner, *Bill Bright*, 98.
74. Chiang Kai-Shek was a Nationalist Party leader in China—and a Protestant—who fought against the Communist Party in China, only to be led into retreat in Taiwan with Mao's success in China.
75. Turner, *Bill Bright*, 98.
76. Marks, *Awakening in Asia*, 21.
77. *My Pastor Joon Gon Kim and CCC* (Seoul: Korea Campus Crusade for Christ, 2005), 209 (translation mine).
78. Marks, *Awakening in Asia*, 21.
79. Marks, *Awakening in Asia*, 21.
80. Marks, *Awakening in Asia*, 22.
81. Hempton, *Methodism*, 5.
82. *My Pastor Joon Gon Kim*, 209 (translation mine).
83. Curtis Evans, "White Evangelical Protestant Responses to the Civil Rights Movement," *Harvard Theological Review* 102.2 (April 2009): 245–273. See also Dupont, *Mississippi Praying*.
84. Butler, *White Evangelical Racism*, 40.
85. Butler, *White Evangelical Racism*, 41.
86. Mary Dudziak, *Cold War Civil Rights: Race and the Image of American Democracy* (Princeton, NJ: Princeton University Press, 2011), 87.

87. Carol Anderson, *Eyes off the Prize: The United Nations and the African American Struggle for Human Rights, 1944–1955* (Cambridge: Cambridge University Press, 2003).
88. Cheng, *Citizens of Asian America*, 147.
89. Cheng, *Citizens of Asian America*, 124.
90. Dochuk, *From Bible Belt to Sunbelt*, 178.

Chapter 3

1. Oh Chiyŏng participated in the first four international tours of the World Vision Korean Orphan Choir: 1961–1962, 1962–1963, 1965–1966, and 1968–1969.
2. Oh Chiyŏng, Oral History Interview.
3. World Vision was established in Korea in 1950, just months after the outbreak of the Korean War. Its initial aim was to provide emergency relief and aid for Koreans and help meet the material needs of widows, orphans, and the impoverished; its founders also sought Korean converts.
4. Oh Chiyŏng, Oral History Interview.
5. Kwon, *The Other Cold War*, 4.
6. Chang Soo Chul was a professor of music at Union Christian College in Seoul who had done his graduate work in the United States.
7. King, "Seeking a Global Vision." 139.
8. See Dunker, *Man of Vision*, for a moving personal narrative regarding her father Bob Pierce's complicated and tragic departure from World Vision.
9. "McFadden and Associates Correspondence," 2. World Vision Inc., Central Records, Monrovia, CA. Founded in 1955, McFadden and Eddy Associates was a public relations firm that worked primarily as the public relations agency for the City of Palm Springs. Frank William McFadden was a partner at McFadden and Eddy Associates from 1955 to 1966, before it merged with another public relations firm to become McFadden, Strauss & Irwin. http://prabook.org/web/person-view.html?profileId= 491580. See "Publicity Firms Tell of Merger," *Desert Sun*, Number 129, January 2, 1964. http://cdnc.ucr.edu/cgi-bin/cdnc?a=d&d=DS19640102.2.16
10. Correspondence from Ted Engstrom to Larry Burr, "Korean Children's Choir," March 10, 1969. World Vision Inc., Central Records, Monrovia, CA. To see the choir's earnings during the 1968–1969 tour, see "Financial Report: Korean Children's Choir Tour," August 1968–February 1969. The choir's records, selling for $2.38 and $3.00 each, included *Ring of Happiness*, *We Sing Because We're Happy with Ralph Carmichael*, and *Christmas Music on Tour with Burl Ives*. World Vision Inc., Central Records, Monrovia, CA.
11. Dudziak, *Cold War Civil Rights*. The international pressures to protect the US global Cold War image meant that domestic civil rights reform was critical. Nations in Asia and Africa decried the hypocrisy of racial segregation in the United States, which threatened to undermine the US global leadership as a democracy.

12. For further background, please see Hilary Kaell's history of the nineteenth century origins of "child sponsorship" in the United States: Hillary Kaell, *Christian Globalism at Home: Child Sponsorship in the United States* (Princeton, NJ: Princeton University Press, 2020).
13. In doing so, this chapter addresses a scholarly concern about how modern American evangelicalism became synonymous with whiteness, for it suggests that US Cold War empire-building projects, mediated through transpacific evangelical humanitarianism, were key. Moreover, in investigating whiteness I also seek to highlight that which has remained "hidden in plain sight," as Butler suggests, in the historiography of modern American evangelicalism. Anthea Butler, "A 'New' History of Evangelicalism—Black Evangelicals and American Evangelicalism," https://www.youtube.com/watch?v=q4UqpBnuCvI, February 13, 2015. Fuller Theological Seminary Online; Tisa Wenger, "The Kingdom of God Has No Borders: Global Evangelicalism Unbound," https://tif.ssrc.org/2018/09/13/global-evangelicalism-unbound/, *The Immanent Frame*, September 13, 2018.
14. Bob Pierce, *The Korean Orphan Choir: They Sing Their Thanks* (Grand Rapids: Zondervan, 1965), 64.
15. The last day of the tour was February 2, 1962. For Immediate Release: "World Vision Korean Orphan Choir in 'Farewell to America' Concert," January 23, 1962. World Vision Inc., Central Records, Monrovia, CA.
16. The Korean War armistice signed in 1953 led to a ceasefire and the division of North and South Korea at the 38th parallel (though not the cessation of the war, which, technically, continues even today).
17. Chung-Nan Yun, *Korean War and Protestantism* (Kyŏnggi-do P'aju-si: Hanul, 2015), 167. As discussed in chapters 4 and 5, Park would go on to govern South Korea as a military dictatorship, belaboring democratic rule, and preserving his administration for eighteen years. The US government wavered in its approval of his rule.
18. Yun, *Korean War*, 183.
19. Eisenhower's administration, much like the Soviet Union, had begun to engage in "people-to-people diplomacy," meaning that everyday people, not just state officials, were crucial to mediating positive diplomatic relations with other nations.
20. Yun, *Korean War*, 210.
21. Yun, *Korean War*, 214. The largest Billy Graham crusade is the subject of chapter 4.
22. Moon Hyangja was part of the choir from 1963 to 1973. Moon Hyangja, Oral History Interview.
23. "Korean Orphans Win City's Hearts," *Los Angeles Times*, October 25, 1961. This tour included twenty-seven girls and seven boys ranging in age from eight to twelve.
24. Yun, *Korean War*, 208.
25. "Welcome Back Little Missionaries! World Vision Korean Orphan Choir on World Tour," *World Vision Magazine*, October 1962, 6. World Vision Inc., Central Records, Monrovia, CA.
26. Tour 1 was approximately three months from October 1961 to February 1962 throughout the United States and Canada. "Fact Sheet: World Vision Korean Orphan Choir," 2. World Vision Inc., Central Records, Monrovia, CA. They were featured on

telecasts such as *Queen for a Day*, Art Linkletter's program, the *Bozo the Clown Show*, and *The Steve Allen Show*.

27. During Tour 2, the choir traveled for seven months from October 1962 to May 1963. Tour 3 was approximately seven months from July 1965 to February 1966.
28. "Financial Report: Korean Children's Choir Tour," August 1968–February 1969.
29. "Financial Report: Korean Children's Choir Tour," August 1968–February 1969.
30. Park Jong Sam, Oral History Interview.
31. "Dr. Bob Pierce Spots—10 sec."; "1962–63 World Vision Korean Orphan Choir Tour." World Vision Inc., Central Records, Monrovia, CA.
32. "Dr. Bob Pierce Spots—15 sec."; "1962–63 World Vision Korean Orphan Choir Tour." World Vision Inc., Central Records, Monrovia, CA.
33. "World Vision Korean Orphan Choir on First U.S., Canada Tour," Pasadena, CA, September 12, 1961. World Vision Inc., Central Records, Monrovia, CA.
34. Pierce, *The Korean Orphan Choir*, 14.
35. Yi Hokyun, Oral History Interview.
36. Park Jong Sam, Oral History Interview.
37. Moon Hyangja, Oral History Interview.
38. Moon Hyangja, Oral History Interview.
39. For further discussion on the role of Christian song and South Korean modernity, see Nicholas Harkness, *Songs of Seoul: An Ethnography of Voice and Voicing in Christian South Korea* (Berkeley: University of California Press, 2014).
40. King notes that the 1960s were the days of "crusades and orphanages," a time when World Vision devoted itself to a "decidedly pro-American Cold War perspective." King, "Seeking a Global Vision," 1.
41. Pierce, *The Korean Orphan Choir*, 13–14.
42. Pierce, *The Korean Orphan Choir*, 64.
43. Pierce, *The Korean Orphan Choir*, 13–14.
44. Pierce, *The Korean Orphan Choir*, 13–14.
45. Wu, *Color of Success*, 2.
46. Wu, *Color of Success*, 171.
47. Pierce, *The Korean Orphan Choir*, 53.
48. World Vision Korean Orphan Choir on First U.S., Canada Tour," Pasadena, CA. World Vision Inc., Central Records, Monrovia, CA.
49. Pierce, *The Korean Orphan Choir*, 24.
50. Pierce, *The Korean Orphan Choir*, 24.
51. Pierce, *The Korean Orphan Choir*, 77.
52. Pierce, *The Korean Orphan Choir*, 77.
53. Lee In Soon was referred to Dr. Ciwa Griffith, of the international HEAR Foundation in Highland Park, who had been successful in equipping children with hearing devices.
54. Pierce, *The Korean Orphan Choir*, 83.
55. Pierce, *The Korean Orphan Choir*, 84. This was at the All Saints Episcopal Church in Pasadena, CA.

56. "On Tour with a Choir of Angels: On Wings of Song and Love," *Life* magazine, International Edition, April 8, 1963, 50. World Vision Inc., Central Records, Monrovia, CA.
57. Pierce, *The Korean Orphan Choir*, 24.
58. Richard Rutt, "Thoughts of the Times," *Korea Times*, January 7, 1966. World Vision Inc., Central Records, Monrovia, CA.
59. Pierce, *The Korean Orphan Choir*, 81.
60. "On Tour," 48.
61. "On Tour," 46–47.
62. "Paragons of Piety" is a phrase that Catherine Brekus uses in reference to the hyperspiritualization of women as a result of the ideology of separate spheres. I am suggesting here that an analogous dynamic of marginalizing by way of uplifting is present with South Korean evangelicals. Catherine Brekus, *Pilgrims and Strangers: Female Preaching in America, 1740–1845* (Chapel Hill: University of North Carolina Press, 1998), 245.
63. Oh Chiyŏng, Oral History Interview.
64. Moon Hyangja, Oral History Interview.
65. Moon joined after the choir had made two international tours with Pierce and conductor Chang Soo Chul, and her first international tour was to North America in 1965–66. Though the choir was called the World Vision Korean Orphan Choir until their fourth international tour in 1968–69 and publicized as such, Moon remembers that children besides her also had parents.
66. Yi Hokyun, Oral History Interview.
67. Oh Chiyŏng, Oral History Interview.
68. Oh Chiyŏng, Oral History Interview.
69. Oh Chiyŏng, Oral History Interview.
70. Oh Chiyŏng, Oral History Interview.
71. Three narratives are from Korean children, the most of any of the nations represented.
72. Emphasis mine.
73. Pierce and Haskin, *Orphans of the Orient*, 51.
74. Klein, *Cold War Orientalism*, 152.
75. Klein, *Cold War Orientalism*, 153.
76. Pate, *From Orphan to Adoptee*, 2.
77. Pate, *From Orphan to Adoptee*, 3.
78. Pate, *From Orphan to Adoptee*, 5.
79. Woo, "Imagining Kin," 42.
80. Woo, "Imagining Kin," 38.
81. Woo, "Imagining Kin," 46.
82. Pierce and Haskin, *Orphans of the Orient*, preface. Emphasis mine.
83. Franklin Graham and Jeanette Lockerbie, *Bob Pierce: This One Thing I Do* (Dallas, TX: Word Publishing Group, 1951), 77.
84. The evangelical tradition has been called a "religion of the heart," and as David Hempton articulates, historians have had challenges in identifying the many elusive

elements that gave the rise to the tradition—that is, to get to the "heart" of a religion of the heart. Hempton, *Methodism*, 5. See also Brekus, *Sarah Osborn's World* for further discussion on evangelicalism and the Enlightenment.
85. Todd Brenneman, *Homespun Gospel: The Triumph of Sentimentality in Modern American Evangelicalism* (New York: Oxford University Press, 2013), 17.
86. Brenneman, *Homespun Gospel*, 20.
87. Woo calls this "Cold War sentimentalism." Woo, "Imagining Kin."
88. Richard Gehman, *Let My Heart Be Broken* (New York: McGraw-Hill, 1960).
89. Tim Stafford, "Imperfect Instrument: World Vision's Founder Led a Tragic and Inspiring Life," February 24, 2005. http://www.christianitytoday.com/ct/2005/march/19.56.html.
90. Dunker, *Man of Vision*.
91. Hamilton, "Historical Study of Bob Pierce," 38.
92. Hamilton, "Historical Study of Bob Pierce," 38.
93. *Other Sheep* was a twenty-minute documentary that showed the "physical and spiritual needs of the masses in the Far East." *World Vision Pictorial*. World Vision Inc., Central Records, Monrovia, CA.
94. Bertha Holt, *The Seed from the East* (Los Angeles, CA: Holt International Children's Services, 1956).
95. "Mercy's Child." BGEA Billy Graham Archives, Wheaton, Illinois.
96. Moon, *Sex among Allies*.
97. "Mercy's Child."
98. Pierce and Haskin, *Orphans of the Orient*, 44. Here we see further evidence of what Hillary Kaell terms "racialized universalim" in chapter 4, "Friends and Friendship: Kin-Like Relations and Racialized Universalism." Kaell, *Christian Globalism at Home*, 100–128.
99. Pierce and Haskin, *Orphans of the Orient*, 55.
100. Oh, *Save the Children*.
101. Correspondence of Ted Engstrom to Jim Franks, August 3, 1970. World Vision Inc., Central Records, Monrovia, CA.
102. Correspondence of Ted Engstrom to Jim Franks, August 3, 1970.
103. Correspondence of Ted Engstrom to Jim Franks, August 3, 1970.
104. Correspondence of Ted Engstrom to Jim Franks, August 3, 1970.
105. Correspondence of Ted Engstrom to Jim Franks, August 3, 1970.
106. Oh Chiyŏng, Oral History Interview.
107. Oh Chiyŏng, Oral History Interview.
108. Oh Chiyŏng, Oral History Interview.
109. Pae Kyungha, Oral History Interview. Pae was a member of the choir from 1981 to 1986.
110. Pae Kyungha, Oral History Interview.
111. Pierce, *The Korean Orphan Choir*, 86.
112. Pierce, *The Korean Orphan Choir*, 86–87.
113. King, *God's Internationalists*.

Chapter 4

1. Kim and Kim, *History of Korean Christianity*, 221.
2. Oh Chiyŏng, Oral History Interview.
3. "Korea Crusade—'73 TV Film."
4. Oh Chiyŏng, Oral History Interview.
5. Newspaper coverage following the 1973 Korea Billy Graham crusade noted that Graham "preached to more than three million people altogether—breaking the record total of his 16-week crusade in New York City in 1957, which was 2.1 million. Associate crusades held at the same time by members of the Graham team in other parts of the country drew an additional 1.5 million people." "Billy Graham's Korean Crusade: Million Heard Him Preach," Religious News Service, Seoul, June 5, 1973. "Korea News 1972–1974," Folder 140–146, Box 140, Collection 17, BGEA–Crusade Activities, Archives of the Billy Graham Center, Wheaton, IL.
6. Cho Miyŏng, Oral History Interview.
7. "Korea Crusade—'73 TV Film."
8. "Korea Crusade—'73 TV Film."
9. "Schedule for Billy Graham," Folder 33-13, "Team Personnel and Procedure," Box 33, Collection 345, 1973, Crusade Media. Archives of the Billy Graham Center, Wheaton, IL.
10. Wacker, *America's Pastor*, 31.
11. Wacker, *America's Pastor*, 30. Wacker identifies the 1973 crusade in South Korea as pivotal evidence of Graham's influence as an evangelist: *America's Pastor*, 21, 137.
12. Lee, *Born Again*, 90. In chapter 3, "Evangelicalism Takes Off in South Korea, 1953–1988," Lee discusses the significance of a series of revivals in this period, beginning with Graham's first revivals in Pusan as well as Pierce's revivals during the Korean War (which I discuss in chapter 1).
13. The transnational framework is an appropriate one to employ not only because it fills a gap in the historiography but also because it keys into an idea circulating among late twentieth-century evangelicals in the United States and South Korea to move beyond borders. Wilson, a Presbyterian missionary, defined the term "transnational" as the "secular word" for an "ecclesiastical term" that signified "mission of the whole Church to all men in the entire world." For Wilson, "transnational" was a term that "stresses the ability to bridge two or more nations in your understanding of life." He thought that an "enlarged understanding of a growing world culture" was as old as the ancient scripture in the Gospel of John: "For God so loved the world that he gave his one and only son, that whoever believes in him shall not perish but have eternal life." To "overstress my nation" as a missionary or as a national was to "invert" a central "motif" in the Christian faith, which was to live a "life for others," as indicated in the Johannine gospel. As Wilson noted, South Koreans were also committed to this religious idea. Stanton R. Wilson, "From All the World . . . to All the World (Some Ideas on the Future of Mission)," October 15, 1971. Box 140, Collection 17, 1971–72, Seoul Folder 140–14, Archives of the Billy Graham Center, Wheaton, IL.

14. Graham's evangelist team was composed of seven Black, white, and Indian American male associate evangelists and numerous South Korean male religious elites.
15. With China's first successful test of nuclear weapons in 1964, Nixon focused on engaging the unexpected rise of China.
16. The US policy of detente resulted in a general strategy of decreasing its military presence in Asia. With Nixon's election in 1969, his Guam Doctrine decreased US troops in South Vietnam from 550,000 soldiers in 1968 to 430,000 by 1970. In Park's 1971 New Year's address, he announced South Korea's military disengagement from South Vietnam. Thereafter, Nixon reduced the US presence in South Korea from 64,000 soldiers in 1969 to 40,000 in 1972. In 1971 South Korea and the US developed a Five-Year Military Modernization Plan with an appropriation of $1.5 billion; the assistance was a way to fill the power vacuum generated from the reduction of troops. Tae-Gyun Park, *An Ally and Empire: Two Myths of South Korea–United States Relations, 1945–1980* (Seongnam-si, Gyeonggi-do: Academy of Korean Studies Press, 2012).
17. Park, *Ally and Empire*, 316.
18. Min Yong Lee, "The Vietnam War: South Korea's Search for National Security," in *Park Chung Hee Era: The Transformation of South Korea*, ed. Byong-Kook Kim and Ezra Vogel (Cambridge, MA: Harvard University Press, 2011), 404–405. Lee elaborates: "Park feared that without U.S. support North Korea would rapidly advance ahead of South Korea. Without the U.S. military presence, South Korea risked creating a 'power vacuum' in the demilitarized zone giving a chance for North Korea to attack South Korea. Though not as polemical as the U.S. context, deploying South Korean troops to South Vietnam posed several political, military risks and domestic political opposition, which Park endured for the sake of building a closer alliance with the U.S." (405).
19. Lee, "Vietnam War," 427.
20. Lee, "Vietnam War," 427.
21. Correspondence from Rev. Chang Suk Young to Billy Graham, August 3, 1968. Folder 151, "Korea Communication, 1968–1975," Box 139, Collection 17, BGEA–Crusade Activities, Archives of the Billy Graham Center, Wheaton, IL.
22. Correspondence from Walter H. Smyth to Rev. Chang Suk Young (Association for a United Church of Korea). Folder 151, "Korea Communication, 1968–1975," Box 139, Collection 17, BGEA–Crusade Activities, Archives of the Billy Graham Center, Wheaton, IL.
23. Correspondence from Loretta White (or Mrs. Elbert White, Project Chairman Colorado District Hearts for Jesus Letterhead: The Colorado District of the Lutheran Church–Missouri Synod) to Billy Graham, November 12, 1970. Folder 140–141, "Korea–Gen 1969–1973," Box 140, Collection 17, BGEA–Crusade Activities, Archives of the Billy Graham Center, Wheaton, IL. White directed the "Hearts for Jesus" program in the Colorado District, which included the promotion of foreign missions for all of the Lutheran children in the district. She desired Graham to come to Korea because she reported that the souls and hearts in Ok So Dong were ready to meet Jesus; the church in her suburb was "growing very rapidly—from a handful to

as many as 300 on a Sunday." She concluded that there was a "remarkable response to the Gospel on the part of the people in OkSooDong. This is a very poor community."
24. Correspondence from Loretta White to Billy Graham, November 12, 1970.
25. Correspondence from Mr. Soon Kim to Billy Graham, November 22, 1970. Folder 140–141 "Korea–Gen 1969–1973," Box 140, Collection 17, BGEA–Crusade Activities, Archives of the Billy Graham Center, Wheaton, IL. Mr. Soon Kim listened to Graham's message on the twentieth anniversary of the beginning of Graham's ministry.
26. Correspondence from Rev. Ihn Kahk Park (Chairman of Asian Christian Layman Association and "Holy Light Society") to Walter Smyth, September 11, 1970. Folder 151, "Korea Communication," Box 139, Collection 17, BGEA–Crusade Activities, Archives of the Billy Graham Center, Wheaton, IL.
27. Wacker, *America's Pastor*, 24.
28. Correspondence from Rev. Kyung Chik Han to Billy Graham, November 20, 1970. Folder 152, "Korea Team," Box 139, Collection 17, BGEA–Crusade Activities, Archives of the Billy Graham Center, Wheaton, IL.
29. "New Neighbors: A Korea Report, February 1973" (hereafter cited as "New Neighbors"). Archives of the Billy Graham Center, Wheaton, IL.
30. Correspondence from Walter Smyth to H. Cloyes Starnes, December 10, 1970. Folder 151, "Korea Communications," Box 139, Collection 17, BGEA–Crusade Activities, Archives of the Billy Graham Center, Wheaton, IL. See also correspondence from H. Cloyes Starnes to Walter Smyth, November 28, 1970. Folder 151, "Korea Communications," Box 139, Collection 17, BGEA–Crusade Activities, Archives of the Billy Graham Center, Wheaton, IL.
31. This report is written anonymously from a "representative in Korea's Report," but most likely it is written by Stanton Wilson, a Presbyterian missionary. Henry Holley circulated the original copy to J. W. White, and two copies went to Walter Smyth, also known as "WHS." "Representative in Korea's Report: New Network of Neighbors," February 1, 1973. Emphasis his. Archives of the Billy Graham Center, Wheaton, IL.
32. Park, *Korean Protestantism and Politics*, 182.
33. "New Neighbors," 5.
34. Kim and Vogel, *Park Chung Hee Era*, 1. As Kim notes, Park's regime remains one of the most "controversial topics for the Korean public, politicians, and scholars both home and abroad." Park is credited for orchestrating the economic "miracle on the Han" at the same time that he committed egregious human rights violations in ruling South Korea as a military dictatorship.
35. Scholars have suggested three phases of Park's rule, from a military government to "democratic interlude" and ultimately to formal authoritarian rule with the amendment of the Yusin Constitution from 1972 to 1979. See Paul Chang, *Protest Dialectics: State Repression and South Korea's Democracy Movement, 1970–79* (Stanford, CA: Stanford University Press, 2015) 3–5; see also Byeong-cheon Lee, *Developmental Dictatorship and the Park Chung Hee Era: The Shaping of Modernity in the Republic of Korea* (Paramus: Homa & Sekey Books, 2006); Myung-sik Lee,

The History of the Democratization Movement in Korea (Seoul: Korea Democracy Foundation, 2010).

36. President Park believed that South Korean military investment in the Vietnam War would provide US support for his domestic politics, which was deemed to be at risk under the Nixon administration's Cold War policy of detente. Min Yong Lee writes that Park desired to "make himself an indispensable strategic ally of the United States in its cold war campaigns, with an eye to discouraging U.S. political forces in an anti-Park transnational coalition." Lee summarizes Park's domestic political aims: "By accommodating the United States' vital security interests, Park thought he could secure U.S. endorsement of his rule and prevent domestic political critics and opponents from building a broad anti-Park coalition with U.S. support." Park's primary geopolitical goal of deploying South Korean troops to South Vietnam was not only to strengthen the US Cold War alliance, but also to protect his domestic politics, which the US largely ignored under Johnson but seemed to make Park vulnerable under the Nixon administration's policy of disengagement. Though it was primarily under Carter's administration in 1976 that Park's domestic politics would come under attack from the United States, the Nixon administration's political disengagement in South Korea did influence Park's domestic politics. Lee, "Vietnam War," 404–40.
37. "New Neighbors," 5.
38. Paul Chang notes that though the 1970s were seemingly a "dark age of democracy," students, Christians, lawyers, and journalists actively responded to state repression with protest in dialectical tension with the state, carrying the torch of democracy in a dark hour; for the specific contributions of Korean Christians, see Chang, *Protest Dialectics*, 79–111.
39. Chang, *Protest Dialectics*, 102.
40. Ogle was trained for an Urban Industrial Mission (UIM) through courses at McCormick Theological Seminary and the University of Chicago. He simultaneously served at the West Side Christian Parish in Chicago (1957–1959), a congregation that was founded on the global spirituality of the worker-priests and primarily served African Americans and Latinos. In the year that Park Chung-hee came to power by coup d'état, the Methodist missionary George Ogle arrived in Inchon, Korea, to begin a chapter of the UIM. The UIM was highly influenced by the French worker-priest movement (1944–1954). "To make the Church spring up in the midst of the proletarian masses," began their mission statement, "taking them with their own attitude of mind, their own way of life and their own organisations." The pope held a tenuous position regarding the ministry and eventually denounced it for its apparently communist connections. While the worker-priest movement largely came to an end in 1954, the spirit of the movement continued through worker-centered ministries, namely the UIM, an ecumenical ministry sponsored by the World Council of Churches, which emerged as a ministry among workers in rapidly industrializing nations in the second half of the twentieth century.
41. Cho Wha Soon, *Let the Weak Be Strong: A Woman's Struggle for Justice* (Oak Park, IL: Meyer Stone, 1988), 89.

42. George Ogle, "Our Hearts Cry with You," in *More Than Witnesses: How a Small Group of Missionaries Aided Korea's Democratic Revolution*, ed. Jim Stentzel (Mequon, WI: Nightingale Press, 2008), 99.
43. Chang, *Protest Dialectics*, 6. In response to Pak's arrest, a group of concerned Christians wrote "1973 Theological Declaration of Korean Christians," which was "an important precedence to Minjung Theology in that it was the first attempt to publicize Christian protest theologically or specifically as a Christian duty." Park's regime actively scrutinized this dissident group of Korean Christians, who later developed a Korean liberation theology called *minjung* theology that argued for Christianity as a religion in service of the oppressed.
44. "Korea Crusade—'73 TV Film." Billy Kim noted: "We need somewhere large enough to conduct a crusade for somewhere that would seat hundreds of thousands. Yoido Plaza used to be a little island right in the midst of the Han River. Plaza was nothing but an old airstrip. Government renovated, and they made a big tar asphalt to have any type of military exercise, military parade, and I believe they didn't realize when they built that plaza that the Billy Graham crusade would do a crusade in that great big plaza."
45. Dana Robert, "The Great Commission in an Age of Globalization," in Orlando E. Costas et al., *Antioch Agenda: Essays on the Restorative Church in Honor of Orlando E. Costas* (New Delhi: Indian Society for the Promotion of Christian Knowledge for Andover Newton Theological School, and the Boston Theological Institute, 2007), 8.
46. Robert, *Christian Mission*, 193.
47. Mayra Rivera Rivera, *The Touch of Transcendence: A Postcolonial Theology of God* (Louisville, KY: Westminster John Knox Press, 2007), 1, 5. See also Joel Robbins, "The Globalization of Pentecostal and Charismatic Christianity," *Annual Review of Anthropology* 33 (2004): 127–130. Robbins discusses the importance of a dualistic Satan-God worldview on which Pentecostals' worldview depends.
48. Robert, *Christian Mission*, 84–95, 193; Robert, "Great Commission," 8.
49. "'Spree'73' Evangelism Gets Severe Criticism," San Juan, *Puerto Rico Star*, August 11, 1973. Archives of the Billy Graham Center, Wheaton, IL.
50. "Billy Graham Irks Black Christians," *Japan Times*, Tokyo, July 20, 1973. Archives of the Billy Graham Center, Wheaton, IL.
51. Kim, *Life of Billy Kim*, 77.
52. Kim Jang Hwan (Billy Kim), Oral History Interview.
53. Kim, *Life of Billy Kim*, 77.
54. "1973 Crusade Media," CN 345, Box 33, Folder 33–37, "Miscellaneous—Korea 1973." Archives of the Billy Graham Center, Wheaton, IL.
55. Among Holley's thank-you letters to the executive committee of the crusade, he sent out a note expressing his "heartfelt appreciation for the privilege" of working with each individual in preparation for the crusade. He expressed that their "cooperation, love, and prayerful support" in executing the revivals were "truly a rich blessing," and he thanked God for the "privilege of co-laboring" with them. He assured them of their prayers for the "follow-up of the many thousands who registered a commitment to Jesus Christ." This letter was sent out to leaders of denominations, parachurches,

military chaplains, the US ambassador, seminaries, military and UN officials, and the head of the Seoul police. A broad swath of Korean society had to cooperate to organize the crusade. Archives of the Billy Graham Center, Wheaton, IL.
56. "1973 Crusade Media." Chang's work shows that in 1973 students were the largest group of protesters.
57. His ideas here echo ideas of Asians in the United States as "model minorities." For a history of the rise of the model minority, see Wu, *The Color of Success*.
58. Anti–Vietnam War protests exploded as Americans learned in the spring of 1970 that Nixon had widened the Vietnam War into Cambodia. See Kruse's discussion of antiwar protests and Graham's connection to Nixon in helping to quell protests. Kruse, *One Nation under God*, 257–263.
59. Han, *Kyung-Chik Han Collection*.
60. "Christian Herald," May 19, 1973. Archives of the Billy Graham Center, Wheaton, IL.
61. "Christian Heritage," June 1973 Africa, "Graham in South Africa." Archives of the Billy Graham Center, Wheaton, IL.
62. Wacker, *America's Pastor*, 130. Wacker observes: "If the 1950s represented two steps forward and the 1960s one step back for Graham's relationship to the civil rights movement, the 1970s and 1980s represented two steps forward. Graham declared that "Christ was neither black nor white but the Savior for all people."
63. Evans, "White Evangelical Protestant Responses."
64. Evans, "White Evangelical Protestant Responses," 249.
65. Wacker, *America's Pastor*, 130.
66. Dupont, *Mississippi Praying*. Dupont argues that "the conservative faith" of her subjects led adherents "inevitably to conservative politics." Dupont acknowledges that "all conservative biblical interpretations do not necessarily dictate right-of-center politics." However, "The specific kind of conservative religion that arose in the racially stratified society of the Jim Crow era did demand these affinities" (11). I suggest here that conservative evangelical faith paired with a conservative politics shored up an authoritarian military regime in South Korea and linked South Koreans to a politics of social change through individual conversions.
67. Wacker, *America's Pastor*, 130. In 1982 Graham was reported to have undergone three conversions—to Christ, to racial justice, and to nuclear disarmament. It was in the 1980s that Graham first publicly declared racism to be a sin.
68. Evans, "White Evangelical Protestant Responses," 250. Michael Emerson and Christian Smith's sociological work shows that contemporary white evangelicals attribute racial problems to prejudiced individuals and personal relationships, not structures of oppression, allowing them to ignore or obfuscate the systems of racialization in the United States. Evans, in particular, notes their observation that "because of the close 'historical and present-day connection between faith and the American way of life,' racial inequality profoundly challenges white evangelical Protestants' 'world understanding' and their 'faith in God and America.'" Here I am suggesting that these linkages between an individualistic evangelical theology and social change in the United States can be extended abroad in South Korea as well, bolstering faith in God and America in foreign nations. Michael O. Emerson and

Christian Smith, *Divided by Faith: Evangelical Religion and the Problem of Race in America* (New York: Oxford University Press, 2000).

69. Billy Graham and Billy Kim preached a series of sermons with passages from the New Testament, and each day of the five days had a theme, including "North Korea Night" and "Military Night." The sermons each day were entitled "The Inescapable Christ," "The Blind Man," "The Prodigal Son," "Rich Young Ruler," and "The Love of God," respectively. Nearly all of the images that Graham and Kim used to illustrate the gospel used men—the blind man, the prodigal son, the rich young ruler—as central characters, establishing a masculine tone.

70. The BGEA and a South Korea–based executive committee, with Han at the helm, organized over two weeks of revival in South Korea from May 16 to June 3, 1973. In the days leading up to Graham's preaching, the multiracial team of BGEA associate evangelists, including Cliff Barrows, Grady Wilson, Howard O. Jones, and Akbar Abdul Haqq, preached in major cities outside of Seoul, such as Pusan and Taejon. Each associate evangelist partnered with a Korean translator and a choir director to preach his own crusades, at which a total of 1.5 million people gathered; the Korean translators were very carefully chosen, with some Korean Americans even applying from the United States to do the work. Akbar Abdul Haqq held revivals in Taejon, May 16–23, 1973; John Wesley White held revivals in Taegu, May 18–25; Ralph Bell held revivals in Kwangju, May 20–27, 1973; Grady Wilson held revivals in Pusan, May 20–27; Cliff Barrows held revivals in Chunchon, May 20–27, 1973; Howard O. Jones held revivals in Chonju, May 20–27, 1973; and Billy Graham held revivals in Seoul, May 30–June 30, 1973. Additionally, Akbar Haqq, John White, and T. W. Wilson held citywide rallies respectively in Chejudo, Suwon, and Inchon. Haqq was the only Indian evangelist; Bell and Jones were the only two African American evangelists, with Jones being the first African American evangelist to join the BGEA; Wilson, Barrows, Graham, and White were the white American evangelists, with the first three being the original evangelists of the BGEA. Each associate evangelist also had a soloist / choir director and accompanist.

71. Graham's 1957 crusade had set a Madison Square Garden record in total attendees, and the Rio de Janeiro crusade drew over two hundred thousand in one sitting, but the 1973 Korea Crusade trumped prior—and future—crusades in sheer numbers.

72. "Korea Crusade—'73 TV Film."

73. Audio 2158, Collection 26. Archives of the Billy Graham Center, Wheaton, IL.

74. "Korea Crusade—'73 TV Film."

75. In addition to the North Korean refugee Kyung Chik Han, Joon Gon Kim and Rev. Billy Jang Hwan Kim were central organizers. As discussed in chapter 2, Joon Gon Kim and Billy Kim had life-changing religious experiences during the war. After Korean communists killed Joon Gon Kim's family, he immigrated to Pasadena, California, to study at Fuller Theological Seminary, where he met Bill Bright and launched Campus Crusade's first international chapter in Korea. As a result of the war, Joon Gon (nicknamed Billy) Kim, who had served as a US military houseboy, immigrated to the US to study at Bob Jones University and then worked as the primary translator at the 1973 Korea Billy Graham crusade. Moreover, as discussed in

chapter 3, the Korean Children's Choir, which began as the World Vision Korean Orphan Choir shortly after the war, served as a special guest for the crusade. Kyung Chik Han, Joon Gon Kim, Billy Jang Hwan Kim, and the Korean Children's Choir—all central to the organization of the 1973 Korea Billy Graham crusade—could not forget the indelible mark that the war had left on their lives.

76. "Korea Crusade—'73 TV Film."
77. Graham, *I Saw Your Sons*, 20.
78. Please see chapter 3.
79. Collection 26, Audio 2158. Archives of the Billy Graham Center, Wheaton, IL.
80. Collection 26, Audio 2158. Archives of the Billy Graham Center, Wheaton, IL.
81. As discussed in chapter 1, Han and Pierce founded World Vision in the midst of the war. They then created the World Vision Korean Orphan Choir in 1957. The first international partnership that Bright created for Campus Crusade for Christ was with Joon Gon Kim who lost his family at the hands of communists during the war.
82. "The Love of God." Binder "Seoul, Korea May 30–June 3, 1973," Box 59, Collection 265, Archives of the Billy Graham Center, Wheaton, IL.
83. Stanton Wilson, "Korea and Christianity," by Stanton R. Wilson Rep in Korea, United Presbyterian Church in the U.S.A. Archives of the Billy Graham Center, Wheaton, IL.
84. As discussed in chapter 2, Billy Kim grew up in the poor Korean countryside, and during the war, worked as a houseboy for US soldiers, running errands and providing entertainment. It was there that he earned his nickname "Billy."
85. In his autobiography, *The Life of Billy Kim*, Kim featured the photo of the 1973 crusade, highlighting the crusade as the pinnacle of his transition from a military houseboy to a world evangelist.
86. As will be discussed later, Billy Kim first framed his partnership with Graham as a "side by side" partnership.
87. As discussed, the Nixon-Park era (1969–1974) of US–South Korean diplomatic relations was one of the more tense periods.
88. This is a reference to Lamin Sanneh's work *Translating the Message*, which argues that indigenous translation of the Bible actually helped non-Westerners to take ownership of the universal message of Christianity. Also, thanks go to Professor Albert Raboteau for his insight on a seminar paper on this section of the chapter, suggesting that both an appeal to the particularity and universality of Christianity was needed for the revival message to take root among the people. Sanneh, *Translating the Message*. Much of the biographical information that follows is discussed at length in chapter 2, but I briefly mention some of the similarities here by way of review.
89. Jang Hwan (Billy) Kim biographical details: Kim, "Education and Cultivation," 83. He was also ordained as a Baptist minister and married classmate Gertrude Stephens (Trudy) before returning together to South Korea in 1959.
90. As discussed in chapter 2, Powers was not himself a Christian, but once Kim converted to Christianity during his time at Bob Jones, he brought Powers into the Christian fold. Kim was productive in his eight years in the United States, graduating with his bachelor's in biblical studies and master's in theology from Bob Jones.
91. Kim, *Life of Billy Kim*, 74.

92. Kim, *Life of Billy Kim*, 74.
93. Kim, *Life of Billy Kim*, 75.
94. Billy Kim, 1974, 6, BGEA Oral History Project, Collection 141, Folder 4-48, Billy Graham Center Archives, Wheaton, IL.
95. "Korea Crusade—'73 TV Film."
96. Correspondence from Bob Jones III to Billy Kim, June 22, 1973. Folder 25–27, Korea Contacts/Communication 1972–74, Box 140, Collection 17, BGEA–Crusade Activities. Archives of the Billy Graham Center, Wheaton, IL.
97. Kim, *Life of Billy Kim*, 77.
98. Kim, *Life of Billy Kim*, 79.
99. Dochuk, *Bible Belt to Sunbelt*, 274.
100. Dochuk, *Bible Belt to Sunbelt*, 279.
101. "Billy Graham South African Crusade," 1973. Online access: https://www.youtube.com/watch?v=HTHxivBCahA. Accessed December 25, 2015.
102. "1973 Pastor Billy Graham and Pastor Kim Jang Hwan, Yoido." Video clip of Billy Graham Crusade in Yoido, South Korea, June 3, 1973. Online access: http://www.youtube.com/watch?v=uFCPTPx5380. Accessed May 1, 2013.
103. Howard O. Jones, *White Questions to a Black Christian* (Grand Rapids, MI: Zondervan Publishing, 1975).
104. Jones, *White Questions*, 13.
105. Kim, *Life of Billy Kim*, 25.
106. Kim, *Life of Billy Kim*, 75.
107. Nicholas Harkness, "Transducing a Sermon, Inducing Conversion: Billy Graham, Billy Kim, and the 1973 Crusade in Seoul," *Representations* 137 (2017): 138. See also Nicholas Harkness, *Glossolalia and the Problem of Language* (Chicago: University of Chicago Press, 2021), 89–121.
108. Kim Jang Hwan (Billy Kim), Oral History Interview.
109. Cho Miyŏng, Oral History Interview.
110. Kim, *Life of Billy Kim*, 80.
111. Billy Kim, BGEA Oral History Project, Collection 141, Folder 4–48. 1974, 7, Billy Graham Center Archives, Wheaton, IL.
112. Billy Jang Hwan Kim, Oral History Interview.
113. "Attendance Records Broken in Korea," June 4, 1973. Collection 544, Box 65, Folder 5, Korea 1973, Archives of the Billy Graham Center, Wheaton, IL.
114. Kim Jang Hwan (Billy Kim), Oral History Interview.
115. Oh Chiyŏng, Oral History Interview.
116. Oh Chiyŏng, Oral History Interview.
117. Oh Chiyŏng, Oral History Interview.
118. Oh Chiyŏng, Oral History Interview. Today, Oh Chiyŏng is an evangelist at a local church as well as a small business owner. With more support for women in ministry, it is possible that she could have become a preacher on the level of the Korean Protestant patriarchs in this book.
119. Paul Yonggi Cho, 1983, 8. BGEA Oral History Project, Collection 141, OH 518, Folder 23-15, Billy Graham Center Archive, Wheaton, IL. Note that Cho's English name is now "David," not Paul.

Chapter 5

1. "Explo '74 Spurs Koreans to Evangelize Their Country," *Texas Methodist*, Dallas, September 19, 1974. In all, 3,400 people from eighty-four other countries and 320,000 Koreans attended the training sessions. The daily attendance for training sessions and evening services averaged 1,090,000 people, and the total attendance for the entire event was 6,550,000 people. An estimated 200,000 participants took their evangelistic training to the streets of Seoul and garnered 272,000 new believers. Lee, *Born Again*, 97.
2. Joon Gon Kim, Explo '72 Speech, Campus Crusade for Christ, Inc. Campus Crusade for Christ International Archives, Orlando, FL.
3. Kim, Explo '72 Speech.
4. Becker, *Fireseeds*, 131. In another account by Nils Becker, he suggests that Bright did know that Joon Gon Kim was going to declare an Explo '74 but that he did not know that Joon Gon Kim would declare a number.
5. "Bailey Marks—Tribute to Dr. Joon Gon Kim," October 3, 2010. The Legacy Project–Campus Crusade for Christ. http://www.youtube.com/watch?v=5yFzRgpjhg4&feature=related. Accessed October 8, 2011. In September 1968 Bailey Marks was appointed director of affairs of the Asia-South Pacific area and served until Joon Gon Kim replaced him, effective 1981.
6. Oh Chint'ak, Oral History Interview
7. Richardson, *Amazing Faith*, 158.
8. Kim, Explo '72 Speech.
9. Turner, *Bill Bright*, 139.
10. Joon Gon Kim, "Stage Set for Awakening." Campus Crusade for Christ, Inc. Campus Crusade for Christ International Archives, Orlando, FL.
11. Lee, *Born Again*, 107.
12. See John Turner's and Darren Dochuk's discussions about Explo '72. See chapter 6, "The Evangelical Bicentennial," in Turner, *Bill Bright*, and chapter 11, "Jesus People," in Dochuk, *Bible Belt to Sunbelt*.
13. To that end, this chapter transnationally extends John Turner's and Nami Kim's analyses, arguing that evangelistic activities were crucial for the rise of conservative Christian politics in both nations. Turner's analysis of Campus Crusade in the United States emphasizes the evangelical conservative activism at Explo '72, which anticipated the rise of the US Christian Right, whereas Nami Kim's analysis focuses on Joon Gon Kim's role in the rise of the Korean Protestant Right in the 1980s/1990s.
14. Judy Douglass, Oral History Interview. See also a discussion about the organization of Explo '72 in Turner, *Bill Bright*, 141.
15. Judy Douglass, Oral History Interview.
16. Oh Chint'ak, Oral History Interview.
17. Turner, *Bill Bright*, 140. There were about eighty-five thousand attendees, far more high school students than the desired college students, and it attracted a more diverse crowd than many evangelical gatherings.
18. Turner, *Bill Bright*, 145.

19. Ed Neibling, Oral History Interview.
20. In 1964, Josh McDowell became a traveling representative for Campus Crusade. McDowell is a Christian apologist and popular evangelical author known for his numerous books, especially *Evidence That Demands a Verdict* (San Bernardino, CA: Here's Life Publishers, 1972) and *More Than a Carpenter* (Wheaton, IL: Tyndale House, 1977).
21. Ed Neibling, Oral History Interview.
22. Ed Neibling, Oral History Interview.
23. Kim, Explo '72 Speech.
24. Kim, Explo '72 Speech.
25. Gertrude Phillips, Oral History Interview.
26. Judy Douglass, Oral History Interview.
27. Gertrude Phillips, Oral History Interview.
28. Gertrude Phillips, Oral History Interview.
29. Notes from conversation with Bailey Marks at Campus Crusade Headquarters, Orlando, Florida, July 2013.
30. "Bailey Marks—Tribute to Dr. Joon Gon Kim."
31. Oh Chint'ak, Oral History Interview.
32. Kim, "Stage Set for Awakening," Campus Crusade for Christ, Inc. Campus Crusade for Christ International Archive, Orlando, FL. Also, in preparation for the main activities, a series of preparatory activities were organized. There were weeklong regional activities outside of Seoul, and Yonggi Cho, the pastor of the Yoido Full Gospel Church, preached. The night before the main event, one hundred thousand women from 15,500 churches stayed up until 4:00 a.m. to pray for the event. On the day of the main event, August 13, people gathered in tents to attend classes, and during the evening services Bright, Kyung Chik Han, Joon Gon Kim, and other conservative religious leaders preached.
33. "World Christian Leaders Lay a Fuse for Evangelism Explosion," *Sentinel*, Waterville, Maine, June 15, 1974; George W. Cornell, "Fuse for Explosion in Evangelism Laid," *Morning Advocate*, Baton Rouge, LA, June 15, 1974.
34. Louise Moore, "Evangelical Christians Focus on South Korea," *Houston Chronicle*, August 3, 1973.
35. Turner, *Bill Bright*, 282. Campus Crusade's emergence as a major foreign missions entity reflected broader trends in foreign missions. Evangelical and fundamentalist organizations accounted for more that 90 percent of North American foreign missions, with the decline of the mainline Protestant contributions.
36. Turner, *Bill Bright*, 282.
37. Judy Douglass, Oral History Interview.
38. Jerry Sharpless, Oral History Interview.
39. Jerry Sharpless, Oral History Interview.
40. Jerry Sharpless, Oral History Interview.
41. Gertrude Phillips, Oral History Interview.
42. Gertrude Phillips, Oral History Interview.
43. Jerry Sharpless, Oral History Interview.

44. Jerry Sharpless, Oral History Interview.
45. Judy Douglass, Oral History Interview.
46. Ronald Yates, "For Explo 74: 800,000 Korean Christians Gather," *Chicago Tribune*, August 19, 1974.
47. Kim, "Stage Set for Awakening."
48. Kim, "Stage Set for Awakening."
49. Kim, "Stage Set for Awakening." Joon Gon Kim went on to equate the revival of Korea with the Protestant Reformation: "Until the Reformation led by Martin Luther, salvation by faith was a truth hidden to the average layman. Likewise, I believe that the clear understanding of the ministry of the Holy Spirit, whose presence and power we appropriate by faith, has been a hidden truth to most Christians." He remarked that at Explo '74 Christians "responded to the challenge to allow the Holy Spirit to control and empower their lives by faith, thus setting the stage for a powerful spiritual awakening that can truly transform our nation and world." He believed that this would be the way that the Great Commission would be fulfilled in his generation. He ended with a vision for the world, not just for Korea: "God wants to do in every heart in every nation around the world which He came to seek and to save."
50. The student movement began to dwindle as US troops were reduced and the communists finally triumphed in Saigon in 1975.
51. Mitchell K. Hall, ed., *Vietnam War Era: People and Perspectives* (Santa Barbara, CA: ABC-CLIO, 2009), 199.
52. William Wei, *The Asian American Movement* (Philadelphia: Temple University Press, 1993), 206.
53. Docuk, *Bible Belt to Sunbelt*, 348–349.
54. Turner, *Bill Bright*, 186.
55. Dochuk, *Bible Belt to Sunbelt*, 347–349.
56. Turner, *Bill Bright*, 123.
57. Dochuk, *Bible Belt to Sunbelt*, 349–350.
58. Turner, *Bill Bright*, 123.
59. Turner, *Bill Bright*, 144.
60. Turner, *Bill Bright*, 142.
61. Turner, *Bill Bright*, 121.
62. Turner, *Bill Bright*, 144.
63. Yoo, *New Spiritual Homes*, 9.
64. Kang, "Evangelical Movement as Revealed," 8. Korea Campus Crusade for Christ Headquarters, Seoul, Korea (translation mine).
65. Chang, *Protest Dialectics*, 55.
66. Chang, *Protest Dialectics*, 62.
67. The People's Revolution Party (PRP) started in 1964 when thirteen individuals were accused of being communists. Chang, *Protest Dialectics*, 74–75.
68. Chang, *Protest Dialectics*, 76.
69. Chang, *Protest Dialectics*, 77.
70. Lee, *Born Again*, 99.
71. Turner, *Bill Bright*, 142.

72. Turner, *Bill Bright*, 142.
73. Inboden, *Religion and American Foreign Policy*, 57.
74. Turner, *Bill Bright*, 190.
75. Paul Chang and Byung-Soo Kim, "Differential Impact of Repression on Social Movements: Christian Organizations and Liberation Theology in South Korea (1972–1979)," *Sociological Inquiry* 77.3 (2007): 326–355.
76. Quebedeaux, *I Found It!*, 191.
77. Quebedeaux, *I Found It!*, 187. *Sojourners'* exposé in April 1976, written by Jim Wallis, used evidence to detail Bright's right-wing associations from the 1950s to the 1970s that appear politically conservative and anticommunist.
78. Dochuk, *Bible Belt to Sunbelt*, 208.
79. Kim, *Gendered Politics*, 8.
80. This is an evangelistic strategy that has appeared in other nations. Freston writes: "Much evangelical politics has shown a calculated caution based on the desire to maximize benefits. We have called this 'corporatism,' because its raison d'être is to strengthen the churches as corporations, to equip them better for their activities, to reward some of their members individually (in terms of employment, financing or prestige) and to strengthen their position vis-à-vis other faiths in the country's 'civil religion.' This basic concern produces a tendency to time-serving and opportunism (since one has to be on the right side of the powers-that-be if concrete results are to ensue), and sometimes even to corruption. . . . It leads to a concern with . . . religious freedom in particular rather than with democracy and human rights in general." Freston, *Evangelicals and Politics*, 294.
81. Kennedy, "Soul Searching in Seoul: Spiritual Explosion." *Mainichi Daily News*, August 24, 1974.
82. Kennedy, "Soul Searching in Seoul."
83. Marks, *Awakening*, 21.
84. Kennedy, "Soul Searching in Seoul."
85. Jerry Sharpless, Oral History Interview.
86. Ed Neibling, Oral History Interview.
87. Ed Neibling, Oral History Interview.
88. Lee, *Born Again*, 97–98. Campus Crusade was a relatively unfamiliar organization to many church leaders who were deeply affiliated with their denominations, namely Presbyterian and Methodist congregations. The most fundamentalist Christians deplored the way that the revival would indiscriminately bring together conservatives and liberals who they feared endorsed communism.
89. Lee, *Born Again*, 97–98.
90. Yates, "For Explo'74."
91. Bright to Joon Gon Kim Correspondence, February 3, 1976. Campus Crusade for Christ, Inc. Campus Crusade for Christ International Archive, Orlando, FL.
92. "Explo '74 Spurs Koreans to Evangelize their Country," September 19, 1974, *Texas Methodist*, Dallas.

93. Bill Bright correspondence with Park Chung Hee, President of the Republic of Korea, September 16, 1974. Korea Campus Crusade for Christ Headquarters. Seoul.
94. Ogle, "Our Hearts Cry with You," 87.
95. Ogle, "Our Hearts Cry With You," 99.
96. Chang, *Protest Dialectics*, 106.
97. See note 4.
98. He was promoted along with Thomas Abraham of India in 1980, to take effect in 1981. Bright says that this transition of leadership had to do with their commitment to indigenous leadership: "I told him that a part of his job description was to work himself out of a job. This is because, in accordance with our indigenous philosophy, an Asian should ultimately be the Director of Affairs for Asia." Marks, *Awakening in Asia*, 20. In 1976, Crusade brought "Here's Life, America" to about 150 cities. Joon Gon Kim was in the midst of planning "Here's Life, Korea" when he was approached by the organizing committee for the World Evangelization Crusade.
99. These media slogans began with Campus Crusade for Christ's "Here's Life, America" campaign in 1975, which was meant to help achieve Bill Bright's vision to evangelize the entire United States by 1976. "Here's Life, World" was a campaign that was meant to be exported outside of the United States to over one hundred countries by the end of 1977.
100. Lee, *Born Again*, 108–109. The last massive evangelistic crusade to take place was the 1988 World Evangelization Crusade, with the Seoul Olympics held in 1988 as the impetus for such a large gathering. The 1988 revival's key characteristic was the rhetoric of Korea as a chosen nation, and therefore, the deliverer of the gospel to the world.
101. Joon Gon Kim also reported his statistics to Bright. Joon Gon Kim to Bright Correspondence, August 22, 1980. Campus Crusade for Christ, Inc. Campus Crusade for Christ International Archives, Orlando, FL.
102. Lee, *Born Again*, 106.
103. Lee, *Born Again*, 107.
104. Lee, *Born Again*, 112.
105. Lee, *Born Again*, 181.
106. Bill Bright, "Report on My Recent Ministry in Korea and China: Two of the Most Important Weeks of My Life and Of Ministry of Campus Crusade for Christ." Campus Crusade for Christ, Inc. Campus Crusade for Christ International Archives, Orlando, FL.
107. Bright, "My Recent Ministry."
108. Bright, "My Recent Ministry." One might surmise that Bright's Calvinistic theology of the Holy Spirit may have helped him to deal with any difficult feelings that the Korean nation was "special" by suggesting that it was all the Holy Spirit's doing.
109. Oh Chint'ak, Oral History Interview.
110. Oh Chint'ak, Oral History Interview.
111. Oh Chint'ak, Oral History Interview.
112. Oh Chint'ak, Oral History Interview.

Chapter 6

1. By the 1980s, approximately thirty thousand Koreans were admitted into the United States per year; Kim to Bright Correspondence, July 18, 1981, Re: June trip in the United States Ministering in Korean Churches. Campus Crusade for Christ, Inc. Campus Crusade for Christ International Archive, Orlando, FL.
2. Deacons went through the Leadership Training Institutes and pastors underwent four-hour training seminars.
3. Kim to Bright Correspondence, July 18, 1981.
4. Kim to Bright Correspondence, July 18, 1981.
5. Bright to Kim Correspondence, September 8, 1981. Campus Crusade for Christ, Inc. Campus Crusade for Christ International Archive, Orlando, FL. Kim ended his letter to Bright echoing a sentiment that the East was the spiritual solution for the secularizing West: "During the next ten years we want to send 100,000 missionaries to Europe, the U.S. and other countries as God opens the doors for our missionaries."
6. Turner, *Bill Bright*, 218. Marla Frederick also provides a detailed account of Black dynamics in an anonymous parachurch organization called "Discipleship Ministries," which provides useful insights into the racial dynamics in evangelical parachurch organizations. See McGlathery and Griffin, "Becoming Conservative, Becoming White," 200.
7. In 1982, Yong Won Kang officially established "KCCC in America" as a nonprofit in the New York metropolitan area, foreseeing a growing ethnic ministry. "Korean Campus Crusade for Christ Los Angeles," accessed October 15, 2011. http://www.kcccla.com/aboutus/ccc.asp. In the 1990s Campus Crusade began to create ethnic specific ministries, for instance, Impact Movement (African Americans), Destino Movement (Latino Americans), and Epic Movement (Asian Americans). See "Impact Movement." Accessed October 10, 2021. https://www.cru.org/us/en/communities/ministries/the-impact-movement.html ; See "Destino Movement" Accessed October 10, 2021. https://www.cru.org/us/en/communities/campus/about-destino.html; "Epic Movement." Accessed November 1, 2011. https://www.cru.org/epicmovement/our-history/
8. Tim Funk, "In Prayer, Franklin Graham Sees Rain at Inauguration as Good Omen for Trump," *Charlotte Observer* January 20, 2017. http://www.charlotteobserver.com/living/religion/article127687134.html.
9. See news coverage on 2016 and 2020 white evangelical vote: "2020 Faith Vote Reflects 2016 Patterns," *NPR* November 8, 2020. https://www.npr.org/transcripts/932263516; Yonat Shimron, "Exit Polls Show Few Changes in the Religious Vote," *Religion News Service* November 5, 2020. https://religionnews.com/2020/11/05/exit-polls-show-few-changes-in-the-religious-vote/
10. Note, however, that there are significant shifts that have also occurred, especially with World Vision, which is a much more ecumenical organization today than it was in the early days of the Cold War. See David King's history of World Vision. This is also why Gary Vanderpol is eager to use World Vision as an example of the social ministry of American evangelicalism. But as I have noted in this book, the early history of World

Vision was critical in shaping American evangelicalism, and it began as a movement with roots in American fundamentalism.

11. Joel Baden, "Franklin Graham Says Immigration Is 'Not a Bible Issue.' Here's What the Bible Says," *Washington Post*, February 10, 2017. https://www.washingtonpost.com/news/acts-of-faith/wp/2017/02/10/franklin-graham-said-immigration-is-not-a-bible-issue-heres-what-the-bible-says/?utm_term=.1e32461cecf7.
12. Erika Lee's history of Chinese immigration is especially helpful in showing the history of exclusion on which American nation-building has depended; she makes connections to the contemporary moment in her conclusion. Lee, *At America's Gates*.
13. Rob Moll, "Missions Incredible," *Christianity Today*, March 1, 2006. https://www.christianitytoday.com/ct/2006/march/16.28.html.
14. Ben Torrey, "The Mission to North Korea," *International Bulletin of Missionary Research* 32.1 (January 2008): 20–22.
15. Kim, *Gendered Politics*.
16. Ju Hui Judy Han, "Shifting Geographies of Proximity," in *Ethnographies of U.S. Empire*, ed. Carole McGranahan and John F. Collins (Durham, NC: Duke University Press, 2018), 205–207.
17. Chen, *Asia as Method*, 120, 177.
18. Han, "Shifting Geographies of Proximity," 211–212.
19. One only needs to examine contemporary newspaper headlines to see the portrayal of North Korea as an irrational, bad, or evil nation. See the following example, in which the North Korean leader Kim Jong Un is portrayed as irrational by the American president. Gerry Mullany, "Trump Warns 'Major, Major Conflict,' with North Korea Possible," *New York Times*, April 27, 2017. https://www.nytimes.com/2017/04/27/world/asia/trump-north-korea-kim-jong-un.html.
20. Viet Thanh Nguyen, "There's a Reason the South Vietnamese Flag Flew during the Capitol Riot," *Washington Post*, January 14, 2021. https://www.washingtonpost.com/outlook/2021/01/14/south-vietnam-flag-capitol-riot/.

Bibliography

Archival Sources

Archives of the Billy Graham Center, Wheaton, IL
Billy Kim Memorial Library, Suwon, Korea
Bob Jones University, Archives Research Center-Mack Library, Greenville, SC
Campus Crusade for Christ International Archives, Orlando, FL
Far East Broadcasting Company, Seoul, Korea
Fuller Theological Seminary, Archives and Special Collections, Pasadena, CA
Han Kyung Chik Memorial Library, Seoul, Korea
Institute for the History of Korean Christianity, Seoul, Korea
Korean Church History Museum, Inchon, Korea
Korea Campus Crusade for Christ Headquarters, Seoul, Korea
World Vision Inc. Central Records, Monrovia, CA
World Vision Korea, Seoul, Korea
World Vision Korean Children's Choir Musical Institute, Seoul, Korea

Oral Histories

Oral History Interviews by the Author
Cho, Miyŏng. Seoul, Korea. August 4, 2016.
Douglass, Judy. Orlando, FL. October 29, 2015.
Kim, Jang Hwan (Billy Kim). Seoul, Korea. April 15, 2016.
Marks, Bailey. Orlando, FL. July 2013.
Moon, Hyangja. Seoul, Korea. April 21, 2016.
Neibling, Ed. Orlando, FL. October 29, 2015.
Oh, Chint'ak. Seoul, Korea. August 4, 2016.
Oh, Chiyŏng. Seoul, Korea. May 28, 2016.
Pae, Kyungha. Seoul, Korea. April 15, 2016.
Park, Jong Sam (Sam Park). Seoul, Korea. April 27, 2016.
Phillips, Gertrude (pseudonym). Orlando, FL. October 29, 2015.
Sharpless, Jerry. Orlando, FL. October 29, 2015.
Yi, Hokyun. Seoul, Korea. August 4, 2016.

Archived Oral Histories
Cho, Paul Yonggi, BGEA Oral History Project, Collection 141. Billy Graham Center Archive, Wheaton, IL.
Kim, Billy. BGEA Oral History Project. Collection 141. Billy Graham Center Archives. Wheaton, IL.
Wong, Gwen. Inter-Varsity Christian Fellowship Archives. Courtesy of Inter-Varsity USA archivist, Ned Hale.

Published Primary Sources

"1973 Pastor Billy Graham and Pastor Kim Jang Hwan, Yoido." Video clip of Billy Graham Crusade in Yoido, South Korea. June 3, 1973. http://www.youtube.com/watch?v=uFCP TPx5380.

"Bailey Marks—Tribute to Dr. Joon Gon Kim." October 3, 2010. The Legacy Project—Campus Crusade for Christ. http://www.youtube.com/watch?v=5yFzRgpjhg4&feature=related.

Becker, Nils. *Fireseeds from Korea to the World: Tribute to Dr. Joon Gon Kim, Founder of Campus Crusade for Christ.* Orlando, FL: Campus Crusade for Christ International, 2007.

"Billy Graham South African Crusade." 1973. https://www.youtube.com/watch?v=HTHxivBCahA. Accessed December 25, 2015.

Cho, Hwa Soon. *Let the Weak Be Strong: A Woman's Struggle for Justice.* Oak Park: Meyer Stone & Co, 1988.

Dunker, Marilee Pierce. *Man of Vision: The Candid and Compelling Story of Bob and Lorraine Pierce, Founders of World Vision and Samaritan's Purse.* Waynesboro: Authentic Media, 2005.

Graham, Franklin and Jeanette Lockerbie. *Bob Pierce: This One Thing I Do.* Dallas: Word Publishing Group, 1951.

Han, Kyung-Chik. *Kyung Chik Han Collection* (in Korean). Seoul: Kyung-Chik Han Foundation, 2010.

Holt, Bertha. *The Seed from the East.* Los Angeles: Oxford Press, 1956.

Jones, Howard O. *White Questions to a Black Christian.* Grand Rapids: Zondervan Publishing, 1975.

Kim, Billy. *Billy Kim: From Military Houseboy to World Evangelist.* Chicago: Moody Publishers, 2015.

Marks, Bailey. *Awakening in Asia.* San Bernardino, CA: Here's Life Publishers, 1981.

My Pastor Joon Gon Kim and CCC. Seoul: Korea Campus Crusade for Christ, 2005.

North American Protestant Ministries Overseas Directory. Waco, TX: Missionary Research Library in cooperation with Missions Advanced Research and Communication Center, 1970.

Pierce, Bob. *The Korean Orphan Choir: They Sing Their Thanks.* Grand Rapids: Zondervan, 1965.

Pierce, Bob. *Orphans of the Orient: Stories that Will Touch Your Heart.* Grand Rapids: Zondervan Publishing House, 1964.

Pierce, Bob. *The Untold Korea Story.* Grand Rapids: Zondervan Publishing House, 1951.

Stentzel, Jim, ed. *More than Witnesses: How a Small Group of Missionaries Aided Korea's Democratic Revolution.* Mequon: Nightingale Press, 2008.

Until Everyone Has Heard: Campus Crusade for Christ International Helping Fulfill the Great Commission, The First Fifty Years, 1951–2001. Orlando: Campus Crusade for Christ International, 2007.

Secondary Sources

Allitt, Patrick. *Religion in America since 1945: A History.* New York: Columbia University Press, 2003.

Ancheta, Angelo N. *Race, Rights, and the Asian American Experience.* New Brunswick: Rutgers University Press, 1998.

Anderson, Carol. *Eyes Off the Prize: The United Nations and the African American Struggle for Human Rights, 1944–1955*. Cambridge: Cambridge University Press, 2003.
Armstrong, Charles K. *The North Korean Revolution, 1945–1950*. Studies of the Weatherhead East Asian Institute, Columbia University. Ithaca: Cornell University Press, 2013.
Azuma, Eiichiro. *Between Two Empires: Race, History, and Transnationalism in Japanese America*. New York: Oxford University Press, 2005.
Balmer, Randall Herbert. *Evangelicalism in America*. Waco, TX: Baylor University Press, 2016.
Balmer, Randall Herbert. *Mine Eyes Have Seen the Glory: A Journey into the Evangelical Subculture in America*. 25th Anniversary ed. New York: Oxford University Press, 2014.
Barstow, Elizabeth. "'These Teen-agers Are Not Delinquent': The Rhetoric of Maturity for Evangelical Young Adults, 1945–1965." PhD diss., Harvard University, 2010.
Bebbington, D. W. *Evangelicalism in Modern Britain: A History from the 1730s to the 1980s*. London: Unwin Hyman, 1989.
Bender, Thomas. *A Nation among Nations: America's Place in World History*. New York: Hill and Wang, 2006.
Bender, Thomas. *Rethinking American History in a Global Age*. Berkeley: University of California Press, 2002.
Bow, Leslie. *Partly Colored: Asian Americans and Racial Anomaly in the Segregated South*. New York: New York University Press, 2010.
Braude, Ann. "Women's History *Is* American Religious History." In *Retelling U.S. Religious History*, edited by Thomas Tweed, 87–107. Berkeley: University of California Press, 1997.
Brekus, Catherine A. *The Religious History of American Women: Reimagining the Past*. Chapel Hill: University of North Carolina Press, 2007.
Brekus, Catherine A. *Sarah Osborn's World: The Rise of Evangelical Christianity in Early America*. New Haven: Yale University Press, 2013.
Brekus, Catherine A. *Strangers and Pilgrims: Female Preaching in America, 1740–1845*. Chapel Hill: University of North Carolina Press, 1998.
Brenneman, Todd M. *Homespun Gospel: The Triumph of Sentimentality in Contemporary American Evangelicalism*. New York: Oxford University Press, 2014.
Brown, Candy Gunther, and Mark Silk. *The Future of Evangelicalism in America*. New York: Columbia University Press, 2016.
Buswell, Robert E. *Christianity in Korea*. Honolulu: University of Hawai'i Press, 2005.
Buswell, Robert E. *Religions of Korea in Practice*. Princeton: Princeton University Press, 2018.
Butler, Anthea D. *White Evangelical Racism: The Politics of Morality in America*. Chapel Hill: University of North Carolina Press, 2021.
Butler, Jon. "The Future of American Religious History: Prospectus, Agenda, Transatlantic Problematique." *William and Mary Quarterly*, 3rd series, 42.2 (April 1985): 167–183.
Carpenter, Joel A. *Revive Us Again: The Reawakening of American Fundamentalism*. New York: Oxford University Press, 1997.
Chang, Paul Y. *Protest Dialectics: State Repression and South Korea's Democracy Movement, 1970–1979*. Stanford: Stanford University Press, 2015.
Chang, Paul Y., and Byung-Soo Kim. "Differential Impact of Repression on Social Movements: Christian Organizations and Liberation Theology in South Korea (1972–1979)." *Sociological Inquiry* 77.3 (2007): 326–355.
Chen, Kuan-Hsing. *Asia as Method: Toward Deimperialization*. Durham: Duke University Press, 2010.

Cheng, Cindy I.-Fen. *Citizens of Asian America: Democracy and Race during the Cold War*. New York: New York University Press, 2013.

Cho, Grace M. *Haunting the Korean Diaspora: Shame, Secrecy, and the Forgotten War*. Minneapolis: University of Minnesota Press, 2008.

Cho, Jane Jangeun. "Immigration through Education: The Interwoven History of Korean International Students, US Foreign Assistance, and Korean Nation-State Building." PhD diss., University of California, Berkeley, 2010.

Cho, Wha Soon. *Let the Weak Be Strong: A Woman's Struggle for Justice*. Bloomington: Meyer-Stone Books, 1988.

Choi, Peter Y. *George Whitefield: Evangelist for God and Empire*. Grand Rapids: Eerdmans, 2018.

Choi, Susan. *The Foreign Student*. New York: Harper Perennial, 2004.

Choy, Catherine Ceniza. *Global Families: A History of Asian International Adoption in America*. New York: New York University Press, 2013.

Cohrs, Rachel. "North Korea's Secret Christians." *The Atlantic*, April 28, 2018.

Cumings, Bruce. *The Korean War: A History*. New York: Modern Library, 2010.

Cumings, Bruce. *The Origins of the Korean War*. Princeton: Princeton University Press, 1981.

Curtis, Heather D. *Holy Humanitarians: American Evangelicals and Global Aid*. Cambridge: Harvard University Press, 2018.

Dochuk, Darren. *From Bible Belt to Sunbelt: Plain-Folk Religion, Grassroots Politics, and the Rise of Evangelical Conservatism*. New York: Norton, 2012.

Du Mez, Kristin. *Jesus and John Wayne: How White Evangelicals Corrupted a Faith and Fractured a Nation*. New York: Liveright Publishing Corporation, 2020.

Dudziak, Mary L. *Cold War Civil Rights: Race and the Image of American Democracy*. Princeton: Princeton University Press, 2011.

Dupont, Carolyn Renée. *Mississippi Praying: Southern White Evangelicals and the Civil Rights Movement, 1945-1975*. New York: New York University Press, 2013.

Emerson, Michael O. *Divided By Faith: Evangelical Religion and the Problem of Race in America*. New York: Oxford University Press, 2000.

Espiritu, Augusto Fauni. *Five Faces of Exile: The Nation and Filipino American Intellectuals*. Stanford: Stanford University Press, 2005.

Evans, Curtis. "White Evangelical Protestant Responses to the Civil Rights Movement." *Harvard Theological Review* 102.2 (April 2009): 245-273.

"Forum: Studying Religion in the Age of Trump." *Religion and American Culture* 27.1 (2017): 2-56.

Freston, Paul. *Evangelicals and Politics in Asia, Africa, and Latin America*. Cambridge: Cambridge University Press, 2001.

Fulop, Timothy Earl, and Albert J. Raboteau. *African-American Religion: Interpretive Essays in History and Culture*. New York: Routledge, 1997.

Gehman, Richard. *Let My Heart Be Broken*. New York: McGraw-Hill, 1960.

Gutiérrez, Gustavo. *A Theology of Liberation: History, Politics, and Salvation*. Maryknoll: Orbis Books, 2017.

Haga, Kai Yin Allison. "An Overlooked Dimension of the Korean War: The Role of Christianity and American Missionaries in the Rise of Korean Nationalism, Anti-colonialism, and Eventual Civil War, 1884-1953." PhD diss., College of William and Mary, 2007.

Hall, Mitchell K. *Vietnam War Era: People and Perspectives*. Santa Barbara: ABC-CLIO, 2009.

Hamilton, John. "An Historical Study of Bob Pierce and World Vision's Development of the Evangelical Social Action Film." PhD diss., University of Southern California, 1980.
Han, Ju Hui Judy. "Shifting Geographies of Proximity." In *Ethnographies of U.S. Empire*, edited by 194–213. Carole McGranahan and John F. Collins. Durham: Duke University Press, 2018.
Hanciles, Jehu. *Beyond Christendom: Globalization, African Migration, and the Transformation of the West*. Maryknoll: Orbis Books, 2008.
Haney-López, Ian. *White by Law: The Legal Construction of Race*. New York: New York University Press, 2006.
Hardacre, Helen. *Shinto: A History*. New York: Oxford University Press, 2016.
Harkness, Nicholas. *Glossolalia and the Problem of Language*. Chicago: University of Chicago Press, 2021.
Harkness, Nicholas. *Songs of Seoul: An Ethnography of Voice and Voicing in Christian South Korea*. Berkeley: University of California Press, 2014.
Harkness, Nicholas. "Transducing a Sermon, Inducing Conversion: Billy Graham, Billy Kim, and the 1973 Crusade in Seoul." *Representations* 137 (2017): 112–143.
Hart, D. G., and Institute for the Study of American Evangelicals. *Reckoning with the Past: Historical Essays on American Evangelicalism from the Institute for the Study of American Evangelicals*. Grand Rapids: Baker Books, 1995.
Hau'ofa, Epeli. "Our Sea of Islands." In *A New Oceania: Rediscovering Our Sea of Islands*, edited by Eric Waddell, Vijay Naidu, and Epeli Hau'ofa, 148–161. Suva: School of Social and Economic Development, University of the South Pacific in association with Beake House, 1993.
Hempton, David. *Methodism: Empire of the Spirit*. New Haven: Yale University Press, 2005.
Hempton, David. *The Church in the Long Eighteenth Century*. London: IB Tauris, 2011.
Herzog, Jonathan P. *The Spiritual-Industrial Complex: America's Religious Battle against Communism in the Early Cold War*. New York: Oxford University Press, 2011.
Hinnershitz, Stephanie. *A Different Shade of Justice: Asian American Civil Rights in the South*. Chapel Hill: University of North Carolina Press, 2017.
Hollinger, David A. *Protestants Abroad: How Missionaries Tried to Change the World but Changed America*. Princeton: Princeton University Press, 2017.
Hong, Jane H. *Opening the Gates to Asia: A Transpacific History of How America Repealed Asian Exclusion*. Chapel Hill: University of North Carolina Press, 2019.
Hong, Young-Gi. "Encounter with Modernity: The 'McDonaldization' and 'Charismatization' of Korean Churches." *International Review of Mission* 92.365 (April 2003): 239–255.
Hsu, Madeline Yuan-yin. *Dreaming of Gold, Dreaming of Home: Transnationalism and Migration Between the United States and South China, 1882–1943*. Stanford: Stanford University Press, 2000.
Hunt, Keith. *For Christ and the University: The Story of Intervarsity Christian Fellowship-USA, 1940–1990*. Downers Grove: InterVarsity Press, 1992.
Hutchison, William R. *Errand to the World: American Protestant Thought and Foreign Missions*. Chicago: University of Chicago Press, 1993.
Inboden, William. *Religion and American Foreign Policy, 1945–1960: The Soul of Containment*. Cambridge: Cambridge University Press, 2008.
Iwamura, Jane Naomi. *Virtual Orientalism: Asian Religions and American Popular Culture*. New York: Oxford University Press, 2011.
Iwamura, Jane Naomi, and Paul R. Spickard. *Revealing the Sacred in Asian and Pacific America*. New York: Routledge, 2003.

Jacobs, Seth. *America's Miracle Man in Vietnam: Ngo Dinh Diem, Religion, Race, and U.S. Intervention in Southeast Asia.* Durham: Duke University Press, 2005.

Jager, Sheila Miyoshi. *Brothers at War: The Unending Conflict in Korea.* New York: Norton, 2013.

Jeyaraj, Daniel, Robert W. Pazmiño, and Daniel Jeyaraj, eds. *Antioch Agenda: Essays on the Restorative Church in Honor of Orlando E. Costas.* New Delhi: Indian Society for the Promotion of Christian Knowledge for Andover Newton Theological School, and Boston Theological Institute, 2007.

Jung, Moon-Ho. *Coolies and Cane: Race, Labor, and Sugar in the Age of Emancipation.* Baltimore: Johns Hopkins University Press, 2006.

Kaell, Hillary. *Christian Globalism at Home: Child Sponsorship in the United States.* Princeton: Princeton University Press, 2020.

Kane, J. Herbert. *A Global View of Christian Missions from Pentecost to the Present.* Grand Rapids: Baker Book House, 1971.

Kang, Woo Suk. "The Evangelical Movement as Revealed in the Life and Thought of Joon Gon Kim." Master's thesis, Chongshin University, 2015.

Kim, Charles R. *Beyond Death: The Politics of Suicide and Martyrdom in Korea.* Seattle: University of Washington Press, 2019.

Kim, Helen Jin. "Gospel of the 'Orient': Koreans, Race and the Rise of American Evangelicalism in the Cold War Era, 1950–1980." PhD diss., Harvard University, 2017.

Kim, Hong Ki. *A History of One Hundred Years of the Korean-American Methodism I, Part I.* Upland: The Committee on Publication of 100 Year History of the Korean-American Methodist Church, 2003.

Kim, Il-sŏng. *On Juche in Our Revolution.* Pyongyang: Foreign Languages PubHouse, 1975.

Kim, Kyung (Isaac) Kyu. "The Education and Cultivation of Intercultural Leaders: A Study of Twelve Prominent Native Born Koreans." PhD diss., School of Intercultural Studies, Biola University, 2009.

Kim, Nadia Y. *Imperial Citizens: Koreans and Race from Seoul to LA.* Stanford: Stanford University Press, 2008.

Kim, Nami. *The Gendered Politics of the Korean Protestant Right: Hegemonic Masculinity.* Cham, Switzerland: Palgrave Macmillan, 2016.

Kim, Nami. "A Mission to the 'Graveyard of Empires'? Neocolonialism and the Contemporary Evangelical Missions of the Global South." *Mission Studies* 27 (2010): 3–22.

Kim, Pyŏng-guk, and Ezra F. Vogel, eds. *The Park Chung Hee Era: The Transformation of South Korea.* Cambridge: Harvard University Press, 2011.

Kim, Rebecca Y. *God's New Whiz Kids? Korean American Evangelicals on Campus.* New York: New York University Press, 2006.

Kim, Rebecca Y. *The Spirit Moves West: Korean Missionaries in America.* New York: Oxford University Press, 2015.

Kim, Sebastian C. H. *A History of Korean Christianity.* Cambridge: Cambridge University Press, 2015.

King, David P. *God's Internationalists: World Vision and the Age of Evangelical Humanitarianism.* Philadelphia: University of Pennsylvania Press, 2019.

Kirby, Dianne. *Religion and the Cold War.* New York: Palgrave Macmillan, 2003.

Kirkpatrick, David C. *A Gospel for the Poor: Global Social Christianity and the Latin American Evangelical Left.* Philadelphia: University of Pennsylvania Press, 2019.

Klein, Christina. *Cold War Cosmopolitanism*. Berkeley: University of California Press, 2020.

Klein, Christina. *Cold War Orientalism: Asia in the Middlebrow Imagination, 1945-1961*. Berkeley: University of California Press, 2003.

Kramer, Paul A. *The Blood of Government: Race, Empire, the United States & the Philippines*. Chapel Hill: University of North Carolina Press, 2006.

Kruse, Kevin Michael. *One Nation under God: How Corporate America Invented Christian America*. New York: Basic Books, 2015.

Kurashige, Lon, Madeline Y. Hsu, and Yujin Yaguchi. "Introduction: Conversations on Transpacific History." *Pacific Historical Review* 83.2 (May 2014): 183-188.

Kwon, Heonik. *The Other Cold War*. New York: Columbia University Press, 2010.

Lahr, Angela M. *Millennial Dreams and Apocalyptic Nightmares: The Cold War Origins of Political Evangelicalism*. New York: Oxford University Press, 2007.

Lee, Erika. *At America's Gates: Chinese Immigration during the Exclusion Era, 1882-1943*. Chapel Hill: University of North Carolina Press, 2003.

Lee, Mary Paik. *Quiet Odyssey: A Pioneer Korean Woman in America*. Seattle: University of Washington Press, 1990.

Lee, Myung-sik. *The History of the Democratization Movement in Korea*. Seoul: Korea Democracy Foundation, 2010.

Lee, Sang Hyun. "Pilgrimage and Home in the Wilderness of Marginality." In Special Issue "Racial Spirits," *Amerasia Journal* 22.1 (1996): 149-160.

Lee, Shelley Sang-Hee. *A New History of Asian America*. New York: Routledge, 2014.

Lee, Timothy S. *Born Again: Evangelicalism in Korea*. Honolulu: University of Hawai'i Press, 2009.

Maffly-Kipp, Laurie. "Eastward Ho! American Religion from the Perspective of the Pacific Rim." In *Retelling U.S. Religious History*, edited by Thomas Tweed, 127-149. Berkeley: University of California Press, 1997.

Mao, Joyce. *Asia First: China and the Making of Modern American Conservatism*. Chicago: University of Chicago Press, 2015.

Marsden, George M. *Reforming Fundamentalism: Fuller Seminary and the New Evangelicalism*. Grand Rapids: Eerdmans, 1987.

Matsuoka, Fumitaka, and Eleazar S. Fernandez. *Realizing the America of Our Hearts: Theological Voices of Asian Americans*. St. Louis: Chalice Press, 2003.

McAlister, Melani. *The Kingdom of God Has No Borders: A Global History of American Evangelicals*. New York: Oxford University Press, 2018.

McGirr, Lisa. *Suburban Warriors: The Origins of the New American Right*. Princeton: Princeton University Press, 2001.

Min, Kyung Bae. *World Vision 50 Year History, 1950-2000*. Seoul: World Vision Korea, Hong Ik Jae Publishers, 2001.

Missionary Research Library. *North American Protestant Ministries Overseas*. Monrovia: MARC, 1970.

Moon, Katharine H. S. *Sex among Allies: Military Prostitution in U.S.-Korea Relations*. New York: Columbia University Press, 1997.

Muehlenbeck, Philip E. *Religion and the Cold War: A Global Perspective*. Nashville: Vanderbilt University Press, 2012.

Ngai, Mae M. "Transnationalism and the Transformation of the 'Other.'" *American Quarterly* 57.1 (2005): 59-65.

Oak, Sung-Deuk. *The Making of Korean Christianity: Protestant Encounters with Korean Religions, 1876–1915.* Waco, TX: Baylor University Press, 2013.

O'Brien, Susan. "A Transatlantic Community of Saints: The Great Awakening and the First Evangelical Network, 1735–1755." *American Historical Review* 91.4 (1986): 811–832.

Oh, Arissa H. *To Save the Children of Korea: The Cold War Origins of International Adoption.* Stanford: Stanford University Press, 2015.

Okihiro, Gary. "Toward a Pacific Civilization." *Japanese Journal of American Studies* 18 (2007): 73–85.

Pak, Chŏng-sin. *Protestantism and Politics in Korea.* Seattle: University of Washington Press, 2003.

Park, Josephine Nock-Hee. *Cold War Friendships: Korea, Vietnam, and Asian American Literature.* New York: Oxford University Press, 2016.

Park, Tae Gyun. *An Ally and Empire: Two Myths of South Korea–United States Relations, 1945–1980.* Translated by Ilsoo David Cho. Seongnam-si, Gyeonggi-do: Academy of Korean Studies Press, 2012.

Pate, SooJin. *From Orphan to Adoptee: U.S. Empire and Genealogies of Korean Adoption.* Minneapolis: University of Minnesota Press, 2014.

Pease, Donald E., and Yuan Shu. *American Studies as Transnational Practice: Turning toward the Transpacific.* Hanover: Dartmouth College Press, 2015.

Priest, Robert J., and Alvaro L. Nieves. *This Side of Heaven: Race, Ethnicity, and Christian Faith.* New York: Oxford University Press, 2007.

Quebedeaux, Richard. *I Found It! The Story of Bill Bright and Campus Crusade.* San Francisco: Harper & Row, 1979.

Rhie, Deok-Joo. *A Study on the Formation of the Indigenous Church in Korea, 1903–1907.* Seoul: History of Christianity in Korea Research Institute, 2000.

Richardson, Michael. *Amazing Faith: The Authorized Biography of Bill Bright, Founder of Campus Crusade for Christ.* Colorado Springs: Water Brook, 2001.

Rivera, Mayra. *The Touch of Transcendence: A Postcolonial Theology of God.* Louisville: Westminster John Knox Press, 2007.

Robbins, Joel. "The Globalization of Pentecostal and Charismatic Christianity." *Annual Review of Anthropology* 33 (2004): 127–130.

Robert, Dana L. *Christian Mission: How Christianity Became a World Religion.* Hoboken, NJ: Wiley, 2009.

Sanneh, Lamin O. *Translating the Message: The Missionary Impact on Culture.* Maryknoll: Orbis Books, 2009.

Shin, Gi-Wook. *Ethnic Nationalism in Korea: Genealogy, Politics, and Legacy.* Stanford: Stanford University Press, 2006.

Sŏ, Chae-jŏng. *Origins of North Korea's Juche: Colonialism, War, and Development.* Lanham, MD: Lexington Books, 2012.

Suh, Chris. "What Yun Ch'i-ho Knew: US-Japan Relations and Imperial Race Making in Korea and the American South, 1904–1919." *Journal of American History* 104.1 (June 2017): 68–96.

Swanson, Paul L., and Clark Chilson. *Nanzan Guide to Japanese Religions.* Honolulu: University of Hawai'i Press, 2006.

Swartz, David R. *Facing West: American Evangelicals in an Age of World Christianity.* New York: Oxford University Press, 2020.

Thomas, Jolyon Baraka. *Faking Liberties: Religious Freedom in American-Occupied Japan.* Chicago: University of Chicago Press, 2019.

Thomas, Todne. *Kincraft: The Making of Black Evangelical Sociality.* Durham: Duke University Press, 2021.
Torrey, Ben. "The Mission to North Korea." *International Bulletin of Missionary Research* 32.1: 20–22.
Turner, John G. *Bill Bright & Campus Crusade for Christ: The Renewal of Evangelicalism in Postwar America.* Chapel Hill: University of North Carolina Press, 2008.
Tweed, Thomas A. *Retelling U.S. Religious History.* Berkeley: University of California Press, 1997.
Wacker, Grant. *America's Pastor: Billy Graham and the Shaping of a Nation.* Cambridge: Harvard University Press, 2014.
Ward, W. Reginald. *The Protestant Evangelical Awakening.* Cambridge: Cambridge University Press, 1992.
Wei, William. *The Asian American Movement.* Philadelphia: Temple University Press, 1993.
Wong, Janelle. *Immigrants, Evangelicals, and Politics in an Era of Demographic Change.* New York: Russell Sage Foundation, 2018.
Woo, Susie. *Framed by War: Korean Children and Women at the Crossroads of US Empire.* New York: University Press, 2019.
Wu, Ellen D. *The Color of Success: Asian Americans and the Origins of the Model Minority.* Princeton: Princeton University Press, 2014.
Wuthnow, Robert. *The Restructuring of American Religion: Society and Faith since World War II.* Princeton: Princeton University Press, 1988.
Vanderpol, Gary. "The Least of These: American Evangelical Parachurch Missions to the Poor, 1947–2005." PhD diss., Boston University School of Theology, 2010.
Yoo, David. *Contentious Spirits: Religion in Korean American History, 1903–1945.* Stanford: Stanford University Press, 2010.
Yoo, David. *New Spiritual Homes: Religion and Asian Americans.* Honolulu: University of Hawai'i Press, in association with UCLA Asian American Studies Center, Los Angeles, 1999.
Yoo, David, and Khyati Y. Joshi. *Envisioning Religion, Race, and Asian Americans.* Honolulu: University of Hawai'i Press, in association with UCLA Asian American Studies Center, 2020.
Yoo, William. *American Missionaries, Korean Protestants, and the Changing Shape of World Christianity, 1884–1965.* New York: Routledge, 2016.
Yuh, Ji-Yeon. *Beyond the Shadow of Camptown: Korean Military Brides in America.* New York: University Press, 2002.
Yun, Chung-Nan. *The Korean War and Protestantism.* In Korean. Kyŏnggi-do P'aju-si: Hanul, 2015.

Index

For the benefit of digital users, indexed terms that span two pages (e.g., 52–53) may, on occasion, appear on only one of those pages.

Figures are indicated by *f* following the page number

Abraham, Thomas, 211n.98
adoption, Korean transnational, 92–94, 100, 186n.98
   adoptees as "tiny ambassadors," 92
   assimilation and, 93–95
   Operation Baby Lift, 97
Ancheta, Angelo, 58–59
anticommunism
   anti-Blackness and, 162–63
   of Billy Graham, 72–73
   Campus Crusade and, 160
   Christianity and, 6–7, 70–74
   civil rights and, 72–73
   Cold War and, 9, 28–29, 70–74, 83–84, 160
   in *Dead Men on Furlough*, 41–44, 97
   decolonization and, 11–12, 73
   evangelicalism and, 11–12, 30–31, 70–74, 168, 182n.38
   fundamentalism and, 13–14, 30–32, 41–42
   of Joon Gon Kim, 66, 67, 70–74, 150–51
   Korean Christianity and, 6–7, 70–74
   Korean War and, 28–29, 49
   martyrdom and, 33–34
   Orientalism and, 162–63
   Protestantism and, 17, 178n.65
   Protestantism, Korean and, 29–32, 53
   race and, 12, 168
   racialization and, 168
   religion and, 3–4
   US Catholics and, 30
   of World Vision, 83
anti-Vietnam War protests, 145, 147–48
Asian American movement, ix

Asians
   educational segregation of, 58–59
   exclusion of, 55–56, 100–1, 213n.12
   integration of, 57, 60
   as model minorities, 78, 84–86, 163, 203n.57
   as perpetual foreigners, 43
assimilation, 84–85
   Asian American evangelicals and, 164
   of Japanese Americans, 85
   of Korean Christians, 164
   of Korean transnational adoptees, 93–95
   of South Koreans, 94–95

Balmer, Randall, 59–60
Barrows, Cliff, 118–19, 188n.16, 204n.70
Bebbington Quadrilateral, 7–8, 175n.32
Becker, Nils, 52, 207n.4
Bell, Ralph, 204n.70
Berkeley Blitz, 136, 145–47
Billy Graham Evangelistic Association (BGEA), 1–2, 3–4, 5, 164, 166
   crusades of, 10, 49
   global rise of, 17–18
   revivals of, 75
   as transpacific network, 36
   See also Graham, Billy; Korea Billy Graham Crusade (1973)
Bob Jones University, 5, 13, 51
   Asian integration at, 60
   Billy Graham, critique of, 188n.17
   Billy Kim and, 58–61, 123–25, 130
   Black exclusion at, 56
   founding of, 54–55
   global mindedness of, 54

Bob Jones University (*cont.*)
  interracial dating ban, 57–58
  nonwhite students at, 56, 189n.26
  Orientalism and, 60, 63
  segregation at, 59–60, 63, 190n.41
Bow, Leslie, 188n.8
Braude, Ann, 179n.82
Braun, Jon, 145–46
Brekus, Catherine, 176n.40, 196n.62
Brenneman, Todd, 96
Bright, Bill, 10, 50, 52, 66–67, 135–36
  civil rights movement and, 56–57
  conversion of, 67
  conversion, salvation through, 148–50
  critiques of, 152–53
  Expo '74, 140*f*, 142, 144
  founding of Campus Crusade, 52, 67–68
  on Korean missionaries, 156, 157
  at 1973 Korea Billy Graham crusade, 119–20
  partnership with Joon Gon Kim, 66–67, 69–70, 74, 191n.66
  politics of, 149–50
  social change through salvation, 148–49, 152–53, 162
  See also Campus Crusade for Christ
Buddhism, 14–15, 167–68, 172–73n.8
Busto, Rudy, ix–x, 179n.82
Butler, Anthea, 8, 194n.13

Campus Crusade for Christ, 2, 5, 51, 54–55, 164
  anticommunism and, 160
  civil rights movement and, 56–57
  critiques of, 210n.88
  ethnic specific ministries, 164, 212n.7
  founding of, 10, 13
  Four Spiritual Laws, 69, 192n.69
  global growth of, 3–4, 17–18, 49–50, 54, 140, 143, 154, 162, 208n.35
  internationalizing of, 69–70, 120, 166, 205n.81
  leftist activism, mitigation of, 145–47, 148
  missionary work of, 140, 141–42, 208n.35
  at 1973 Korea Billy Graham crusade, 119

  revivals of, 75
  support for Explo '74, 136–43
  transpacific networks of, 3–4, 159–60
  See also Bright, Bill; Explo '72; Explo '74
Cash, Johnny, 137
Challberg, Roy, 105
Chang, Paul, 154, 201n.38
Chang Soo Chul, 76, 196n.65
Chang Suk Young, 110–11
Chi Haksun, 148
Chiang Kai-shek, 70–71, 192n.74
China
  rise of, 109–10
  US relations with, 199n.14
Chinese Americans
  in *Dead Men on Furlough*, 43–44
Cho, David Yonggi, 3, 133
Cho, Grace, ix
Cho Mansik, 25
Cho, Miyŏng, 108, 128–29
Cho Wha Soon, ix–x, 113–14, 153
Choi, Susan, 27–28, 51
Chon Tae'il, ix, 147–48
Chosun Seminary, 66, 68, 147, 190n.56
Choy, Catherine Ceniza, 187n.103
Christian Children's Fund (CCF), 92
Christian Coalition of America, 17, 178n.66
Christian Council of Korea, 17, 178n.66
Christian Democratic Social Party, 29, 182n.28
Christianity
  anticommunism and, 6–7, 70–74
  in Japan, 15–16
  modernist, 2–5, 183n.45
  race and, 99
  See also Protestantism
Christianity, Korean
  anticommunism and, 70–74
  erasure of, 32–33
  as evangelical movement, 175n.28
  globalization of, 155
  growth of, 177n.58
  history of, 14–19
  martyrdom and, 32–33
  triumphalism of, 155–56
  See also Protestantism, Korean; Protestantism, South Korean

Christianity, North Korean, 3, 172–73n.8
Christianity, South Korean, 2–4, 165–66, 172n.6
  anticommunism and, 6–7
  in US, 161
  See also Christianity, Korean; Protestantism, Korean; Protestantism, South Korean
Chun Doo-hwan, 157
civil rights
  anticommunism and, 72–73
  Billy Graham and, 72, 115, 117–18, 203n.62
civil rights movement
  anticommunism and, 72–73
  Bill Bright and, 56–57
  Campus Crusade and, 56–57
  Cold War and, 77, 193n.11
  fundamentalism and, 72–73
Cleage, Albert B., 127
Cold War
  anticommunism and, 9, 28–29, 70–74, 83–84, 160
  civil rights movement and, 77, 193n.11
  detente, 199n.16, 201n.36
  empire and, 64
  evangelicalism and, 2–4
  Orientalism and, 44, 53, 175n.30
  Protestantism and, 16–17
  racial democracy and, 5–6, 53–54, 61–64, 65–66, 98
  sentimentalism and, 92, 96
  South Korea and, x
  US empire building and, 64
Cold War, religious, 11–12, 18, 160
  anticommunism and, 3–4
  white fundamentalism and, 23
Cold War Orientalism, 53–54, 78, 92, 165–66
  Asian integration, politics of, 57
  "orphans" and, 93
communism
  evangelicalism and, 5
  religious Cold War against, 3–4
  See also anticommunism
Cone, James H., 127
Confucianism
  in Korea, 14–15, 167–68, 172–73n.8
  rank in, 22

conversion
  of Bill Bright, 67
  of Billy Kim, 13, 61–63, 65–66, 204–5n.75
  of Carl Powers, 65–66, 65f
  evangelicalism and, 31
  Great Commission and, 54
  of Indians, 174n.21
  of Joon Gon Kim, 13, 70–71
  orphans and, 91–92
  as pilgrimage, 190n.46
  salvation through, 148–50, 162–64
  social change and, 117–19, 136, 157, 164
  South Korean Protestantism and, 18
Costlin, James, 115
Cowan, Kathleen, 97–98
Crowe, Philip, 114–15
Cumings, Bruce, 27

Dead Men on Furlough (film), 23, 40–44
  anticommunism in, 41–44, 97
  Chinese Americans in, 43–44
  martyrdom in, 42–43
decolonization, 9
  anticommunism and, 11–12, 73
  missionaries and, 165–66
  movements for, 165–66
  nationalism and, 53
Dochuk, Darren, 3, 178n.70
Douglass, Judy, 136–37, 138, 140
Douglass, Steve, 136–37
Dulles, John Foster, 182n.38
Du Mez, Kristin, 38
Dunker, Marilee Pierce, 24–25, 48
Dupont, Carolyn Renee, 203n.66

Eisenhower, Dwight D., 3–4, 5–6
  fundamentalists and, 50
  people-to-people diplomacy of, 53–54, 194n.19, 195n.41
empire, US
  Cold War and, 64
  Korean War and, 24
  World Vision and, 47
empire, US evangelical, 22, 165–66
  Korean War and, 7–11, 22–24
  1973 Korea Billy Graham crusade and, 2, 7

empire, US evangelical (*cont.*)
  rise of, 7–11, 120, 135, 163
  South Korean Protestants and, 3–4, 14–18, 45, 135, 136, 163–66
  WEC '80 and, 155–56
  whiteness and, 12–13, 165
Engstrom, Ted, 76, 101–2
Epic Movement, 164, 212n.7
erasure
  of Kim Ch'anghwa, 48–49, 187n.103
  of Korean Christianity, 32–33
  of Korean Protestantism, 23, 25, 32–33, 36, 40
  of Koreans, 40, 163
  of Kyung Chik Han, 45, 48–49, 187n.103
  martyrdom and, 43, 45, 186n.93
  of Paek Okhyŏn, 48–49, 187n.103
  racialization and, 12
  of Tabitha Widow's Home, 187n.103
evangelicalism, ix–x, 171n.5
  anticommunism and, 11–12, 30–31, 70–74, 168, 182n.38
  Christian Right and, x
  Cold War and, 2–4
  communism and, 5
  conservatism and, 146
  conversion and, 31
  corporatism and, 210n.80
  defined, 7–8
  diversity of, 8–9
  evangelicals of color, 165
  global mission of, 61–62, 73–74
  Great Commission, 3–4, 7, 14, 49
  mainstreaming of, 77–78, 81, 94–95
  masculinity and, 8
  neo-evangelicalism, 2–3, 54–55, 68, 72, 77–78, 94–95, 99, 190n.56
  politics and, x, 8, 157–60, 210n.80
  race and, 12, 17
  racism and, 8
  as "religion of the heart," 96, 196n.84
  revival of, 10–11
  sentimentalism and, 94–101
  social change and, 159
  as transnational, 6–7, 175n.28
  as transpacific, 6, 40, 120
  as white male movement, 2

  whiteness and, 2, 8–9, 12, 13–14, 23–24, 78, 194n.13
  white supremacy and, 165
  See also fundamentalism
evangelicalism, US
  global context of, 18–19
  Korea and, 9–11
  See also evangelicalism
evangelicals, Asian American
  assimilation and, 164
  in evangelical American institutions, 164
  as model moral minority, ix–x, 164
  politics of, 8, 167–68
  race and, 8, 12, 168–69
  transpacific history of, x, 164–66
Evans, Curtis, 203–4n.68
exceptionalism
  American, 19–20, 65–66, 99–100, 135–36, 143, 156, 159–60, 166
  Korean Protestant, 32–33, 135–36, 156, 175n.32
Explo '72, 114–15, 119, 136–39, 145, 168, 207n.1
  attendance, 207n.17
  as Christian Woodstock, 137, 207n.17
  conservative activism at, 146–47
  as foil to leftist movements, 146
  Nixon support for, 146
  political scandal and, 151–52
Explo '74, 16–17, 66–67, 119–20, 135, 139–45, 140f, 207n.1
  attendance, 144
  authoritarian politics of, 150–54
  Campus Crusade support for, 136–43
  critiques of, 152–53, 210n.88
  political scandal and, 151–52
  preparatory activities for, 208n.32
  resistance to, 142
  See also Joon Gon Kim

feminist theology, 3
Foner, Eric, 178n.69
Franks, Jim, 101–2
Frederick, Marla, 212n.6
Fuller Theological Seminary, 5, 13, 51
  founding of, 54–55, 190n.56
  global mindedness of, 54

fundamentalism, 2–3, 4–6
  anticommunism and, 13–14, 30–32, 41–42
  civil rights movement and, 72–73
  mainstreaming of, 81
  See also evangelicalism
fundamentalist-modernist controversy, 4–5, 31, 52–53, 54–55, 67, 68
fundamentalists, ultraseparatist, 54–55, 57–58, 77, 123

Gandhi, Indira Nehru, 80
Gehman, Richard, 96–97
Graham, Billy, 3–4
  anticommunism of, 72–73
  antiwar protesters, opposition to, 116–17
  "Christmas in Korea" 1952, 36–40, 37*f*, 120–21
  civil rights and, 72, 115, 117–18, 203n.62
  color-blind conservatism of, 125–26
  critiques of, 114–15
  diplomacy of, 108
  Explo '72 and, 137
  as Great Legitimator, 111
  individualistic theology of, 72–73, 115, 117–18, 126–27
  Madison Square Garden crusade, 54–55, 77, 188n.17, 204n.71
  Martin Luther King, Jr., conflict with, 72, 117–18
  parachurch of, 6
  Park Chung-hee, defense of, 116–18
  politics of, 167–68
  race and, 126–27
  on racism, 203n.57
  revival of evangelicalism, 10–11
  Talking Pictures album, 39*f*, 40
  See also Billy Graham Evangelistic Association (BGEA); Korea Billy Graham crusade (1973)
Graham, Franklin, 21, 95–96, 105–6, 164–65
  anti-refugee sentiment, 166
Graham, Ruth, 36, 107, 123
  at 1973 Korea Billy Graham crusade, 108
Great Commission, 135–36, 209n.49
  conversion and, 54
  evangelicalism and, 3–4, 7, 14, 49

Habib, Philip C., 108
Halversen, Richard, 96–97
Hamilton, John, 97, 183n.49
Han, Ju Hui Judy, 167–68
Han, Kyung Chik, 10, 12–13, 18, 24–26, 204n.70
  alliance with Bill Pierce, 22, 24–25, 26, 44–45, 46–47, 98–99, 180n.2
  early life, 25–26
  erasure of, 45, 48–49, 187n.103
  as "friendly," 44–45, 49
  immigration to US, 187–88n.7
  letter to Billy Graham, 111–12
  martyrdom of, 23
  1973 Korea Billy Graham crusade, 111–12, 204–5n.75
  orphanages of, 75–76
  social welfare ministries, 24–25
  World Vision, founding of, 24
  World Vision Korean Orphan Choir, founding of, 75–76
  See also World Vision; World Vision Korean Orphan Choir
Hanciles, Jehu, 17
Haqq, Akbar Abdul, 204n.70
Harvey, Don, 43
Hempton, David, 178n.70
Hirsch, Dean, 46–47, 186n.96
history
  transnational turn in, 18–21, 178n.69
history, transpacific, 179n.74
  religion in, 18–21
Hoelkeboer, Tena, 46
Holley, Henry, 200n.31, 202–3n.55
Holt, Bertha, 97–100
Holt, Harry, 97–100, 186n.98
  race and, 100–1
Hyun, David, 52, 73

immigration, Korean, 13, 161, 212n.1
  of Billy Kim, 51–53, 55–56, 57–58, 62–63, 65–66, 187–88n.7
  of Joon Gon Kim, 51, 52, 55–56, 66, 187–88n.7
  of Kyung Chik Han, 187–88n.7

immigration, Korean (cont.)
  post-Korean War, 51
  waves of, 55–56
immigration laws, US, 52, 55–56, 188n.19
  Asian exclusion, 55–56, 213n.12
imperialism
  postcolonialism and, 31
imperialism, cultural, 14–16
individualism, ix
  theological, 72–73, 115, 117–18, 126–27
Inter-Varsity Christian Fellowship, 183n.45
Iwamura, Jane, 186n.93

Jager, Sheila Miyoshi, 28
Japan
  annexation and colonization of Korea, 15, 28
  Christianity in, 15–16
  as Shinto state, 177n.55
Jesus '82 revival, 161
Joh Dong Chul, 115–16
Johns, Bob, 68–69, 71
Jones, Bob, Jr., 54–55, 60
Jones, Bob, III, 124–25
Jones, Howard O., 204n.70
  color-blind theology of, 127
Jones, Marlin, 87
Joy Mission, 107
Juche ideology, 3, 29, 181n.27

Kane, J. Herbert, 29–30, 182n.32
Kang, Yon Won, 212n.7
Kendall, Bob, 69
Kerr, Clark, 145–46
Kim, Billy Jang Hwan, 3–4, 10, 65f, 187n.5, 205n.85
  Bob Jones University, education at, 58–61
  Bob Jones University, severing of ties with, 123–25, 130
  color-blind gospel of, 128
  conversion narrative of, 13, 61–63, 65–66, 204–5n.75
  crusade of, 21
  democracy, defense of, 63–66, 74
  immigration to US, 51–53, 55–56, 57–58, 62–63, 65–66, 187–88n.7
  integration of, 57

  mimicry of Billy Graham, 125–26
  1973 Korea Billy Graham crusade, 1–2, 2f, 7, 108, 118–19, 120–22, 129f, 204–5n.75, 205n.85
  1973 Korea Billy Graham crusade, aftermath of, 128–34
  politics of, 167–68
  superseding of Graham, 128–30
  translating of Billy Graham, 1, 123–26, 128–30
Kim Ch'anghwa, 12–13, 44
  erasure of, 48–49, 187n.103
  martyrdom of, 22–23, 33–35, 40
  See also Dead Men on Furlough (film)
Kim Chongnyŏl, 152–53
Kim Dong Whan, 164
Kim Duck Hei, 35
Kim, Gertrude (Trudy), 57–58, 123
Kim Hwallan (Helen Kim), 187–88n.7
Kim Il-sung, 26–27, 28
  Juche ideology of, 29
Kim Jae Jun, 66, 147, 190n.56, 191n.64
Kim Jong Pil, 115–16
Kim, Joon Gon, 10, 50, 187n.5, 207n.5
  anticommunism of, 66, 67, 70–74, 150–51
  Bill Bright, partnership with, 66–67, 69–70, 74, 191n.66
  Christian liberalism, critique of, 67, 68–69
  conversion, salvation through, 148–50, 162–64
  conversion narrative of, 13, 70–71
  critiques of, 152–53
  denouncing of Chosun, 147
  Explo '74 declaration, 137–40, 207n.4
  founding of Korean NAE chapter, 147
  immigration to US, 51, 52, 55–56, 66, 187–88n.7
  integration of, 57
  Korean War experience, 70–72, 204–5n.75
  1973 Korea Billy Graham crusade, organizing of, 204–5n.75
  organizing of Explo '74, 119–20, 135, 140f, 142, 143–45
  politics of, 149–51
  on social change, 148–49, 152–53

social program, lack of, 161–63
support for Park regime, 154, 162–63
as WEC '80 chair, 155–57
See also Explo '72; Explo '74
Kim Keum Ja, 86–87, 88–91
Kim, Nadia, 38–39
Kim, Nami, 7, 136, 149–50, 178nn.65–66, 207n.13
Kim, Rebecca, 177n.63
Kim Sang Yong ("Peanuts"), 13, 103*f*
suicide of, 77, 101–4
Kim, Soon, 110–11, 200n.25
Kimm, Diamond, 52, 73
King, David, 178n.70, 187n.103
King, Martin Luther, Jr., 72–73
Kissinger, Henry, 109–10
Klein, Christina, 9, 53–54, 92, 93
Korea
  Christianity in, 172–73n.8
  Confucianism in, 14–15, 167–68, 172–73n.8
  division of, 27–28
  evangelicalism, US and, 9–11
  Japanese annexation of, 28
  Japanese colonization of, 15
  revival of, 144–45, 209n.49
  US militarization of, 11–12, 23, 49
  US occupation of, 28
  See also Christianity, Korean; South Korea
Korea Billy Graham Crusade (1973), 1–2, 2*f*, 16–17, 107, 113–14, 115, 129*f*, 178n.70, 202n.44
  attendance, 1, 7, 108, 172n.4, 198n.5
  invitations for, 110–12
  Korean ascendancy and, 125–31
  Korean War and, 120–22
  lead-up events, 118, 204nn.69–70
  Park Chung-hee regime cooperation with, 115–16
  politics and diplomacy of, 115–18, 122
  transpacific significance of, 7, 50, 108–9, 118–20, 198n.12, 203–4n.68
Korea Campus Crusade for Christ in America, 164, 212n.7
Korean Americans
  racialization of, 161
  religious demographics, ix–x

Koreans
  agency of, 16
  erasure of, 163
  integration of, 13
  model minoritization of, 163
  racialization of, 58
Korean War, x
  anticommunism and, 28–29, 49
  armistice, 194n.16
  casualties of, 9–10
  as forgotten war, 11, 18, 49, 169
  as holy war, ix
  Joon Gon Kim, experience of, 70–72, 204–5n.75
  national unity and, 24
  1973 Korea Billy Graham crusade and, 118
  orphans and, 98–99
  as religious war, 32
  theological significance of, 120–22
  US evangelical empire and, 7–11, 22–24
Kramer, Paul, 176n.45

Lee, Erika, 213n.12
Lee Hokyun, 47, 82, 90
Lee In Soon, 87–90, 195n.53
Lee, Sang Hyun, 190n.46
Lee, Timothy, 172–73n.8, 175n.28, 198n.12
liberation movements, 145
liberation theology, ix, 2–3, 5, 147, 171n.5
Loo, Richard, 43, 185–86n.81
Love, Charles, 87
Luke, Keye, 43, 185–86n.81

MacArthur, Douglas, 15–16
Maffly-Kipp, Laurie, 20, 179n.82
Mao Tse-tung, 11–12, 28
March First Movement, 26–27
Marks, Bailey, 135, 138–39, 192n.71, 207n.5
Marsden, George, 190n.56
martyrdom, Korean, 48
  anticommunism and, 33–35
  in *Dead Men on Furlough*, 42–43
  erasure and, 43, 45, 186n.93
  of Kim Ch'anghwa, 22–23, 33–35, 40
  Korean Christianity and, 32–33
  of South Korean Protestants, 40

232 INDEX

masculinity
  evangelicalism and, 8
  militarized, 38
Massey, Kundan, 192n.71
May, Henry, 179n.79
McAlister, Melani, 176n.40
McDowell, Josh, 137
McFadden and Eddy Associates, 193n.9
McGovern, George, 146
Mears, Henrietta, 67, 69, 191n.59, 192n.73
  anticommunism of, 70–71
Mercy's Child: Holt Children (film), 97–100
Metamorphosis, 164
Methodism, 175n.29
migration, post-World War II, 9–10
  See also immigration
Miller, Perry, 179n.79
minjung theology, ix, 147, 202n.44
missionaries
  American Protestant, 4–5, 174n.22
  Asian, 143–44
  college students, 52–53
  colonialism and, 114
  decolonization movements and, 165–66
missionaries, Korean, 3, 7, 17, 143–44, 156, 161, 167–68, 212n.5
  global mission of, 155–56
missionaries, US, 143, 167–68, 177n.58
  Campus Crusade and, 140, 141–42, 208n.35
  to Korea, 10, 15, 32
  US imperialism and, 147
missions, Korean, 29–30, 156, 167–68, 182n.32
model minority myth, 78, 84–86, 203n.57
  Asian American evangelicals and, ix–x
  Koreans and, 163
  racialization and, 12
Moffett, Samuel, 25–26
Moon Hyang Ja, 79–80, 82–83, 90, 196n.65
Moon, Katherine, 179n.72
Morton, David, 23, 36
Moynihan Report, 85

National Association of Evangelicals (NAE), 54–55, 188n.18
  Korean chapter, 68, 147
  social reform through evangelization, 149
  statement of faith, 191n.64
nationalism
  decolonization and, 53
  developmental, ix
nationalism, Korean, 26–27, 183n.53
  evangelicalism and, 133–34
Nehru, Jawaharlal, 80
Neibling, Ed, 137, 142, 154
  support of military dictatorship, 151
neo-evangelicalism, 2–3, 54–55, 68, 190n.56
  mainstreaming of evangelicalism, 77–78, 94–95
  rescue narrative of, 94, 99
  white fundamentalists and, 72
  See also evangelicalism
Nethery, Ray, 192n.71
new evangelicalism
  See neo-evangelicalism
Nguyen, Viet Thanh, 168
Niebuhr, Reinhold, 30, 182n.37
1973 Korea Billy Graham Crusade
  See Korea Billy Graham Crusade (1973)
Nixon, Richard, 145
  detente policy, 109–10, 199n.16, 201n.36
  Nixon Doctrine, 110, 112
  relations with South Korea, 109–12, 205n.87
  support for Explo '72, 146
North Korea, 213n.19
  evangelizing of, 21

Ockenga, Harold, 54–55, 72
Ogle, George, 113–14, 153–54, 201n.40
Oh, Arissa, 184n.56, 187n.103
Oh Chint'ak, 66–67, 135, 138–39
Oh Chiyŏng, 13, 75–76, 78, 89–91, 103f, 193n.1
  born again experience of, 91, 107, 131–32
  Joy Mission Women's Choir founding, 132–33
  on "Peanuts," 102–4
  politics of, 157–59
  on World Vision Korean Orphan Choir, 104
Orientalism, 30
  anticommunism and, 162–63

INDEX   233

Bob Jones University and, 60, 63
Cold War and, 44, 53, 175n.30
transpacific critique of, 20
Orientalism, Cold War, 53–54, 78, 92, 165–66
Asian integration, politics of, 57
"orphans" and, 93
orphanages, 34–35, 75–76, 184n.56
orphans, 12, 13
  Asian exclusion and, 100–1
  conversion and, 91–92
  Korean War and, 98–99
  as metaphor, 92–93
  See also World Vision Korean Orphan Choir
Other Sheep (film), 97, 197n.93

Pae Kyungha, 104–5
Paek Okhyŏn, 12–13, 22–23, 34–35, 34f, 44
  erasure of, 48–49, 187n.103
  World Vision sponsorship of, 36, 45
  See also Dead Men on Furlough
Pak Hyong-kyu, 113, 148
parachurches, 2, 6, 21, 74, 164–66, 193n.90
  See also Billy Graham Evangelistic Association (BGEA); Campus Crusade for Christ; World Vision
Park Chung-hee, ix–x, 2, 78–79, 108–9
  assassination of, 157
  Billy Graham defense of, 116–18
  Explo '74 support for, 152
  martial law declaration, 148
  military dictatorship of, 112–13, 147–48, 151, 194n.13, 200n.34, 200–1n.35
  religious suppression under, 113–14
Park, Chung Shin, 172–73n.8
Park, Ihn Kahk, 111
Park, Josephine, 44–45
Park Jong Sam (Sam Park), 45, 47, 80, 82–83
Park, Tae Gyun, 179n.72
Pate, Soojin, 93
People's Revolutionary Party (PRP), 148, 152, 209n.67
Phillips, Gertrude, 138, 141–42, 154
Pierce, Bob, 24–25
  alliance with Kyung Chik Han, 22, 24–25, 26, 44–45, 46–47, 98–99, 180n.2

anticommunism and, 30–31
departure from World Vision, 105–6
as entrepreneur, 80–81
films of, 40–44, 97–101, 185n.73
on Kim Ch'anghwa, 33–34
missionary work of, 32–33
orphanages of, 75–76
racial imagination of, 98–99
sentimentalism of, 95–97, 98–99
travel to Korea, 10, 12–13
World Vision, founding of, 22–23, 180nn.1–2
World Vision Korean Orphan Choir, founding of, 75–76
See also World Vision; World Vision Korean Orphan Choir
Powers, Carl, 51, 57, 58, 60, 62–63, 65–66
  conversion of, 65–66, 65f
Protestantism
  nation building and, 29
Protestantism, Korean
  anticommunism and, 29–32, 53, 178n.65
  erasure of, 23, 25, 36
  waves of, 187n.5
Protestantism, South Korean, ix–x
  anticommunism and, 17, 178n.65
  challenge to US evangelicalism, 136
  during Cold War, 16–17
  conversion and, 18
  indigenous practices of, 32–33
  Korean nationalism and, 133–34
  revivals of, 13, 17
  US evangelical empire and, 3–4, 14–18, 45, 135, 136, 163–66
Protestants, Korean
  agency of, 14, 17
  erasure of, 40
  integration of, 52–53, 67
Provost, Ray, 185n.70

race, 84–85, 168
  anticommunism and, 12
  Asian American evangelicals and, 8, 12, 168–69
  Billy Graham and, 126–27
  Christianity and, 99
  evangelicalism and, 12, 17
  post-World War II, 84–85

234 INDEX

race (cont.)
  racial interstitiality, 60, 212–13n.10
  US as racial democracy, 98
  whiteness and, 162–64
  World Vision Korean Orphan Choir and, 86
racialization
  of anticommunism, 168
  erasure and, 12
  integration and, 12
  of Korean Americans, 161
  of Koreans, 58
  model minoritization and, 12
  38th parallel and, 11
racism
  Billy Graham on, 203n.57
  evangelicalism and, 8
Reagan, Ronald, 2–3, 159–60
  color-blind conservatism of, 125–26
religions, Asian American, 180n.84
religious history, American, 20, 179n.79, 179–80nn.82–83
  of women, 179n.82
rescue
  new evangelical narrative of, 94, 99
revival
  in America, 5
  of evangelicalism, 10–11
  in Korea, 14, 16–17
  of Korea, 144–45, 209n.49
  South Korean Protestant, 13, 17
  transpacific, 2, 3–4
Rhee, Syngman, 26–27, 40, 178n.65, 207n.1
  Methodism of, 29
  ousting of, 79, 147–48
Rhie Deok-Joo, 187n.5
Rivera, Mayra Rivera, 114
Robbins, Joel, 202n.47
Robert, Dana, 114, 177n.58
Robertson, Pat, 17, 178n.66
Roddy, Clarence, 191n.59
Ross, Dick, 41, 185n.74

Samaritan's Purse, 105–6, 164–65
Sanneh, Lamin, 177n.58, 205n.88
Scopes Trial, 5
segregation, educational, 56–57, 58–60, 190n.41
  at Bob Jones University, 59–60, 63, 190n.41
  Brown v. Board of Education, 56, 58–59, 60
sentimentalism
  of Bob Pierce, 95–97, 98–99
  Cold War sentimentalism, 92, 96
  evangelicalism and, 94–101
  World Vision Korean Orphan Choir and, 95
shamanism, 167–68, 172–73n.8
Sharpless, Jerry, 141, 142, 143, 151–52, 154
Shin, Gi Wook, 27
Shinto, 177n.54
  in Korea, 15
Smith, Christian, 203–4n.68
Smyth, Walter, 110–12, 200n.31
South Korea
  Buddhism in, 14–15, 167–68, 172–73n.8
  as center of Christian power, 138–39
  Cold War and, x
  Confucianism in, 14–15, 167–68, 172–73n.8
  economic development of, 159
  inseparability from US, 9, 176n.45
  Nixon Doctrine and, 110
  Nixon-Park era, 109–12, 205n.87
  Protestantism in, 29–30
  religious demographics of, 14–15, 172–73n.8
  revivals in, 14, 16–17
  See also Korea
sovereignty, Korean, 26–27, 28
Stalin, Joseph, 28
Student Christian Movement, 183n.42

Tabitha Widow's Home (Tabitha *mojawŏn*), 24–25, 34–35, 36, 184n.59
  erasure of, 187n.103
Tan, Henry, 164
Thomas, Jolyon, 177n.54
Thompson, Jerry, 61–63
Torrey, R. A., 78
transnationalism
  evangelicalism and, 6–7, 175n.28
  in history, 18–21, 178n.69
  38th parallel and, 11

Truman, Harry, 3–4
  Cold War policies of, 28–29
  fundamentalists and, 50
Trump, Donald, 165
Turner, John G., 136, 175n.28, 207n.13

University Bible Fellowship (UBF), 177n.63

Vanderpol, Gary, 187n.103
Vietnam War
  antiwar protests, 116–17, 145, 147–48
  South Korean troops in, 110, 199n.18, 201n.36

Wacker, Grant, 108–9, 111, 178n.70
Wallis, Jim, 149–50
Ward, W. R., 175n.28
WEC '80 (1980 World Evangelization Crusade), 16–17, 155–60, 211nn.98–99
  attendance, 211n.100
  Joon Gon Kim as chair, 155–57
  leftist movements, opposition to, 157
Wesley, John, 96, 114–15
White, John, 204n.70
White, Loretta, 110–11, 199–200n.23
Whitefield, George, 114–15
whiteness
  American Protestantism and, 37–38
  evangelicalism and, 2, 8–9, 12, 13–14, 23–24, 78, 194n.13
  race and, 162–64
  sacralization of, 36, 37–40, 48–49
  US evangelical empire and, 12–13, 165
  World Vision Korean Orphan Choir and, 78
white supremacy
  evangelicalism and, 23
  US militarization of Korea and, 37–38
  white evangelicalism and, 165
Wilson, Grady, 23, 36, 185n.70, 204n.70
Wilson, Stanton R., 121, 198n.13, 200n.31
Wilson, T. W., 204n.70
Wong, Brent, 164
Wong, Janelle, 8
Wong, Jean, 43, 185–86n.81
Wong, Leila, 164

Woo, Susie, 93, 94, 96, 187n.103
World Vision, 2, 3–4, 5, 164, 165–66, 212–13n.10
  anticommunism of, 83
  child sponsorship program, 35, 36, 45, 46–47, 184n.56
  erasure of Kyung Chik Han, 45, 48–49, 187n.103
  expansion into BGEA, 23
  founding of, 10, 22–23, 33–34, 46, 120, 205n.81
  global rise of, 17–18, 83
  Korean origins of, 46–50
  mainstreaming of, 81, 94–95
  at 1973 Korea Billy Graham crusade, 119
  origins of, 12–13, 18
  orphan metaphor, 92–93
  politics of, 167–68
  US empire and, 47
  White Jade myth, 46, 48
  See also Han, Kyung Chik; Pierce, Bob
World Vision Korean Orphan Choir, 10, 75–92, 104–6, 107, 205n.81
  critiques of, 87–88
  earnings of, 76–77, 80, 89–90, 193n.10
  as "Korean Children's Choir," 76, 94, 119
  as "little ambassadors," 75, 76, 78, 81, 83–85, 106, 119
  as "little missionaries," 81
  as national treasure, 29–30
  at 1973 Korea Billy Graham crusade, 119
  orphanages of, 75–76
  as orphan-less, 90, 93
  race and, 86
  sentimentalism and, 95
  tours of, 78, 79–80, 86–87, 105, 194n.15
  whiteness, expansion of, 78
  See also Oh Chiyŏng
World Vision Pictorial, 38–39, 185n.70
Wu, Ellen D., 84–85

Yellow Peril, 84–85
Yi Kwangsun, 47–48
Yi Sŭnghun, 25
Yoido Full Gospel Church, 3
Yoo, David, 179n.82

Yoo, William, 44
Young Nak Presbyterian Church, 32, 45
Youth for Christ (YFC), 23, 31, 32, 46, 183n.45

Yu, Margaret, 164
Yun Chi'ho, 26, 187–88n.7
Yun, Chung-Nan, 79
Yung, Victor Sen, 43